Working with the Professionals

to create the home you want

The moderns
Golden Hit Parade
PANAMARENKO
LIVING IN MO
LE CORF DU MANO

Working with the Professionals

to create the home you want

John Warde
Consulting editor

Mike Lawrence

Paul Hymers

Jeff Howell

TIME® LIFE BOOKS

ALEXANDRIA, VIRGINIA

TIME® LIFE BOOKS

Time-Life Books is a division of Time Life Inc.

TIME LIFE INC.
President and CEO Jim Nelson
TIME-LIFE TRADE PUBLISHING
Vice President and Publisher
Neil Levin
Senior Director of Acquisitions and Editorial Resources Jennifer Pearce
Director of New Product Development Carolyn Clark
Director of Trade Sales Dana Coleman
Director of Marketing Inger Forland
Director of New Product Development Teresa Graham
Director of Custom Publishing
John Lalor
Director of Special Markets
Robert Lombardi
Director of Design Kate L. McConnell
Project Manager Jennie Halfant

Originated in Singapore by PICA
Printed and bound in Portugal by Printer Portuguesa

10 9 8 7 6 5 4 3 2 1

TIME-LIFE is a trademark of Time Warner Inc., and affiliated companies.

Library of Congress Cataloging-in-Publication Data

Warde, John, 1947
   Working with the professionals ; to create the home you want / John Warde, Jeffrey Howell, Michael Lawrence, Paul Hymers.
      p. cm.
ISBN 0-7370-0313-8 (softcover : alk. paper)
   1. House construction—Planning—Amateurs' manuals. 2. Contractors—Selection and appointment—Amateur's manuals. I. Lawrence, Michael, 1947- II. Hymers, Paul. III.Time-Life Books. IV. Title.

TH4812 .H68 2000
690'.837—dc21   99-089108

Books produced by Time-Life Trade Publishing are available at a special bulk discount for promotional and premium use. Custom adaptations can also be created to meet your specific marketing goals. Call 1-800-323-5255.

A Marshall Edition
Conceived, edited, and designed by Marshall Editions
The Orangery
161 New Bond Street
London W1Y 9PA

Project Editor Theresa Lane
Art Editors Fehmi Comert, Simon Wilder
Photo Researcher Claire Taylor
Copy Editor Katherine Ness
Proof Reader Constance Novis
Editorial Assistant Emily Salter
Indexer Jill Dorman
Managing Art Editor Patrick Carpenter
Editorial Director Ellen Dupont
Art Director Dave Goodman
Editorial Coordinator Ros Highstead
Production Anna Pauletti
DTP editor Lesley Gilbert

Contents

Finding a contractor
(pp. 16–17)

Interior improvements
(pp. 34–35)

Redecorating rooms
(pp. 36–39)

Interior improvements
(pp. 34–35)

Converting garages
(pp. 92–93)

Introduction

Knowing where to start and how to proceed with home improvements can be a mind-boggling experience. Although some people love to do the work themselves, plenty of homeowners simply don't have the knowledge, skill, inclination, or time to take on do-it-yourself home-improvement projects. *Working with the Professionals* is for those people. This book is divided into three main chapters: it explains how to hire and manage professionals to do your home improvements, what types of improvements can be made to your home, and how your house works.

An expert can advise on the best way to achieve the maximum storage space in any room in your home, especially in the living room (above, top) and the kitchen (above).

Choosing a professional is not difficult once you know how to go about it. The first step is to decide on the scope of the work you want done so that you can select the right type of professional—for example, an architect for a major renovation or an addition, a designer who specializes in bathrooms for a bathroom remodeling, a contractor to oversee a standard basement conversion, or a carpenter to replace your kitchen cabinets. If you have trouble choosing colors and deciding on an overall plan for your home improvements, some of these professionals, such as an architect or designer, will be able to present the best available options based on both your budget and tastes.

One area that professional designers seldom overlook is the small details— for example, the handles on these kitchen units.

Your task doesn't stop with choosing a professional—you must also think about getting estimates, creating budgets, signing contracts, and plans that will meet building regulations, as well as how to work with the professionals on a day-to-day basis once the work proceeds. Understanding what's involved beforehand will make the whole process go more smoothly. Unfortunately, disputes do sometimes occur, and if you find yourself in this situation, you should know the best way of handling it.

Knowing what options are available will make it easier for you to decide how to improve your home. This book explains how the experts can make home improvements, both inside and outside a house. They may be decorative, such as replacing a floor covering, or practical—for example, adding to your house's existing wiring. Whether you want to create a large open-plan room from two small adjoining rooms, convert your garage, or update your bathroom, you'll learn about the materials that you can choose from, whom you should hire, how the work should proceed, and when you should inspect the work.

Working with the experts will inevitably involve discussing technical details, which can be confusing. To help you understand the terminology and, in general, how your house works, you need to learn about the sections of the house that the experts will be renovating. This information will help ensure that you recognize good workmanship. It will also explain why the experts have to make changes in certain ways; for example, why a load-bearing wall cannot be knocked down without first strengthening support for the structure above it. Finally, a reference section with forms and contracts, a glossary, and a list of resources rounds off all you need to know in order to work with the professionals.

An architect goes through years of education and training to ensure that your home renovation is practical, safe, and attractive.

A designer who specializes in bathrooms (top) or kitchens (bottom) will know the latest—and best— materials available to provide you with an original room that will meet your tastes.

1

Choosing and managing the professionals

The easiest part of renovating your home is making the decision to change certain features that you don't like or find inadequate. Determining what you do want and who should make the improvements, however, can be a baffling experience. This chapter will explain what the professionals do, how to get them to do what is best for you and your home, and how to ensure that you don't incur any financial or legal problems along the way.

A desirable, innovative living space can be yours by hiring an architect who will design the renovation and choose materials to suit your tastes.

1 Architects

Like attorneys and physicians, architects are licensed professionals. Their qualifications include five to seven years of studying architectural design, structural engineering, and related subjects such as mathematics and physical sciences.

After getting a bachelor's or master's degree in architecture, the candidate must spend three years of internship working under the supervision of licensed architects; then comes a state licensing examination. No professional is more qualified to handle projects involving the siting, construction, remodeling, and landscaping of buildings than an architect.

What architects do

First of all, an architect can get you past the primary stumbling block in any construction project—coming up with a workable plan. With their broad training and experience, architects can help you define what you want to build, then turn your ideas into reality. They can suggest options for designs, materials, and methods you might never have thought of on your own, and they are expert at managing building costs so you get the most from your construction dollar. Architects also are trained in seeing "the whole picture"; that is, how a particular building project will fit into or affect its larger context. This kind of consideration can result in advantages ranging from savings on energy bills to increased home resale value. Most of all, it usually pays off in construction that is pleasing and comfortable to live in.

Architects specify or approve the building materials and techniques to be used in a project and are qualified to and often manage the construction process in its entirety. Besides drawing construction plans, the architect is in charge of all legalities such as obtaining planning and zoning approvals and variances. He or she may help select or hire contractors and other specialists to perform the work, and will oversee the project, visiting the site to make sure the plans are being followed and that the quality of the job meets the standards stated in the contract.

Your representive

Finally, and in many cases most importantly, an architect represents your interests—personal and legal—in the building project. He or she is your agent, bound by law and professional ethics to work on behalf of the building owner, not the contractor. Through an architect you can keep accurately informed on the progress and costs of a project, and can also be sure that contractors will not be paid until they have fulfilled to the architect's satisfaction all obligations pending. Should disputes arise involving the municipality or any construction business involved in a project, it is the architect's job to intercede in your place, shouldering all responsibility. Should defects occur in a structure owing to mistakes in design or construction specifications, the architect is liable, not you.

Choosing an architect

Architects tend to have individual styles and specialties, so often the best way to begin your search is to ask other homeowners for names of architects they may have used for projects similar to what you are planning. Many architects are also members of the American Institute

The architect works with the homeowners at all stages to ensure they will be happy with the final results.

Adding an addition to the house and creating an open-plan arrangement between the old and new sections is best left to an architect, whose training and education should ensure the structural integrity of the building.

of Architects (AIA). This organization maintains over 300 chapters nationwide and can furnish you with lists of members and descriptions or photos of their work (see pp. 168–171).

Making a short list

Compile a list of likely architects; then contact them to describe your project and ask if they are available to take it on. If they are, ask them to send you information about their firm, including their qualifications and experience with projects like yours. If they are not available, ask them to recommend another firm.

After winnowing your list, interview the candidates that remain. If a firm has several architects, be sure to speak with the person who will handle your project. Ask what the architect sees as the important challenges of your project, how he or she will approach it, how busy the architect is with other projects, and what services are provided and how fees are charged.

Study the architect's portfolio of work to determine whether the style suits your taste. Ask to visit an actual completed project. Obtain the names of some of the architect's past clients and follow up on them.

If the architect is a member of the AIA, you can obtain from your local chapter an Architect's Qualification Statement verifying the architect's credentials. In the end, however, remember that you are buying a service, not a product. Your final choice should be a person with whom you get along well and whose creativity, technical skills, and judgment you trust.

Architects' fees

Fee structures vary, based on the project and the size and type of the firm you hire. Some architects charge by the hour, others by the square footage (or meters) of the project, by a percentage of the construction costs (from 5 to 15 percent), or by a flat fee for itemized services.

The architect should explain how he or she calculates the fee; afterward, the two of you will negotiate the amount and the payment schedule before signing the contract (see pp. 20–21). The AIA publishes standardized contracts that most architects use. These detail the specifics of the agreement—services, schedules, deadlines, fees, and the responsibilities and liabilities of both parties. As with any contract, be sure you understand it before you sign it.

As a rule, designers take on smaller, simpler, and more specific projects than architects. They often provide exactly the right service for homeowners who don't need an architect's comprehensive (and more expensive) expertise.

The homeowner who needs help formulating remodeling plans that are beyond a contractor's ability will benefit by hiring an interior designer. There are designers who specialize in everything from kitchens to decks. They have less training than architects, and the profession is less regulated. If your project involves multiple rooms, structural challenges, or a lot of calculations and engineering decisions, hire an architect. For simple renovations and conventional additions a designer will do.

What designers do

Interior designers specialize in room design. Their skills are aimed toward creating spaces that function well and suit a client's preferences. As well as having technical knowledge of construction systems, building materials, codes, and other standards and practices, interior designers are proficient in space planning, traffic flow, the use of patterns, furniture selection, and layout.

Building and remodeling designers are often associated with general contracting firms or are contractors themselves. Their education and training consists of a mix of architectural and engineering studies and on-the-job construction experience. Consider one for structural remodeling such as building an addition, enclosing a porch, or converting a garage. Building and remodeling designers often specialize in specific construction projects or areas of a house, as well as in special interests such as historical preservation.

Kitchen and bath designers specialize in designing, remodeling, and equipping kitchens, bathrooms, and home spas. As with interior designers, they are highly trained and proficient, especially in space planning and the functional use of these rooms. Kitchen and bath designers have a wide knowledge of available equipment, fixtures, furnishings, and decorative materials. Many specialize in creating gourmet kitchens, for example, and in designing kitchens and baths to be accessible to elderly or mobility-impaired occupants.

Lighting designers, who are often also interior designers, specialize in providing effective, pleasing lighting in various situations. They have technical knowledge of lighting systems and expertise in choosing lighting for function and decorative impact, and for meeting special needs.

Other specialist designers include closet and storage designers, home office designers, porch and deck designers, and sunroom designers.

Choosing a designer

States vary in requiring designers to be licensed or accredited. To learn the requirements where you live, contact your local building inspector. Industry associations such as the American Society of Interior Designers (ASID) offer certification programs that provide design pro-

Don't forget !

- A designer may charge a flat fee, or a fee based on an hourly rate or square footage (meters). The fee should include an initial and subsequent design consultation and a site visit, leading to sketches and final drawings.

- When a building permit is required, the drawings may first need approval by an architect.

- Contracts vary in format and terms. Be sure you understand the contents before signing one.

Ask yourself

- Does the designer have a specialty? For example, does he or she develop designs with mostly ethnic elements or in Shaker style, and does he or she design only bathrooms or another type of room?

- Does the designer have a certificate from the American Society of Interior Designers? What are his or her training background and professional affiliations?

- Can the designer provide references from recent customers?

- How does the designer charge for the work involved?

fessionals with credentials showing they have met industry agreed-upon standards for competency and ability. Six years of combined college-level education and work experience are required (two years of course work and four years on the job), in addition to passing an examination.

The way to find a designer is by word of mouth. Ask friends, neighbors, and colleagues for recommendations, especially if any have had work done that is similar to what you want. Or call a local architect or contracting and construction company specializing in the type of project you have in mind; they often know qualified designers. If you're look-

ing for an interior designer, bath or kitchen designer, or lighting designer contact the ASID, the National Kitchen and Bathroom Association (NKBA), or the American Lighting Association (ALA; see pp. 168–171).

After compiling a list of candidates, arrange short interviews with them to describe your project and to find out if they are interested. Discuss the designer's experience and professional affiliations, and look at any portfolio of completed projects. Obtain the names of past clients and talk to them before making a decision. You will want someone you can trust and with whom you can establish a good rapport.

The designer and homeowner have agreed on a Mexican theme for this kitchen. The paint colors chosen for the walls are based on typical Mexican colors, and the colors of the pottery above the cabinets complement the color scheme.

The chunky cabinets have the feeling of old-world Mexico. The designer has chosen handles and hinges that are contemporary in style, yet they easily blend in with the cabinets.

The designer has taken great steps to obtain this Mexican theme but, at the same time, the kitchen must be practical. The kitchen island functions as a work surface and includes the stove and burners for cooking.

1 Rules and regulations

Most remodeling beyond simple repair and maintenance requires permission from the local building authorities—your city or county building department. Many remodeling projects also require inspection to ensure that the work is safe.

Permission generally comes in two parts. Adding onto structures on the property may require a building permit from the building department, and these may also have to meet with approval by zoning authorities.

Zoning ordinances

Municipal zoning ordinances regulate how residental and commercial property is used. In the case of residential property, for example, they might prevent you from converting a garage into an apartment—even a so-called self-contained apartment (see pp. 104–105)—if you live in a neighborhood zoned specifically for single-family residences. In addition, height restrictions govern how tall a building may be, and setback ordinances restrict how close a building may be extended toward the street and other property lines.

When the application for your building permit is submitted, it will be forwarded for zoning review, if necessary. Should any aspects of the proposed project violate the local statutes, you may be allowed to ask for exceptions—called variances— or you may be told to modify your plans to bring them into compliance with the statutes. Obtaining a variance can be either a routine procedure or what may seem like a prolonged battle.

When planning a remodel, one good reason to hire a professional, such as an architect or designer, is to avoid zoning and setback problems from the start. Their expertise should mean that they can come up with plans that do not conflict with existing ordinances—including many you may not know of.

Inspections

Obtaining a building permit sets in motion an inspection process to make sure the work performed complies with local code specifications. The number of inspections required will depend on the project; each inspection is intended to monitor construction at each phase. Starting a new phase cannot proceed until the previous phase has been examined by a building inspector and approved. Ignor an inspection at your peril; the inspector can order the work torn out to the stage at which the inspection was to have been performed. If an inspection turns up code violations, they must be corrected and reinspected—this can be a very costly procedure.

The cost of inspections is figured into the cost of the building permit. However, scheduling inspections must be done as work progresses.

Ask yourself	?

Ask yourself

- Will your project require a building permit? If you have hired an architect for a large renovation, he or she will seek permission. However, if you have hired someone for a small project, such as a carpenter to erect a fence, then you should seek permission before buying the materials. In this case, there could be a restriction on the height of the fence.

Normally, this is the responsibility of whoever is in charge of the project as a whole and is likely to be the same person whose signature appears on the building permit. Ownership of this task, too, should be written clearly into the contract.

Certificate of occupancy

A certificate of occupancy is proof that a project has been formally inspected and is in compliance with applicable building codes and other regulations. It also constitutes legal permission to live in the building.

Obviously, you can't obtain a certificate of occupancy without first obtaining a building permit, but after the work is done, the certificate is the more valuable of the two documents and is the one you should preserve in your files. You may need it if you sell your house— as proof that remodeling was done correctly—and you might also need it to win damages from your home-

---

Don't forget

- Always seek permission from the appropriate authorities before undertaking a remodeling project. Rules and regulations change from region to region; a renovation you liked when visiting a friend elsewhere may have to be adjusted before it is given permission in your locality.

- Make sure that you file the certificate of occupancy in a safe place. It can be a valuable asset if you sell your home at a later date.

This addition required a permit before work could begin. At various stages of the construction, an inspector visited the site to ensure the work met with the standards set by the local building codes.

owner's insurance company in the event of a fire or other catastrophe that insurance representatives could blame on either faulty or illegally performed workmanship.

Building codes

The collections of local laws, specifications, and recommendations that set minimum safety standards for residential and commercial construction are known as building codes. Besides structural considerations, building codes address plumbing, electrical and mechanical systems (heating, ventilation, and air conditioning), and fire safety. They also spell out the qualifications professionals and, sometimes, even homeowners need in order to perform certain types of work such as electrical wiring.

Codes vary from one region to the next. However, in practically all cases, local codes are derived from larger so-called model codes written by one of several organizations. These include:
• Building Officials & Code Administrators International, Inc. (BOCA);
• International Conference of Building Officials (ICBO);
• International Code Council (ICC);
• National Fire Protection Association (NFPA, authors of the National Electric Code, or NEC);
• Southern Building Code Congress International, Inc. (SBCCI). (For addresses and details on these organizations, see pp. 168–171.)

A single model building code, the International Residential Code, which was developed by the ICC, will supercede codes written prior to 2000. States will have three options: to adopt the new code as it is written; to adopt it with modifications; or to not adopt it. Local and model building code texts are available in public libraries.

When the time comes to actually have remodeling work performed—after the planning is completed and the building permit and other permissions are obtained—you will need to hire contractors and subcontractors to do the work.

If you plan only to put a new coat of paint on the walls, then a contractor is not for you. However, if your project requires representatives of more than three trades, say a carpenter, an electrician, a drywall installer, and a painter (about what you'd need for an ordinary room makeover), your best course is probably to hire a general contractor. That person, in turn, will hire and oversee the individual specialists, who are called subcontractors, specialty contractors, or tradespeople.

Hiring the right general contractor and understanding what his or her job and responsibilities are, as well as knowing your own rights and obligations, is crucial in any home renovation. Making the wrong choice or not understanding what is expected of either side can turn even a simple project into a bitter and potentially costly affair.

What contractors do

A general contractor is usually skilled in at least one of the building trades; however, his or her main occupation is organizing and supervising entire construction projects. When you hire a general contractor, essentially, you place him or her in complete charge of the building phase of your project, which will be subject to the terms of the contract (see pp. 20–21) and any additional input you—or your architect or designer (see pp. 10–13)—might have along the way. With a project for which an architect or designer has created plans, a general contractor normally enters the picture when the finished plans are let out for bids (see pp. 18–19).

In the case of smaller projects, the contractor might draw up plans and would be selected at the outset. In either case, at the earliest possible stage the contractor will compile an estimate of all the labor and materials involved, as well as the overall cost of the project (which will include the contractor's profit). Afterward, it will normally be the general contractor's responsibility to secure all building permits, to order all the materials necessary, and to hire, schedule, and oversee each subcontractor; he or she will also have to schedule inspections (see pp. 14–15). Finally, the general contractor is usually in charge of handling any final corrections before the project is signed off.

Ask yourself ?

- Does the size of your renovation project warrant hiring a contractor? If you'll use less than four people, probably not; yes if you use more.

- Does a potential contractor have a license, or has he or she been in business for at least four years?

- Does a potential contractor have adequate insurance and bonding to protect you in the case of any accident, shoddy work, or breach of contract?

- Does the contractor have experience working on projects that are similar to yours?

Choosing a contractor

The best way to locate a general contractor—or, indeed, anyone in the building trades—is by asking friends, colleagues, neighbors, and relatives, especially any who have had work done that is similar to what you are planning. Other fairly reliable sources for recommendations are local lumberyards and

In a home renovation where a wall is knocked down and replaced by floor-to-ceiling windows, the contractor will be responsible for hiring and overseeing a number of professional tradespeople.

building suppliers who cater to professional customers. Sometimes, too, you may obtain help (although you shouldn't expect any direct referrals) from your state's contractor's licensing bureau, the local building inspector's office, and the local headquarters of relevant trade unions and builders associations. Even insurance agents and realtors

can be a source. Unfortunately, unlike architects and designers, contractors do not belong to a trade association that can furnish lists of qualified members.

Obtaining credentials

After gathering a list of potential contractor candidates, you need to verify that they are in good professional standing. This is not easy, because licensing and certification requirements vary from state to state and, in some cases, from county to county and city to city. Call your local building department for details on regulations where you live; then verify with the contractors you select as candidates that they meet those requirements. In states requiring contractors to be licensed, obtain a contractor's license number and confirm with your state or local contractor's licensing bureau that the license is valid.

Since there are few established minimum standards, you should look for contractors who have been in business for at least four years (six years is even better), who have experience in the sort of project you are planning, and who are willing to give the names of former clients. You should speak to these clients to verify that they were satisfied with the contractor's performance. You might also want to ask for local bank and business references—you can call these to see if any have complaints about past payment problems. Finally, you can often learn of any consumer complaints against a contractor by calling your local Better Business Bureau.

Financial protection

Be sure to verify that the contractors you are considering are adequately insured and bonded. The contractor should also have workers' compensation insurance to protect you from being sued if a worker is injured on your property. Bonding gives you

Facts & figures

For your protection, as well as the contractor's, property damage and liability insurance should be comprehensive and generally in excess of $200,000. (However, some areas require contractors to carry only $100,000 in liability insurance.)

In areas where bonding is required, the amounts vary from approximately $3,000 to $10,000.

legal recourse if the work performed by the contractor does not meet building code standards. However, in some cases you may also make claims against the bond for breach of contract. If bonding is not a requirement where you live, you should still seek contractors who will post a bond voluntarily.

Once you've verified the credentials and qualifications of potential candidates, final selection of a general contractor is made by evaluating the bids each candidate submits (see pp.18–19).

Subcontractors

Subcontractors specialize in a single trade; for example, plumbing, painting, bricklaying, or roofing. They are often self-employed individuals, or they may be a small company whose workers all do essentially the same thing (a plumbing subcontractor, for instance, may be a business operated by a master plumber who has journeymen and apprentice plumbers working for him or her). If you hire a general contractor, all subcontractors should be hired and supervised by the general contractor. If you have only a small or specialized project or act as your own general contractor, you may hire subcontractors yourself. Use the same selection methods as for hiring a general contractor.

1 Inviting estimates

If you have hired an architect or a designer to help you with your project, a simple way to proceed is to ask him or her to organize and oversee the construction work as well. This will mean that he or she will handle soliciting bids.

The architect or designer will ask three contractors to bid for the work. The bid is based on his or her detailed drawings of the project and a written specification, also called a "spec" or call-out sheet. The spec lists the work to be carried out, the materials to be used, and any information about the project in as much detail as possible—enough for contractors to submit a realistic price for completing it.

Submitted estimates

After interviewing and verifying the credentials of the contractors (see pp. 16–17), a copy of the drawings and specification is presented to each candidate, often during a visit to your house. After receiving the information, each contractor submits an itemized bid, which should be compared point by point. It is up to you, and your architect or designer if you've hired one, to study all the bids and make the final decision.

Estimates submitted at bidding are not binding without prior agreement. Bids for construction projects must, therefore, be scrupulously studied. Bidding is also a gamble for contractors—it takes time and must be done free of charge in areas where the building business is competitive. Only truly interested contractors will submit a bid, which should be accurate if they were given enough detailed information.

Comparing bids

Evaluating bids from contractors takes skill and close observation by an architect or designer; as the client you will be the final arbiter. If you

Don't forget !

Be sure bids include as much information as possible:

- Contractor's qualifications and credentials (obtain the contractor's business license number, if required in your area, and proof of both general liability and workers' compensation insurance)
- Fees for permits, rental equipment, and utilities if appropriate
- Fees for demolition, cleanup, and debris removal
- Fees for site work, including grading, tree removal, and landscaping
- Fees for project construction (including itemized costs and allowances for all work and materials)
- Fees for finish work (also itemized as described above)
- Fees for materials and services not covered above

are hiring a contractor on your own, you need to be completely knowledgeable about what is involved.

Compare the total, or bottom line, prices of each bid. Contractors' bids are the sum of materials, labor, and overhead costs, plus a profit of 10 to 30 percent. Because all the bids are for the same job and are from local contractors who work, buy materials, and hire subcontractors within the same geographical area and business environment, you should expect the figures to be about the same, varying by no more than about 10 percent.

Don't discount low or high bids. Analyzing what each bid includes, and therefore what underlies each final price, is the crucial step. Study the details. You can check costs of materials by visiting home centers and building supply stores; a contractor usually qualifies for profes-

sional discounts and can obtain materials from wholesale suppliers, so the costs shown on the bid should be lower than the prices you see in the stores. However, if they are substantially lower—more than 50 percent—it is worth questioning. The contractor may be proposing to use a lesser grade of something shown on the call-out sheet, or to supply a "contractor-grade" (low-quality) item for something the sheet does not identify by grade, brand, or model.

Setting allowances

Examine bid allowances carefully. These are the amounts contractors "allow" for products, materials, and labor whose specifications have not been finalized at the time of bidding. Be sure you clarify the details of the allowances and have them stated in the bid. Check the quality of the product or material the contractor has based the allowance figures on, and the number of items or amount of a material the allowance includes. Also make sure the allowances are comprehensive, including trim, preparation and final finish work, and installation fees.

Be sure it is clear who will be doing the work—the contractor or employees of the business, or will subcontractors be hired? The contractor is responsible for carrying out the project satisfactorily, but it will help you come to a hiring decision to know who will be employed.

The final choice

Before deciding on a contractor, consider whether the bid seems fair and honest, and whether it reflects the professionalism you expect. Find out the degree to which the candidate will commit to handling your project exclusively (many contractors divide their time between projects), how quickly the work can be scheduled and performed, what policies apply regarding changes requested during construction, and what provisions apply for making corrections after the work is done.

If you receive positive answers, that candidate is your best choice. A big part of deciding which contractor to hire will depend on which person you trust, respect as a professional, and feel you can get along with.

Ask yourself ?

- Do the quantities and quality of materials differ between bids?

- Do they differ from those indicated on the drawings or specification?

- Are any steps or materials left out, intentionally or by mistake?

- What about the prices quoted for materials or products; are they accurate and reasonable?

The bid for this bathroom included work and materials supplied by a plumber, electrician, carpenter, and tiler. With so many tradespeople and materials involved, the details of such a bid should be closely scrutinized.

Inviting estimates 19

1 Drawing up the contract

After you have hired a contractor for your project, the next steps are to negotiate and draw up a formal contract. A contract is a legally binding business agreement for the supply of goods or services at an agreed-upon price.

In the construction and remodeling industry, it is customary for all jobs, no matter how small, to be performed by contract only, even if the contract amounts to nothing more than a simple work order.

Work orders are usually reserved for minor repairs—unblocking a sink, for example, or replacing an electrical outlet. They often contain only a perfunctory description of the job, the agreed-upon price, and the signatures of the contractor and homeowner. By contrast, most contracts for home improvement projects, especially those involving a general contractor and subcontractors, are lengthy and detail every aspect of the work, the idea being to protect both parties by communicating the exact responsibilities of each.

Contract forms

You don't have to come up with the contract forms; the contractor will supply them, or if you've commissioned an architect, he or she may supply the forms. (This can often be to your advantage because it places the contractor, not you, in the defensive position of having to initiate changes to the prewritten contract wording.) Contractors use standardized forms written in plain language that can be understood without an attorney; however, if your project is very expensive, obtaining an attorney's advice on the contract is recommended (see pp. 164–167).

Take your time filling out the contract, and never sign a contract that contains blanks. Make sure you understand and agree to each point, and that the contract accurately represents your complete agreement with the contractor. Everything in a contract is open for discussion and negotiation. If you encounter wording you aren't comfortable with, you can supply other wording for the contractor's approval. Contracts can take days, weeks, or months to complete, depending on the project; and discussions between contractor and homeowner leading up to the final version clarify for everyone the actual nature of the project.

Before signing a contract, make sure it includes details of all the work involved in the project, as well as who is responsible for doing the work. Besides new materials, this kitchen renovation required a plumber, electrician, flooring expert, and carpenter.

A contract should contain a complete description of the work to be done, with particular emphasis on the exact services to be performed and materials to be used, including quality, quantity, size, color, brand, and model if appropriate. All fees to be paid and any stipulations regarding payment should be included, as should written versions of any verbal agreements made during preliminary discussions. Contracts vary according to the complexity of the project and the structure of the business arrangement.

Contract types

Homeowners and contractors can enter into any of several business arrangements, each represented by a different contract type:

- Fixed-price, or lump-sum, contracts name a specific sum as the total payment due the contractor for performing the contract terms. A work order is the least detailed form of fixed-price contract.
- Cost-plus-fee, also called time-and-materials, contracts specify payment for actual time worked and materials used, plus a profit that can be either a fixed amount or a percentage of costs. "Cost-plus" contracts, as they are often called, are used for jobs too small to justify formal bidding and where the full cost cannot be accurately determined up front, such as repairs to plumbing or electrical wiring concealed in walls.
- Cost-plus-fee contracts with a not-to-exceed clause limit the amount of markup the contractor can charge.
- Labor-only contracts limit contractor responsibilities to furnishing and supervising labor. Materials are supplied by the homeowner.
- Management-fee-only contracts pay a contractor to supervise a construction project; payment of subcontractors and materials is done by the homeowner or a representative.
- Design-build contracts cover projects for which the contractor is also the designer. The best of these for the homeowner consist of two parts: a preconstruction agreement covering design, and a fixed-price agreement covering construction. The latter should be based on estimates under the terms of the former.

Signing a contract

After all negotiations are finished and the contract is drawn up, read it carefully to make sure it contains everything you believe it should; that you understand all of the wording; and that you agree with every point. Ask yourself a final time whether you truly want to proceed. If the answers to all of these considerations is yes, take a deep breath, sign the contract, and get an exact copy, also signed.

Don't forget !

Here are key items to look for in any contract, where they apply:

- Contractor's name, business address, and licensing details
- Provision for obtaining building permits and legal permissions
- Binding estimate of costs
- Full, complete price for the job
- Payment schedule
- Plans and specification sheet
- The project start date, any interim deadlines, and the formal completion date
- Description of change-order policies (change orders address requests for alterations to the project after the contract has been signed)
- Provision for removing or saving old building materials
- Specification of any work to be done by the homeowner
- Provision for cleanup and site restoration
- Warranties by the contractor to remedy defects in materials and workmanship (this extends to the subcontractors)
- Provision for lien releases (to release the homeowner from lien claims by subcontractors, contractor, and suppliers)
- Hold-back clause (withholds a portion of the contract price until the job is completed to the homeowner's satisfaction)
- Arbitration clause (agreement to submit disputes to arbitration)
- Acceptance clauses (describe responsibilities of the signers)
- Places for signature by the homeowner and the contractor

1 Creating a budget

Deciding to have building work done on your home is perhaps the easiest step. Making decisions on how much money to spend on it—and making sure that the money is spent efficiently—is perhaps one of the most difficult steps.

Building is not an exact science, and when alterations or additions are taking place on a home, it is not uncommon for unexpected difficulties to arise during the work. In fact, it is common for jobs to cost more and take longer than the original estimates; it is not excessive to budget an extra 25 percent for increased costs over the estimates to avoid distress. If the extra costs never materialize, you will certainly find a use for the money.

Small loans

There are several ways to obtain the money for home improvements. For small jobs, the most obvious is to use cash from savings or investments. The chief merit is that you avoid paying interest charges.

More often, home improvement costs are financed by loans from banks, credit unions, and savings and loan associations. There are several different types. For a small amount, consider a passbook or personal loan. With a passbook loan you can borrow money by using the amount you have in your savings account as collateral. With a personal loan— usually available only from the bank in which you keep the majority of your accounts—you can sometimes obtain money on the basis of your signature. You will need something of value as collateral; if not a savings account, then securities, jewelry, or other valuables that can be sold by the bank if you default.

If you have a life insurance policy, you could borrow against it. The interest rate will be lower than for most bank loans, and you don't have

The renovation on this kitchen included installing ventilation for the stove (which was moved to the island), new cabinets, lighting, and flooring, and a new window.

to pay the money back in regular installments. However, taking a loan on an insurance policy reduces the amount the policy will pay by the amount you owe until you repay it.

Facts & figures

Interest payments on home equity credit spending are tax deductible up to the first $100,000 of borrowed funds, provided the money is used for home improvements. (Always check with a tax adviser before counting on deducting interest from home equity credit line payments.)

Like a first mortgage, interest payments on home equity loans are generally tax deductible.

Don't forget !

- Always add an extra 25 percent to the estimated budget to cover any unforeseen expenses.

- Decide what the best method of payment will be for your situation. Are you comfortable using your house as collateral to finance the work?

- Set up a separate account to handle all the project transactions.

- Make sure there is a reasonable payment schedule. Do not pay too much money at the start of the project, but pay installments on time.

A source of small loans are HUD and VA loans, available from banks. HUD loans are backed by the U.S. Department of Housing and Urban Development (HUD). VA loans are backed by the Veterans Administration (VA) and are available to veterans of the U.S. armed services. Both require less security and carry lower interest rates than ordinary loans.

Larger loans

A popular way of financing home improvements involving medium and large sums is taking out a home equity loan—or second mortgage—or establishing a home equity line of credit. A home equity loan lets you borrow a fixed amount up to the value of your home minus the amount you owe on the first mortgage; the house serves as collateral. Second mortgage interest rates are higher than first mortgage rates but lower than the rate for bank loans. A home equity line of credit lets you borrow irregular amounts of money on an open-ended basis up to a portion of the value of your home; you repay it at regular intervals. Again, your house serves as collateral.

You can also raise money by refinancing your home with a new first mortgage for a larger amount than you owe. This method might be worthwhile if you have paid off much of the original sum and if interest rates have gone down at least three points from the level you

are paying. Refinancing this way will involve closing and appraisal costs, as if you were buying the house.

Payment schedules

To simplify record keeping, set up a separate checking account to handle project transactions. (Many remodeling costs are tax deductible when you sell the house.) Small projects of under $3,000 are paid upon completion. Larger projects are paid in installments, called draws or progress payments; the timing is in the contract. Draws are paid on signing the contract, on completion of specified stages of construction, and on completion of the entire job.

The amount paid out during the project should correspond with the amount of work performed. Resist an initial payment over 10 percent of the contract amount (in some states it is unlawful for a contractor to ask for more). Also make sure the contract defines "completion" as it relates to the construction stages.

Delays in draws are a hardship to contractors, who use the money to pay employees, subcontractors, and materials suppliers. Contracts include penalties for late payments, so make sure you pay on time.

Have a check, including the cost of any change-order amounts up to that point, ready when each stage is met, as written in your contract. If the money for draws is coming from a bank or other lender, the contractor must submit a request to you or to the lender. After it is approved, the funds are made available by deposit directly into your checking account or that of the contractor, or by check, which may be made out to you, the contractor, or both of you. On large jobs, loan money is deposited with an independent funding control company, which disburses it to the contractor on approval of the draws.

Less money was spent on this renovation than the one shown to the left. The cabinets are more basic and fewer were needed; the stove was replaced in the same position as the old one, so there was no need to move utilities.

Deciding on the order of work

The sequence of operations involved in any building project can be vital in getting the job completed on time, within the budget, and to a professional standard—so it is important that your contractor carries out the work in a specific order.

To understand how various construction tasks follow each other, consider how a platform-framed home is constructed (see pp. 134–135). Not all of the operations may apply to the job you have in mind, but some of them certainly will, and if you are employing professional builders, then they will expect things to follow a roughly similar pattern.

Preparing the site

The first task in any house-building project will be site clearance, including the demolition of any existing structures and removal of trees. Any materials from the demolition that are to be saved or recycled will have to be separated, cleaned off, and stored in a suitable location.

Smart builders know extra work can be avoided by storing both recycled and new building materials sensibly; once stored, they should only need to be moved to their point of use when needed. The storage area should be easily accessible, yet it shouldn't interfere with the operations later on. A good contractor will also time the deliveries of any new materials to arrive only when they're needed.

Site work is the general term for the operations that follow site clearance. With a new house, these include leveling the site, removing topsoil, rough-grading the soil to prepare for paths, driveways, and patio areas, and excavating for footings and any underground service supplies such as water, gas, electricity, and telephone. All of this is followed by pouring the footings, foundation walls, basement floor, and any aboveground slabs—for example, the garage floor. Foundation walls made of concrete block are also erected at this time.

Building the frame

Framing the house begins by installing the sills, first-floor joists, and subflooring to cover the foundation. After that, the exterior walls and floor framing of each story are assembled and sheathed; stairways are built between floors; interior load-bearing walls are erected; the rafters or roof trusses are installed; and the roof is covered with sheathing. Windows and doors are not installed during this phase of construction, which builders call closing in; nevertheless, the result is an enclosed building inside which materials can be stored and work can proceed, regardless of weather conditions.

Generally, the construction crew is large enough that the so-called building shell—the outer walls and roof—can be completed while interior construction is begun. Enclosing the shell consists of adding the finish roof covering and flashing, installing windows and doors, and installing siding and trim, including

Home addition progress chart

	NUMBER OF WEEKS											
	1	2	3	4	5	6	7	8	9	10	11	12
Demolition and site preparation	■											
Foundation excavation		■										
Pour footings			■									
Foundation walls/slab floor				■								
Drainage work					■							
Backfill					■							
First-floor construction						■						
Walls to roof						■	■					
Roof structure							■					
Roof coverings								■				
Windows/doors								■				
Break through to existing house								■				
Electrical rough-in									■			
Plumbing rough-in									■			
Close walls										■		
Molding and trim										■		
Electrical finish											■	
Plumbing finish											■	
Pressure test (plumbing system)											■	
Decorating											■	
Gutters, weatherstripping, caulking												■

A combination dining room and sunroom was gained by building an addition over part of an underutilized yard. The site had to be cleared of an old concrete patio and steps before building work could begin.

vents, soffits, and skylights if they are planned for your addition.

Indoor construction begins with erecting partition walls. After that, services—these are plumbing, heating, and electricity delivery components—are roughed in, insulation is installed, and all the interior framing is covered with wallboard or other material and painted. Plumbing and electrical fixtures, kitchen and bathroom cabinets, such built-in units as shelves, finish flooring, and such last-minute hardware as doorknobs complete the house.

Kitchen and bath remodeling

For a smaller job, such as a kitchen or bathroom remodel, site work is obviously less; however, the job usually involves at least some demo-lition, such as removing old cabinets, tearing up old flooring, and taking out a partition wall or two. If a load-bearing wall is removed, the structure above it must be secured (see pp. 136–137). Sealing off the room from the rest of the house to contain dust is also an important preliminary step.

When construction starts, new wall framing is erected first; the concealed portions of electrical wiring and plumbing runs are installed, then the framing is covered and painted or otherwise decorated. Completing the project is the same as described earlier—plumbing fixtures, lighting, switches, and so forth are installed to complete the service installations; cabinets, countertops, and built-in units are installed, usually followed (rather than pre-ceded) by finish flooring; then any appliances such as dishwashers are brought in and connected.

Dormers

Building a dormer or other attic addition involves cutting through the roof. The first step is erecting temporary frames to support the ends of the rafters that must be cut through to create the opening. Next, the roof is opened in sections by sawing through it between the rafters. Then the rafters are severed and the unwanted segments removed.

Construction starts with erecting the dormer's front wall frame and securing it with temporary braces. Next, the dormer's roof frame is constructed and sheathed. At this stage, the roof opening can be covered with a tarpaulin in the event of rain and the attic protected until work can resume.

Framing and sheathing the side walls and sheathing the front wall come next, followed by installing any windows or skylights. With the shell completed, work can proceed indoors. Ceiling joists must be installed; then electrical wiring, insulation, and the finish wall covering follow. On the outside, flashing, finish roofing, siding, and trim complete the job.

Most of the worst building stories concern the tribulations of trying to carry on a normal life while having remodeling work done at home. With a large-scale project, it is not unreasonable to stay somewhere else for a few days or even a few weeks.

To avoid the inconvenience of living on a building site, some people schedule the work to coincide with a vacation, but many people remain at home and the job proceeds with the house occupied. Some inconvenience should be expected. You and your builder should discuss this issue and write a few policies into the contract to ensure that disruption is kept to a minimum and the job proceeds as smoothly as possible.

There are projects that take place outside the living area—for example, building a garage or kitchen addition. These involve only minor intrusion into the home. However, there may be issues to be resolved such as noise, dust, and obstruction of access.

Limiting noise

Regarding noise, the builders should make it clear what their working hours will be (often 8:00 AM until 5:00 PM) and agree that they will not work outside of these hours without permission. Working hours are often specified in the contract to avoid any misunderstandings.

Ask yourself ?

- During what hours does the contractor plan to work?

- How does the contractor plan to keep dust and construction debris to a minimum?

- Has the contractor made plans for the work in such a way that access to your home will not be blocked?

Along these same lines, many builders like to have a radio playing while they work. If this disturbs you or the neighbors, especially if anyone is studying or working at home, raise this issue. Most builders are reasonable people, and as long as your requirement is presented as a firm request and not an order, you should expect that they will do their best to compromise.

Don't start by assuming the worst. Greet workers anytime you come face to face, and communicate with them to break the ice and establish a rapport. However, remember that subcontractors work for the contractor, not you. If you have complaints relating to behavior or anything else, take them up directly with the contractor.

Restricting dust

There is always a certain amount of dust or mess involved in building work, and most contractors will do their best to ensure that this does not intrude into the living areas. Responsibility for preventing dust and construction debris from escaping the work zone is often written into the contract. Where dust is unavoidable, such as when an interior wall or ceiling is taken down, the builder should seal off the area from the rest of the house by fastening polyethylene sheeting over doors and windows and along passages used by workers to the outside. Carpets and other floor coverings are best removed first, but if this is not possible, they should be covered with drop cloths or other protective material. One method is to cover the floor with two layers of polyethylene sheeting; at the end of each day the top layer can be disposed of with any debris and a new layer set down for the next day's work. When demolition is involved, plywood panels can be arranged on top of the plastic to protect the floors from chunks of debris and to make it easier to shovel up any waste. Dust levels can be kept low by regular vacuum cleaning.

Avoiding obstructions

Maintaining safe, unobstructed access to the property during construction is important for everyone, so builders should be instructed to do their best not to block paths, driveways, and passageways with materials and to keep them clean and free of litter and debris. By the same token, your contractor may have you agree to a clause in the contract requiring you and others, including pets, to stay out of the work area at all times unless you are with the contractor and to enter work zones with increased awareness of the inevitable safety hazards.

During working hours, stay out of the way and let the professionals do their work. Resist the urge to look over their shoulders and to complain about small issues. You should respect the skills of the professionals involved by letting the work proceed without interference.

Complete remodeling of a kitchen or bathroom may mean making other arrangements for eating and bathing until the work is finished.

Don't forget !

- Write into the contract any agreed-upon policies that will keep interruptions to a minimum.

- Ensure that measures are taken to limit the amount of noise created before 8:00 AM and after 5:00 PM.

- Allow the professionals to do their work with as little interference from you as possible.

1 Handling disputes

Getting construction work done on your home sounds like a relatively simple process—a building contractor does the work and you pay him some money. But, unfortunately, in real life construction is a complicated job.

Every building situation is somewhat different, and contractors and homeowners often have differing interpretations of what is expected and of how a project is proceeding. Even the best contracts cannot capture every detail and provide for each and every eventuality.

Avoiding problems

Open and frequent communication is the best way to avoid problems. Discuss issues as they come up. If a dispute does arise, to prevent it from getting out of hand, take pains to settle the matter calmly.

You should consider the following: A contractor's reputation is crucial to his or her livelihood, and for that reason more than any other, he or she will usually be reluctant to pursue an issue that will foster ill feeling with a client, even if the client is actually at fault. In addition, a dispute that escalates so much that it involves attorneys and legal maneuvers can quickly become expensive and time consuming for both parties. However, bear in mind that construction projects are often accomplished on small margins and under tight deadlines with regard to payrolls and subcontractor availability; and any unresolved disputes that threaten a contractor's ability to pay bills and complete a project on time will generate justifiable attempts for legal recourse.

Requesting changes

Probably the most frequent sources of conflict are requests for changes to the work during the course of a project. Homeowners may want to

The more involved a renovation is, the more likely that problems will arise. You can avoid confrontation with the professionals by going over all the details thoroughly during the early stages and throughout the project.

make changes because they prefer using a more attractive—and more expensive—material, for example; or the cost of the project may be rising too sharply due to unforeseen problems, so they may want to reduce the scale of the project.

Contractors may also request a change to the project—for example, if conditions behind walls are worse than expected or different than described in the contract.

Change orders

It is crucial that all requests for changes be made in writing and not simply communicated verbally. A well-written contract (see pp. 20–21) will include a clause requiring all change requests, however large or small, to be written up and signed off on by both parties prior to the work being performed.

Although a change order can be written on ordinary paper or onto the contract, most contractors will prefer to use a printed change-order form, which clearly describes the change, its effect on the contract price, and the date when payment for the change is due. (Payment is usually due when the work is completed or at the time of the next progress payment. This should be specified in the contract.)

Most changes add to the contract price; however, some changes—for example, opting for a lesser-grade material than is specified in the contract—may decrease the price; the contractor should credit the homeowner. Some changes may not affect the contract price at all; that fact, too, should be stated in writing.

Legal recourse

What if a dispute does become insurmountable? Any well-written contract will stipulate agreed-upon courses of action. Where small amounts of money are involved, small-claims court is usually the best answer (see box, below) once negotiation has failed.

If the dispute is complicated or involves more money than the limit for small claims court, arbitration is often the resolution method specified. Lawyers may be present for both parties, which automatically raises the costs of seeking settlement, and there is a healthy administrative fee charged by the state or arbitration association for bringing the case together. Nevertheless, arbitration hearings are a less expensive and less time-consuming option than full-blown civil court litigation.

In arbitration, instead of a judge, arguments are heard by either a state-appointed or a contract-specified construction arbiter, who is often a member of the American Arbitration Association (see pp. 168–171). Ample time is given to hearing and weighing the issues, and the whole

process often takes only a few months compared with the one or two years it frequently takes to move such cases through the civil courts.

Depending on the language of the construction contract, arbitration can be binding or nonbinding. With binding arbitration, both sides agree to abide by the arbiter's decision on how to resolve a case. With nonbinding arbitration, or mediation, neither side has to accept the arbiter's decision; however, specifying this type of resolution in a contract does provide both sides the opportunity to present grievances in front of an unbiased third party, which often clears the air sufficiently for the dispute to be resolved.

If you do decide on civil court litigation—which is not the recommended course of action—be prepared to spend a considerable sum of money on legal and court fees; also, you could wait years instead of months for settlement.

Alternative choices !

Small claims court is the bottom rung in the state civil court system. In most states, the amount cannot exceed $5,000, and, in some states, the amount is even less. Persons pursuing judgments in small claims court may not be allowed to bring attorneys; in many states the proceedings involve only the plaintiff, defendant, and a judge.

The advantages of small claims court are that it is economical and speedy once a court date is scheduled, which may take 60 to 90 days. The disadvantages are that on a busy day neither side may get more than a few minutes to present his or her side of the case, and plaintiffs who lose cannot appeal to a higher court.

At the end of a remodeling project, both the homeowner and the contractor need to assess the work. The latter, who generally has the experience of many similar jobs to draw on, may declare the work substantially finished, but the former may not agree.

The contractor will come to a point where he or she perceives the work as substantially finished by the terms of the contract and so wants to be paid off, with the understanding that a few return visits may be needed to take care of minor follow-ups. (Callbacks, as they are called, are routine, especially after major work.)

However, the homeowner may spot problems that seem anything but trivial. If he or she is unsure of what "substantially finished" is, he or she may justifiably believe the problems should be remedied before the final payment is made, in case the contractor vanishes afterward.

Settling up

Both parties generally have legitimate arguments. A well-written contract can save the day. There are two general ways to deal with settling up at the end of a project. One is to agree on delaying the final payment by a reasonable time period—often 10 to 30 days—past the date the contractor declares the project substantially finished. (The definition of "substantially finished," as it relates to the project, should be clearly spelled out in the contract.) This period allows time for the homeowner, or the architect or designer if one is hired, to inspect the project in detail and create a so-called punch list of items to be completed before the final payment is made. (In practice, a punch list often is started much earlier in the project by the contractor as a way of keeping tabs on subcontractors' work.)

Unfinished work and missing items such as hardware belong on the punch list; so do reminders to obtain all remaining inspections and the

Rules & regulations

Expect any contractor to guarantee the quality of all work performed and materials used, including labor and materials supplied by subcontractors. The terms of the warranty should be detailed in the contract.

A warranty lasts for one year from completion and may include implied warranties imposed by state laws. Many materials carry manufacturers' warranties that provide for replacement (but not labor costs) if they are defective. The contractor should give you all warranty certificates and other information supplied with these items.

certificate of occupancy, if needed, to receive all warranty certificates, owner's manuals, and other literature for equipment or materials that have been installed, and to obtain signed lien releases from all potential claimants. The contractor and homeowner or homeowner's representative then go over the punch list and agree on the tasks that need finishing; some may not fall within the contract and others may be covered by warranties that legally can take longer to fulfill. When the items are completed, the final check is written.

Hold-back clause

The second way to settle up is to make the final payment on time, but to withhold a portion of it—usually about 5 percent—until the punch list items are completed. A so-called hold-back clause can be written into the contract to allow this. While it may not provide as much incentive for a contractor to complete the punch list promptly as delaying the entire final payment, if you have a good relationship with the contractor and trust that the work will get done, then this alternative is the most equitable. Generally, a hold-back clause allows the contractor to pay the remaining subcontractors and suppliers, close the books on the project, and get on with the next one, while still guaranteeing that he or she will return to perform the finishing touches.

Liens

Most states allow contractors and others who furnish labor or materials to your home to file a claim—called a mechanic's lien—against your property if they are not paid. You can find yourself subjected to a mechanic's lien even if you have paid your contractor on time and in full. If the contractor has not paid his or her subcontractors or suppliers, they can seek restitution from you, despite your having already paid the contractor money that was intended for them. In some extreme cases, foreclosure proceedings can be instituted to sell your house to generate the funds.

As the homeowner, you are legally responsible for seeing that all bills relating to the construction on your house have been completely paid. You must, therefore, make sure that the ability of the contractor to expose you to liens is kept

The workers may pack up their tools and clear the site before the final details are applied. Although the caulking and weatherstripping of this addition occurred a week after the site clearance, there was no reason not to occupy it.

When to inspect !

- As the renovation progresses, inspect the project for general quality of workmanship, but also keep an eye open for the finishing details.

- After the tradespeople clear the work site, thoroughly check all the details. Make a list of any missing items and incomplete or unacceptable work.

- With the project "substantially finished," look through all your paperwork to ensure that you have all the documentation necessary; this should include the certificate of occupancy and any warranties.

to a minimum. The best way to do this is to make sure certain clauses appear in your contract.

Lien release documents

Stipulate in the contract that as progress payments are made and before the final payment is made, you are to receive signed lien release documents from all subcontractors, materials providers, and others stating they have been paid in full, and that each of those potential claimants releases you from lien claims.

Even with this clause in your contract, you may receive so-called preliminary lien notices from subcontractors and suppliers during the course of the project. These documents simply state the right of those providers to claim a lien if circumstances warrant. Laws in most states stipulate that such notices must be delivered within certain time limits or else the claimant loses the right to file a lien at a later date, so these notices are routinely sent out. As long as the clause is in your contract, there is no need to be alarmed.

How the experts can improve your home

2

Whether you've just moved into a new house or have been in your home for a few years, there are bound to be ways that you want to improve it. Home improvements can be simple—perhaps simply a new coat of paint on the walls. However, the more ambitious homeowner may want to add or knock down walls, convert a basement or attic, build on an addition, or upgrade the wiring or heating. Whatever the changes are, the experts are often the best ones to do the work for you.

Incorporating new details into a room—such as the wall-mounted lighting fixtures, the borders framing the walls, and the patio door in this living room—are best achieved with professional help.

2 | Interior improvements

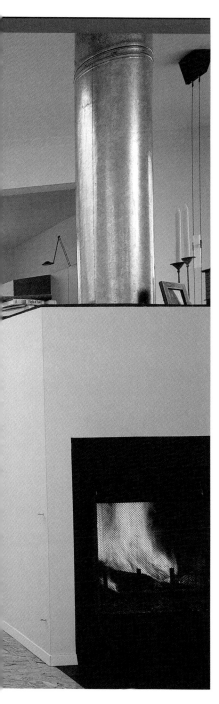

The typical modern home has rooms designed for a vast array of activities, from an eat-in kitchen and exercise room to an entertainment center and home office. With the activities in these rooms come furniture, equipment, and other belongings, so interior improvements must be carefully planned to be practical, as well as to provide ample storage space.

However, for most people the home is also a special retreat. It is equally important to develop a style that will enhance its appearance and comfort, as well as reflect your personal taste. A professional can help you decide on a plan that incorporates all of these elements, creating a home that meets the needs of each member of the family.

Having a well-equipped and tastefully decorated kitchen (far left) adds to the pleasure of preparing meals for the family. An open-plan area comprising of a dining room and living room (left) creates a feeling of spaciousness that cannot be experienced in two separate rooms.

Despite the popularity of do-it-yourself—home decorating in particular—there are many people who either do not want to do the job themselves or feel that their skills are not polished enough to achieve the finish they want.

For those people who don't want to redecorate a room themselves, the answer is to call in the professionals. Their expertise will help create a room to suit your taste.

Choosing the scale

You first have to think about the scale of the work you want a professional decorator to do for you. You may simply have a room that needs brightening with a coat of new paint on the walls and ceiling and perhaps a change of color for the woodwork. A more ambitious plan could involve stripping the old wallpaper and hanging something new, along with perhaps the addition of a decorative crown, chair, or picture rail molding. The most extensive task would be a complete indoor makeover—new decor throughout the house—perhaps after moving into a new property or simply as a serious update to a house you have occupied but not redecorated for several years.

Color selection

If you have a clear idea of the paint colors and wallpaper patterns you want to use, simply give them to your decorator and let him or her do the estimating and purchasing. The advantage to this plan is that a professionally licensed decorator can often obtain the materials at a greater discount than you can; your cost will probably be less, even after allowing for the markup the decorator adds as profit. Also, any errors made in quantities will be the decorator's responsibility—not yours.

If you are unsure about color and pattern, a good decorator will be happy to give you advice. He or she may try out a range of paint colors, possibly applying them to the walls and woodwork in small patches, and will bring wallpaper samples for you to look at in place. Inspect colors in both natural and artificial light, and take your time deciding what looks best. Think carefully before making your final choice. If you do not like the results and want them changed, your costs will escalate.

A large room can handle strong colors such as the green used on these walls. To prevent the color from becoming overpowering, white is used on the ceiling and wood trim, as well as in the drapery and bed linen.

Rules & regulations

Federal standards regulate VOC levels in coatings manufactured in the United States. The standards are expressed in pounds of VOCs per gallon. Containers of paint and finishes manufactured in compliance with the standards must display the date of manufacture and either the amount of VOCs contained or the VOC content limit with which the coating complies.

If you experience unpleasant side effects when exposed to fresh paint or other finishes, ask the decorator to use ones that are lower in VOCs than the standards specify.

DIY jargon !

VOC An abbreviation for volatile organic compounds, which are carbon-based chemicals similar to those found in gasoline. They are used as solvents in paints and are now regarded as harmful if inhaled regularly or in large quantities. Traditional gloss and semigloss paints, and clear finishes, have very high VOC levels, while in latex and other water-based paints the levels are much lower.

Neutral colors provide a calm setting for this living room. The designer has used various shades of white and beige to create the look. Natural materials, such as the rattan furniture, also have a calming effect.

Technical advice

If you are looking for dramatic changes, you can trust your own taste or seek the help of an interior designer. He or she can offer complete remodeling and decoration, including carpets and soft furnishings such as drapery and upholstery.

Apart from getting help in making the right choice of color scheme, you may also need professional advice about choosing the best types of decorating materials. In particular, knowing the pros and cons of the various options will guide you toward making informed choices instead of relying on guesswork. For example, if you have small children, you should have walls decorated with materials that are tough, stain-resistant, and easy to keep clean. In kitchens and bathrooms, you should be looking for hygienic and waterproof surfaces that help to discourage condensation and mold.

If you have had previous problems, such as flaking paint, stains, or discoloration, that seem to have come from within in the house, a professional decorator or an interior designer will be able to guide you on product choice and suggest solutions to these problems to avoid them recurring in the future.

Choosing paints

Materials for interior decorating fall into several categories: paint for walls and ceilings; paint for wood and metal; clear finishes for wood; wallcoverings (see pp. 38–39); tiles for walls; and tiles and sheet materials for floors (see pp. 40–43).

Latex paint is the standard choice for walls and ceilings. Paint from the best-selling brands is relatively inexpensive, but designer colors from specialist paintmakers can be expensive. Latex paint is quick-drying and has a low VOC content.

There are several levels of paint sheen: gloss, semigloss, satin (or low-luster), eggshell, and flat (or matte). Gloss or semigloss paint is the traditional finish for wood trim and metal. Until recent years, these paints were solvent-based, with a high VOC content. Today, the trend is toward using water-based paints for trim and metal, as well as for walls, and the latest formulations are as durable as their solvent-based relations. When specifying the finish you want, remember that a high gloss highlights any imperfections in the surface, and a less reflective finish is more forgiving.

Wood finishes

Clear finishes for wood can be applied to existing woodwork, either as a new layer over an existing clear finish or as a new finish on stripped or refurbished woodwork. Varnishes are basically paint without pigment, and like paint can be solvent- or water-based. The finish may be a high gloss or a softer satin look. Both give a durable and easy-to-clean finish. If you want to color the wood grain but not obscure it, an all-in-one stain sealer will give a medium depth of color, while a wood stain followed by clear varnish will give a stronger effect.

Selecting a wallcovering !

While there is an almost endless variety of wallcovering patterns, the types of wallcoverings available fall into only a few groups.

PAPER WALLPAPER
pros: Least expensive type of wallcovering; vinyl-coated type is easy to strip
cons: Tears easily

VINYL WALLCOVERING
pros: Easy to wipe clean; solid vinyl type is available for high-moisture areas
cons: Expensive

EXPANDED VINYL WALLCOVERING
pros: Good for uneven walls
cons: Medium durability; moderately expensive

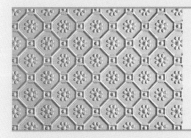

HIGH-RELIEF WALLCOVERING
pros: Hides uneven wall surfaces, especially on plaster walls; durable; can be painted
cons: Needs expert installation

SILK WALLCOVERING
pros: Some types have luxurious patterns with better detail than paper or vinyl wallcoverings
cons: Very expensive; requires professional installation

Wallcoverings

In general, wallcoverings—which are also called wallpapers—are either covered with a printed design or textured. Most are intended to provide a decorative finish, but some are used either as a backing for fragile wallpapers or to strengthen and mask failing plaster.

Printed wallcoverings may be just paper, washable wallpaper (printed paper with a clear surface coating that can be wiped clean), or vinyl (printed plastic with a paper backing); see the chart, left, for more details. Prices vary widely, especially for designer-printed wallpapers and luxury vinyls. Specialty wallcoverings include materials such as silk and grass cloth. They are very expensive, so they are usually hung for effect in small feature areas.

Ceramic tiles

Although paint and wallcoverings decorate most walls in the house, there are two rooms—the kitchen and bathroom—where another material, ceramic tile, is often used. There are ceramic floor tiles too, plus a range of other floor coverings available in unit and sheet form (see pp. 40–43).

Tiled surfaces are immensely durable. Ceramic wall tiles come in a huge range of colors and designs. Because of their small size, they are easy to install, although tiling a large area and grouting (filling) the joints between the tiles can be time-consuming. The only major drawbacks to tiles are that, due to their cold surface, tiled walls can create condensation in steamy rooms and that the tiles themselves are expensive when compared with other decorative materials. `

Standard wall tiles are available in 4½ x 4½-inch (115 x 115-mm)

Wallcoverings with a subtle pattern can add color to a room and provide a background for furnishings.

Tiled surfaces are waterproof and easy to clean, making them an ideal choice for bathrooms and kitchens.

Unusual paint effects can be created with special techniques that are best achieved by a skilled professional.

squares, 6-inch (150-mm) squares, and 4½ x 6-inch (115 x 150-mm) rectangles; they are ⁵⁄₁₆ inch (8 mm) thick. Sheets of about 64 tiles, uniformly spaced and mounted on a permanent backing, are also available; they are considerably quicker to install. There is also a wide range of border and motif tiles that can add to the attractiveness of tiled walls.

Final choices

Although the major skill an interior designer brings to the job is the ability to turn a client's vague ideas into reality, he or she will also have access to manufacturers' catalogs, as well as industry-only suppliers, not available to nonprofessionals. The designer will be able to draw on a huge database to find the products you want in the colors and patterns you like. However, don't expect the service to be inexpensive, especially if you take a long time to agree on a color scheme or if you use a designer who commissions or refers you to professional decorators to do the work.

The designer will visit your home, discuss your intentions, and take note of any existing furniture, furnishings, and decorative features that are to be incorporated in the new color scheme. By the next visit,

sketches, color cards, sample fabric swatches, and design suggestions will have been developed, and your comments will be invited. Sooner or later you will arrive at a color scheme you like, and final designs (or a computer-generated printout) will be provided for your approval.

When work starts

The worker—painter, wallpaperer, or carpenter—will need unrestricted access to the rooms being decorated, at least during working hours. The first job will be to move the furniture, either out of the room if it's easily portable or into the center, where it will be covered with drop cloths—as will the floor. The next step will be to take down any wall or ceiling fixtures, such as shelves and lighting, and mark their positions so they can be replaced later. Any surfaces that aren't being decorated will be masked off. It's a good idea to remove valuable items, take down curtains and blinds, and disconnect home entertainment equipment yourself before work starts.

What happens next depends on the scale of the job. For repainting, washing the walls and ceiling and repairing surface defects are all that is necessary before work can begin.

For wallpapering, the paperer may have to strip an existing wallcovering or treat painted walls with sizing before hanging the new material. With painting or papering, ceilings are normally done first, then walls, trim, and items such as radiators.

When to inspect !

- It is best to inspect the work at the end of each day, after the worker has left.

- Check newly painted surfaces for any signs of runs, bits of bristle or debris in the surface film, incomplete coverage, and any other imperfections.

- With wallcoverings, look for lifting seams and poorly trimmed ends, and for large blisters that are often the result of incomplete pasting. Don't panic if you discover a rash of small blisters; these disappear as the paper dries out, leaving a completely flat surface.

- Don't be afraid to point out any defects to the worker and ask for them to be fixed. Any faults not corrected now will only annoy you in the future.

All floor coverings have a finite life, and there comes a time when you will need replacements. Furthermore, colors and designs tend to become unfashionable as interior design tastes change.

Whatever your reason for wanting new floor coverings, there is a strong case for calling in professional help. A professional undoubtedly costs more, whereas your own labor is free, but a professional does guarantee that there will not be any expensive mistakes, such as cutting sheet materials in the wrong place or having tiles lift and wood floors warp. Poor do-it-yourself workmanship soon shows and is hard to fix.

High-quality work

Ensuring that the floor covering is laid properly is particularly important in the case of wall-to-wall carpet. The carpet has to be laid under slight tension, with the edges anchored over tackless strips fitted around the perimeter of the room. Without this tension, the carpet will stretch slightly underfoot and will be wrinkled by furniture being moved over it. Getting the tension right involves hooking one edge of the carpet onto its tackless strip and then using a special tool called a knee kicker to stretch it, first down the length of the room to the opposite strip, then out to the strips along the side walls.

Sheet vinyl also requires a professional hand if it is to be laid and fitted well. The sheet has to be accurately trimmed to fit snugly against the perimeter walls, and it has to be fitted neatly around any floor-level obstacles such as toilets, washbasin pedestals, and kitchen cabinets. It then has to be cemented around the edges and at door openings with flooring adhesive or double-sided tape.

DIY jargon !

Tackless strip A narrow strip of plywood with short nails punched through it so all the points are angled toward one edge of the strip. It is designed to anchor the edges of wall-to-wall carpet once it has been laid and stretched. Strips are installed around the room at a distance of 1 inch (25 mm) from the baseboard, with their teeth facing the wall; they are nailed to wood floors and cemented to solid ones with adhesive. Special all-metal strips are installed at doorways.

While vinyl tiles are suited to do-it-yourself installation, it is wise to leave ceramic and quarry tiles to the experts. The subflooring (see pp. 142–143) needs careful preparation to ensure smoothness and stability; otherwise tiles may crack. The tiles themselves must be evenly bedded in the appropriate adhesive, and the joints filled with grout once the adhesive has set. As long as the job is done properly, the resulting floor should last a lifetime.

Vinyls and tiles

Floor coverings come in quantities of individual units or in rolled sheets. "Unit" materials include ceramic floor tiles and vinyl tiles.

Ceramic floor tiles are thicker than wall tiles. They may be glazed with a single color or a printed design, or they may be unglazed. A popular variety of unglazed floor tile is called quarry tile. All ceramic tile is extremely durable but also cold and noisy underfoot. Ceramic floor tiles come in a variety of square, rectangular, and interlocking shapes.

Vinyl tiles are squares of solid plastic designed to be cemented to the floor. Less expensive types are usually plain colors or simple printed patterns; more expensive varieties can imitate other floor coverings such as parquet, brick, and mosaic. They form a durable floor that's easy to keep clean.

Sheet vinyl is the modern replacement for linoleum. It comes in a variety of designs and thicknesses, with and without cushioned backing. This relatively inexpensive flooring is waterproof, resilient, and comfortable underfoot, especially if a cushioned type is chosen. Sheet vinyl is sold by the linear yard (meter) in standard widths of 6 and 12 feet (1,830 and 3,660 mm), enabling you to have a seamless floor in all but the largest rooms.

Wood flooring

Decorative wood flooring is available in two main forms—tiles and boards—and in a wide variety of wood types. Strips are boards less than 3 inches (75 mm) wide; they are either solid or laminated, with tongue-and-groove edges that interlock to form a flat, stable decorative surface. Wider boards are known as planks. The boards can be nailed down or held together by a system of hidden clips. The resulting floor is attractive, long-lasting, and easy

Durable and exquisite, a slate floor will last the life of a kitchen. Slates are available in both regular and irregular shapes.

Ask yourself

• What type of room will the floor covering be in? For example, avoid carpet for floors exposed to moisture, such as in kitchens and bathrooms.

• How often do people walk in and out of a room? Rooms that are used a lot should have a durable floor covering.

• Have you thought about colors? Dark carpets are more likely to hide stains but light colors can make a small room seem larger.

to keep clean, making it a popular alternative to wall-to-wall carpets.

Parquet tiles are made by bonding small fingers of wood (usually presealed) to a fabric backing. Alternatively, the fingers can be joined by splines (thin strips of wood) and glue. The tiles are available in a range of sizes. Parquet flooring is cemented to the subfloor (or to an underlayment attached to the subfloor) to create a smooth surface.

Carpets

One of the most common forms of roll, or sheet, flooring materials is carpet. Carpeting is, of course, made in plain colors and in an enormous range of woven designs. It offers a floor surface that is warm and luxurious underfoot, as well as durable. You should select an appropriate grade; for example, rooms that will get heavy traffic—where people go in and out of the area often—need durable carpets. Carpet is sold by the linear yard, in standard widths of 9, 12, and 15 feet (2,745, 3,660, and 4,575 mm).

The biggest drawback to carpet is that it can harbor dust and house mites, both potential causes of allergic reactions in sensitive people.

Replacing floor coverings

Selecting a floor covering !

Before choosing one of the variety of floor coverings available, consider which material best suits the needs of the room it will be in.

CERAMIC FLOOR TILES
pros: Durable; water resistance makes them a good choice for kitchens and bathrooms
cons: Cold and noisy to walk on

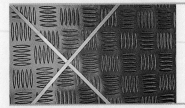

VINYL TILES
pros: Inexpensive; easy to lay
cons: Prone to lifting at edges

SHEET VINYL
pros: Inexpensive; some have a cushioned backing—they are more comfortable to walk on
cons: Can be slippery when wet; susceptible to damage

CARPET
pros: Comfortable; quiet; suitable for most rooms
cons: Harbors allergens; better-quality ones are expensive

SISAL
pros: Warm, natural appearance; durable
cons: May need to be woven with wool to make it softer, but this increases price

WOOD FLOORING
pros: Natural beauty; ages gracefully; solid types can be refinished
cons: Can be noisy to walk on; easily damaged by water

Before work starts

Choosing what type of floor covering to have is only part of the selection process. Being aware of what will be involved in laying different floor coverings will help you to understand the scale, complexity, and expense of the job, and will enable you to inspect the end result knowledgeably when it is finished.

Rooms where new floor coverings are being laid have to be cleared of all standing furniture and other items. Find out beforehand whether this chore is your responsibility or whether it is part of the job you will be paying the installer for.

Removing old flooring

Once the floor is cleared, the first step will be to remove the old floor covering. With carpet, the installer or an assistant will free it from the tackless strips and roll it up; then he or she will lift and remove the old padding. (It is false economy to retain this, as crumbling old padding will cause the new carpet to wear prematurely.) The installer may also decide to replace the tackless strips or to install additional ones.

With sheet vinyl, if it cannot be left in place (see facing page), the installer will slice it into strips, which will then be rolled as they are lifted. Older sheet vinyl (installed prior to 1986) may contain asbestos. In that case, the same procedure will be used but extra precautions will be taken to eliminate airborne dust during the removal process and to thoroughly vacuum the area afterward. If you think your vinyl flooring contains asbestos, make sure that your installer is experienced in removing it safely and is properly qualified to do so if regulations in your community specify this.

A floor with plain tiles can be enhanced by setting them off with inset tiles that fit in the corners.

A wooden floor can be left unstained but protected by a varnish, or it can be stained.

Laying ceramic tiles

Ceramic and quarry tiles are usually arranged, or "dry-laid," on the floor to ensure proper spacing and to keep border tiles (they may be cut to fill the edges) the same width along opposite walls. If the tiles are going over a wood floor, the tilesetter will cover it with a substrate layer of plywood or cement backer board to provide a stable surface for the tiles. The setter will find the center of the room, plan the layout, and fasten wood guide strips to the floor in one corner of the room to provide an accurate starting point. He or she will lay the whole tiles in sections from the starting point toward the doorway of the room, and leave the floor to harden overnight before returning to cut and fit the border tiles and grout, or fill, the joints. Quarry tiles are finished by applying sealer to them after the grout has cured.

Vinyl flooring containing asbestos and most cemented resilient flooring, such as cork, vinyl, and asphalt tile, is often best left in place beneath the new flooring. If necessary, latex floor-leveling compound can be spread over the old flooring to provide a smooth surface for the new flooring, or plywood underlayment (usually ¼ inch/6 mm thick) can be installed instead.

Ceramic and quarry tiles have to be either broken away one by one—a job that is costly and extremely labor-intensive—or else covered with floor-leveling compound if there are no problems with raising the floor level slightly by adding the new floor covering on top of the compound.

Floor preparation

Once the subfloor is exposed, the installer will check that the floorboards are secure, nail down any that are loose, and sink below the surface any nails that have worked upward and could damage the new floor covering. If a dusty concrete floor is being prepared, it will be sealed to stop dust from rising through carpeting and to improve the adhesion of sheet vinyl and floor tiles.

Laying carpet

Before the carpet goes down, new padding must be laid. This is cut to fit against the inside edges of the tackless strips and should be slightly beveled with a knife so it can't ride up onto the stips when the carpet is being stretched. Padding is stapled to the floor at 6-inch (150-mm) intervals around the perimeter and butt-joined where pieces meet. Some installers use double-sided tape under the seams. The carpet itself is cut roughly to size, then stretched into place before trimming.

Laying sheet vinyl

Sheet vinyl is laid in a similar way, being rough-cut, then trimmed to fit and cemented down at the edges, seams, and thresholds. The exception is when it is fitted in a bathroom or kitchen, where the sheet has to fit closely around basin pedestals, tubs, toilets, and base cabinets. Some installers can scribe and cut vinyl freehand around these obstacles, but others make a paper template of the whole floor, then scribe the room's perimeter and obstacle outlines onto the sheet before cutting it out and dropping it into place.

When to inspect !

- When the job is finished, make sure that carpet edges are neatly tucked into the gap between the tackless strips and the baseboard, and that the seams are well matched and securely bonded to the carpet tape beneath.

- Check that sheet vinyl is perfectly trimmed all around, with no overcuts visible, that it is lying flat, and that it is securely fastened beneath threshold strips at doorways.

- Inspect ceramic and quarry tiles by laying a straightedge across the surface to check that all the tiles are level, and check that all the grout lines are evenly filled.

- Where appropriate, check that doors have been shortened enough at the bottom to clear a new floor level comfortably.

Remodeling kitchens

One of the most popular home improvements is remodeling the kitchen. A well-designed layout makes the kitchen work far more efficiently and accommodates your family's needs. It can be expensive, but it is a good investment if you sell your house.

Ask yourself ?

• Is the kitchen where your family and friends socialize?

• How active are you in the kitchen—do you use it just to heat convenience foods or are you a gourmet cook who requires plenty of work space?

• Do you use mostly fresh food, canned food, or frozen food? This will affect your storage space—you may need more cabinets, a larger freezer, or extra vegetable storage space.

• Have you thought about where to place essential elements? Are they within easy reach of your work area or near other items you often use with them?

Cabinets provide storage for everything from tableware to dry goods such as cereal. Baking items are best stored near the oven, while glass and china should be stored near the sink. Doors and drawer fronts may be solid wood or veneered with wood or plastic, and they can be stained or painted. Glass doors are an option on wall cabinets if you want to display the contents.

The surface behind the stove and sink and the countertop where you prepare food should be made of a durable material to withstand food spills and water splashes. Ceramic tiles are an ideal choice; other materials to use are post-form laminate and synthetic stone.

In a large kitchen, an island provides additional storage and countertop work space. Some islands have a protruding edge, so that people can sit around it on high stools to eat an informal meal.

Ceramic floor tiles made for heavy-traffic areas are ideal in kitchens because they won't be stained by dropped food or spills; however, they can be noisy to walk on and cold to bare feet in the winter. Other materials to consider include laminated wood flooring and sheet vinyl—but choose a stain-resistant vinyl.

The complete remodel

The most common kitchen remodel involves stripping out everything in the room and starting over from scratch. You should choose this option if your kitchen is poorly laid out or has out-of-date equipment. Professional kitchen installers will provide a complete package deal, including new built-in cabinets, countertops, and appliances.

They start by planning the layout of the new kitchen and selecting the type and arrangement of the kitchen units. The planning is often done using a computer program, which allows you to see how the room will look from various angles and lets you refine the plan until you are satisfied with the proposals. The installers then order all the components and carry out the work.

The facelift

If the cost of a complete remodel is too high or your kitchen works well but looks a little old-fashioned, consider giving it a simple facelift. Practically all kitchen cabinets are built the same way, from materials that last for years under most circumstances. Because the style of most cabinets is determined by the design of the doors and the drawer fronts, replacing or refacing these is often enough to produce a completely different look, which can be further enhanced by replacing the countertops. A facelift will update your kitchen for far less than the cost of a complete remodel, and with far less upheaval—the work may take no more than a day.

Extending the kitchen

Your kitchen may be too small for your needs. The kitchens in many older homes were designed solely for cooking, and no amount of clever planning can find space in them for an eating area. Today's appliances also require more room.

The only solution is to enlarge the kitchen, either by adding an addition, if you have room to build one, or by borrowing floor space from an adjoining room. For example, some older houses have a pantry next to the kitchen; the dividing walls could be removed to create extra space. If the dining room is next door, knocking through the wall between them would enable you to turn the two rooms into a large combination kitchen-and-dining room.

Using another room

The last resort is to tear out what you have and install a new kitchen in another room. For example, a larger dining room could become the kitchen, leaving the smaller room for the occasional use most dining rooms get. You could use a living room as the kitchen, and knock through the existing kitchen and adjacent room to create a large living space. The difficulty with this type of relocation lies in rerouting wiring and plumbing, which can be challenging and expensive.

DIY jargon !

Carcass The wood, metal, or plastic "skeleton" frame of a kitchen unit, or cabinet, to which the decorative surface and door is attached.

Carousel Storage device installed in a cabinet; it pivots from a central point, giving more efficient access to the cabinet's contents. It is useful in cabinets placed in a corner, where items are normally difficult to retrieve.

Post-form laminate A material used in kitchens as a counter-top; it consists of a core (a less attractive, inexpensive material) covered with a decorative veneer, or thin top layer.

Planning the kitchen

If you decide a complete renovation is what your kitchen needs, there is a lot of homework you can do before calling in the professionals. You may think this job is theirs, but the process will help you answer many questions you'll be asked and will also make it easier for you to decide on the final results.

The first issue to think about is the layout of your kitchen. The aim of all kitchen planning is to keep the size of the work triangle, the area between the three essential food preparation centers—the sink, range, and refrigerator—to a minimum. This will be determined primarily by the shape of the room, unless you decide to extend it (see p. 45).

Typical kitchens

The smallest of kitchens can only have cabinets and appliances along one wall. A larger rectangular room with a doorway at each end works best as a galley kitchen, with cabinets and appliances against the two long walls and enough room in between to work at the units. In a more square room, cabinets and appliances

Facts & figures

Prebuilt face-frame base cabinets are 34 inches (865 mm) high (36 inches/ 915 mm high with the countertop) and 24 inches (610 mm) deep to suit American appliances; they come in several widths. Euro-style cabinets are slightly deeper. Be sure prebuilt or ready-to-assemble (RTA) Euro-style cabinets suit the height and depth of your kitchen appliances or that your installer will build out walls or add shims to bring all surfaces flush.

against adjacent walls in an L-shape is a practical layout. All the working traffic is confined to the triangular area within the L. The classic U-shape can fit in a large kitchen.

Some homes combine the kitchen and a living area in one large room. The kitchen units are placed along one wall and an island separates the kitchen area from the living area. The island, which can also be used in a large kitchen, can be a counter-top with a built-in range or cooktop with a ventilation hood above it (unless the cooktop is equipped with a downdraft ventilator), a counter-top and sink, a butcher block, or simply a sturdy table plus chairs.

Washing up

Sinks fit best against an outside wall, beneath a window, but corner sinks are available and sinks can be installed in islands. You can select from dozens of bowl and faucet combinations. Whether you choose a single-, double-, or triple-bowl sink, make sure at least one bowl is large enough to allow you to fill big pots with water and to wash large dishes and pans with ease, even if you have a dishwasher. Dishwashers

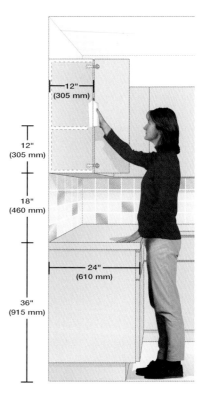

12"
(305 mm)

12"
(305 mm)

18"
(460 mm)

24"
(610 mm)

36"
(915 mm)

The countertop should be at a comfortable height for preparing foods; the wall-hung cabinets should be high enough to provide space for working on the countertop below, yet within reach to store items in them.

should be near a sink for easy connection to its drainpipe. Consider a waste disposal unit installed under the sink if your municipality allows them. (Disposals are not recommended if you have a septic system.)

Kitchen appliances

Refrigerators and freezers can go almost anywhere, but be sure the doors open without obstructing other appliances.

In cooking equipment, you have the option of a freestanding, slide-in, or drop-in range, or a separate cooktop and oven—or ovens. Freestanding ranges rest directly on the floor and fit between cabinets. Slide-in ranges rest on the floor and have finished sides, but they require a custom-built backsplash. Drop-in ranges are similar to slide-ins but must be installed in a base cabinet designed for them. Cooktops also require a special base cabinet. Freestanding ovens, either single or double, are installed in walls. Most ranges are all-gas or all-electric; but some "gourmet" ranges feature gas cooktop burners and electric ovens.

Choosing cabinets and countertops

Kitchen cabinets can be purchased ready-made or can be custom-built. Conventional face-frame cabinets consist of partitioned units made of plywood or particleboard, to the front of which is attached a frame of thin hardwood lumber. Cabinet doors are attached to the frame with surface hinges; drawer and door fronts match the frame. Modular or Euro-style, cabinets are becoming popular. These are individual boxes installed side by side and feature specially hinged flush doors.

Standard countertops are made of plywood, medium-density fiberboard (MDF), or particleboard faced with plastic laminate. Better-quality countertops include ceramic tile and synthetic stone (see p. 48).

In addition to determining what will fit in the room, you should consider the placement of the appliances, cabinets, and other features to make working in the kitchen easier.

If your kitchen is rectangular and narrow, all the cabinets and appliances must be along one wall. Work space will be at a minimum, so consider investing in ways to increase it such as installing a pull-out chopping block that fits into a drawer.

The U-shaped kitchen has cabinets and countertops arranged against three walls, with one key appliance in each section—usually the sink and dishwasher beneath the window, the range to one side, and the refrigerator to the other. The sink or range is sometimes incorporated into a kitchen island.

Selecting a countertop

There are a variety of countertop materials to choose from, some of which come in an extraordinary range of colors and patterns.

GRANITE
pros: Natural, durable, heat-resistant, can be cut to desired shape
cons: Needs expert installation

STAINLESS STEEL
pros: Hygienic; high-tech appearance
cons: Costly; prone to scratching

SYNTHETIC STONE
pros: Tough, beautiful, durable
cons: Costly; needs expert installation

POST-FORM LAMINATE
pros: Inexpensive; comes in a variety of colors and patterns
cons: Prone to scratching

SOLID WOOD
pros: Beautiful, natural material
cons: Hot pots and pans can leave marks; ultraviolet light can change color of wood

CERAMIC TILE
pros: Beautiful, durable
cons: Grout is prone to staining and mold

When work begins

Remodeling a kitchen can last a few days, a week, or longer. On the day work starts, the team's first job is to disconnect all power, water, and waste connections to the appliances, so you will need to make alternative eating arrangements. They will then remove the wall and base cabinets.

Electricity and plumbing needs

New electricity circuits may have to be run if you are switching from a range to a cooktop and separate oven, and new outlets for additional appliances may be desired, both above and below the countertops. Codes require at least two 20-amp appliance circuits in kitchens, arranged so that adjacent appliances are plugged in on separate circuits. Stationary appliances, such as a dishwasher and refrigerator, require individual, or "dedicated," circuits supplying power only to them (but codes recommend that refrigerator and freezer circuits contain an outlet for an electric clock, so that power outages affecting perishable foods can be easily detected). New lighting circuits may be part of the job.

The position of the pipes for the plumbing may need to be altered if the sink and dishwasher are moved. At the same time, you should have shutoff valves installed on any older kitchen supply lines lacking them, and have any plumbing relocated that runs through outside walls (a problem only in old houses).

Passing inspection

Any changes to plumbing and electricity must meet local building code requirements and pass inspection by an official (see pp. 16–17). Appliance installations may have to be

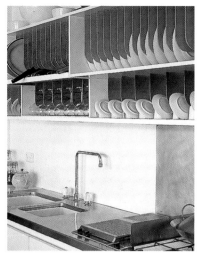

Under-the-counter wicker baskets are suitable for storing fresh vegetables that will be used within a few days.

Display racks are ideal for showing off china. Each piece has its own place, making it easier to store.

The built-in boxes for spices and wire baskets for vegetables make these shelves a decorative feature.

inspected to ensure that they meet fire-safety regulations. Obtaining building permits and scheduling inspections is often the installer's responsibility (see pp. 22–23).

Installation sequence

The new base cabinets can now be installed. Each unit will be set in place, often working away from the corners, and will be leveled before it is attached to the wall against which it stands. Neighboring units are screwed together to ensure stability.

The countertops are cut to length and secured with screws and brackets. Joining runs at right angles is one job professionals are better at than amateurs, because of the precision required. Countertop joints should be bonded with adhesive to ensure that no water penetrates the substrate, causing it to swell.

Cutouts are made for sinks and cooktops at this stage, and the cut edges may need to be sealed to prevent water penetration. Then the sink and cooktop are installed. Sinks are surrounded by a flexible sealing gasket and the junction between the rim and the countertop is usually also

sealed with silicone or another specialized caulking compound. A cooktop will be connected to its power or gas supply, and if the cooktop is gas-fueled, any necessary wiring will be connected to supply the automatic ignition. Built-in ovens are installed in the same way as cooktops, in wall openings created for them.

Next the wall cabinets are hung. With individual units (Euro-style or others), the general practice is to install them loosely to the wall framing and the adjacent units, then to tighten them during final alignment.

The finishing touches

The plumber will connect the supply and waste pipes to the sink and dishwasher; the electrician will complete alterations to the lighting, install appliances such as the range hood, and make the final connections to the stationary appliances. The carpenter will hang and align the cabinet doors, install the drawers, and attach the hardware. Unless new flooring is to be installed (often a final step to avoid marring it), he or she may also cut and attach baseboard and cornice or crown

molding where the cabinets touch the floor and ceiling.

Final steps include painting the walls, tiling the backsplashes, sealing the countertops with caulking compound, and sealing tiled surfaces after the grout between the tiles has cured. Test everything before you agree that the kitchen remodeling is finished.

When to inspect !

- Inspect the progress at the end of each day, especially work that will be concealed such as wiring and plumbing.

- When the cabinets are in position, check that each is secured both to the wall and to adjacent cabinets.

- Use a carpenter's level to check that countertops are horizontal, both along their length and from front to back.

- Finally, check that doors and drawers are accurately lined up, and that they open and shut easily.

Remodeling a bathroom

Traditionally, bathrooms have been regarded as purely functional. However, changing habits and tastes mean that more emphasis is now placed on upgrading bathroom fixtures, layout, and decor than ever before.

Remodeling a bathroom can range from a simple project with modest costs to one that is challenging and expensive. The easiest remodels are those that do not involve rerouting or installing extra plumbing. In terms of increasing a home's resale value, adding a second bathroom in a house that has only one will bring a greater return on investment than simply remodeling the existing facilities. However, if your home is already well equipped with two or three bathrooms, remodeling the master bath instead of adding yet another bathroom usually pays the most dividends.

Like-for-like remodeling

The most basic bathroom renovation, short of simply repainting the walls and changing the rugs and shower curtain, is to replace existing fixtures with new ones. This gives you the opportunity to choose the latest styles and colors, and often to take advantage of newer, more efficient, and, sometimes, safer technology. For example, you could swap a vanity and countertop basin for an airy pedestal unit (or vice versa), and choose a low-profile, water-saving toilet to replace an inefficient and bulky two-piece model. You can also upgrade older double-handle faucets to maintenance-free single-handle models, and replace conven-

Modern bathroom designers often place emphasis on materials and utilizing space, making a once mundane room a room of luxury.

tional bathtub and shower faucets with antiscald versions that protect bathers against burns from hot water.

Changing the layout

Rearranging bathroom fixtures to make the room work better is a bigger project than a like-for-like remodeling, but the rewards are greater. For example, you can replace an older large rectangular bathtub with a space-saving corner bath or shower enclosure to gain more floor area. Swapping the positions of the basin and toilet may also generate additional space. You could rehang the bathroom door so it opens outward instead of inward.

Ask yourself

- Are you happy with your bathroom layout but find the decor dated? A simple solution is to change the fixtures and repaint the room.

- Are you always bumping into things in your bathroom? By rearranging the components, you may create more space.

- Does it seem that there is always someone else in the bathroom when you want to use it? Consider adding another bathroom to your home.

Remodeling that involves changing the layout is where professional bathroom designers come into their own. They can offer a wider range of options than you're likely to think of, and most professionals have access to computer programs that can juggle bathroom components for the best fit and the optimum use of floor space. With help from a professional, you may find you even have room for additional fixtures such as a bidet, or twin basins so two people can wash at the same time during the morning rush hour.

Enlarging a bathroom

If the bathroom cannot hold the facilities you want, you should consider enlarging the room. This may or may not be complicated. For example, newer houses are often designed with closet space next to the master bath; all that is necessary is to break out the wall separating the rooms. However, enlarging a bathroom may mean reducing the size of adjacent rooms or "bumping out" an exterior wall.

You should consult with a professional who can advise on the structural implications of the alterations. You will also need a building permit and someone to do the work. A bathroom designer may be useful for planning the enlargement, but a contractor will probably be your best friend when it comes to seeing the project through to completion.

Different rooms

Another option is to create a new bathroom by converting an existing room or by carving out space as described above. How feasible this is depends on the position of the house soil stack (see pp. 154–155), to which you'll need to connect the new fixtures. In a home with more than one stack, the choices for locating a new bathroom are greater; you or your designer should consult a plumbing contractor before going too far with your planning.

(see pp. 154–155)

DIY jargon !

Bidet A bathroom fixture on which the user sits astride to clean his or her anatomy after using the toilet.

Soil stack A vertical pipe through which the waste from plumbing appliances, such as basins, bathtubs, and toilets, travels to the sewer line.

When designing a new bathroom, consider who will use it. Homes with children need bathrooms that can be used by more than one person at a time. Partitioning the toilet from the washing area will help eliminate the morning lineup when getting ready for school. In adult-only homes, a second bath may be used by guests and visitors. It should be located where it can be reached from a guest bedroom and living areas.

Choosing materials

Many tubs are made of porcelain-enameled cast iron, but tubs made of molded fiberglass and of acrylic are gaining popularity because of their variety, light weight, and lower cost. Economical enameled steel tubs are also available. Molded fiberglass and acrylic are used for the majority of shower stalls and combination tub-and-shower enclosures.

Washbasins set in a countertop are molded of polyester plastic, often mixed with stone chips to make so-called synthetic, or cultured, stone resembling marble, onyx, and other varieties. Drop-in basins set in a countertop also come in other materials, such as porcelain, enameled cast iron, enameled steel, and stainless steel. Freestanding basins, or lavatories, toilets, and bidets are porcelain.

Bathroom counter surfaces, like those in kitchens, are durable laminated, solid plastic, or ceramic tile. Floors are usually tile or sheet vinyl.

Whom to hire

If your project involves only replacing old fixtures with new models, hire a plumber to do the changeover. You may also need a painter to repaint or to hang wallpaper, and a tile setter or flooring installer. If you have a complete remodeling done by a bathroom design firm, they will contract or carry out all the work.

A simple change of fixtures will take a plumber no more than a day or two. Replacing a bathtub and repairing rotted flooring near a toilet may add more time to the project.

Removing the toilet

Once the plumber has turned off the water supply to the fixtures, he or she will flush the toilet to empty the bowl and tank as much as possible; any remaining water is sponged out.

If the toilet is a two-piece model, the plumber will disconnect the tank from the bowl (some tanks must also be detached from the wall). He or she will then unscrew the bowl from the floor and disconnect it from the soil pipe. To prevent odors, the opening of the soil pipe will be temporarily plugged with a rag; any wax or putty around the pipe will be scraped off.

Basin and bathtub

Removing the basin and bathtub are next. For a basin, the plumbing is disconnected and the unit is either removed from a vanity cabinet or lifted free from a bracket holding it to the wall.

Always choose a paint that has been formulated for bathrooms.

Removing a bathtub can be easy or difficult, depending on how accessible the plumbing connections are and whether or not the tub rests on feet on the floor or is built into the wall and surrounded by paneling. The procedure involves exposing the plumbing, if necessary, and disconnecting it, then freeing the tub from any mountings on the floor or wall.

The tub must be maneuvered out of the bathroom and the house. This can be difficult if the tub is heavy or hard to fit through doorways. Acrylic replacement bathtubs are available that fit over existing rectangular tubs, eliminating the need to remove them.

Installing a bathtub

The first fixture to be installed will be the bathtub, due to its size, then the toilet and basin. A new bathtub may require adding supports to the wall and repairing or modifying the floor and the frame beneath the tub. With the tub in position, the waste

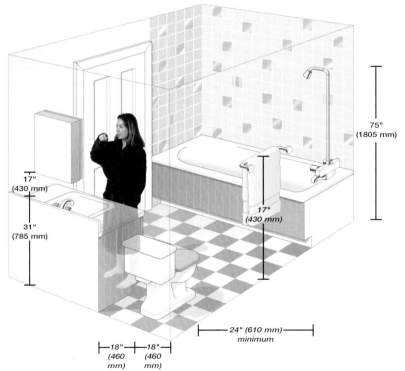

A bathroom should be planned with enough space for leg room at the toilet, and with the mirror, shower head, and towel racks at comfortable heights.

Two basins in the bathroom will reduce a large family's waiting time during the morning rush. A heated towel rack supplies warm towels in winter.

Ceramic tiles can be used to finish the sides of a bathtub.

and overflow assembly will be connected to the drainpipe. Afterward, the wall will be repaired and refinished, and paneling may be installed to conceal the sides of the tub. The final step is to caulk the seam where the tub and walls meet.

Installing a toilet

If you are replacing both the flooring and the toilet, the flooring should be installed first. Afterward, installing a new toilet involves preparing the soil pipe over which the toilet bowl rests by installing new closet bolts and a new wax gasket, or ring, in the soil pipe opening. The bolts anchor the bowl to the soil pipe and the wax ring provides a leakproof seal. Next, the plumber and a helper will lower the toilet bowl over the bolts and onto the wax ring. The bolts are tightened so that the wax ring is under constant compression. With a two-piece toilet, the tank is attached after the bowl is anchored to the floor. The final step is to attach the toilet's water supply tube to the fill valve inside the tank.

Sealant may be applied around the base of a toilet; this may be required by building code. Ask your plumber to delay applying sealant for a few days until you are sure the toilet does not leak where it enters the soil pipe.

Installing a basin

A basin is installed by attaching it to the top of the vanity cabinet if it is part of a one-piece countertop model, by securing it in a countertop cutout if the basin is a drop-in model, or by mounting it to the wall framing by means of a special bracket if it is a wall-mounted or pedestal unit. Afterward, the basin's drain assembly is connected to the household drain system and the faucets are installed and connected to the household water supply.

Bathroom redesign

If you are having a redesign done by a firm of bathroom specialists, they will follow the same sequence the plumber uses to remove the fixtures. As soon as this is done, the team will carry out any alterations to the sup-

ply and waste pipes that are necessary to reach any repositioned fixtures. They will also add any wiring needed for shower or spa bath pumps and for new lighting and wall outlets.

When to inspect !

- Inspect the work during the installer's breaks and at the end of the day. Look for neat workmanship; check fixtures, hardware, and surfaces for signs of damage—scratched chrome or chipped porcelain.

- Make sure every fixture is secure by gripping it and attempting to move it.

- Check that silicone sealant has been used to waterproof areas between fixtures and walls.

- When the job is finished, wipe a paper towel around all plumbing connections and look for signs of a leak on the paper. If you find any, contact the installer.

Your living room is where you spend more of your waking hours than anywhere else in the house. It is also the main room your visitors see, so you have plenty of reasons to want it to look its best.

The best way to achieve the look you want in a living room is to call in the professionals. Which professionals you employ will depend on the scale of the work you want carried out. You may need painters and wallpaperers to tackle the walls, ceiling, and woodwork; carpet installers; a flooring contractor to lay tile, resilient, or natural wood flooring; drapery installers to hang new curtains or blinds; and cabinet installers or cabinetmakers to handle ready-made or custom-built storage and display units. If you're planning a complete remodel, you may be better off calling in an interior designer or decorator. He or she can coordinate the entire operation, subcontracting stages of the work to different tradespeople as the project proceeds.

Redecoration

The living room is one area of the home where you may well decide to choose more expensive decorating materials and furnishings than you would select for other rooms. For example, you may want an unusual painting style such as rag rolling or stenciling on your walls, and executing these well on a large scale can be difficult for an amateur. Similarly, exotic wallcoverings such as silks can transform a room and give it a luxurious look, but they are expensive and can be ruined if hung by an inexperienced paperhanger. Professionals may cost you more money, but the quality of the results that they achieve will outweigh the extra expense. They can also be held responsible for any shortcomings—a type of insurance that would not be possible if you attempt to do the work yourself (see pp. 38–41).

Storage and display

A living room is not only a home's location for entertaining—it is also the family's showcase of treasures, a trait that has evolved from the Victorian era when many homes had parlors or "best rooms" reserved for special guests and occasions. Coping with these requirements usually means the room needs some carefully planned storage and display units. These will also be needed if the room is to contain home entertainment equipment—for example, an audio system and CDs, cassette tapes, and records; a television, videocassette recorder, and tapes; and computer equipment.

You have two choices in providing these units. The first is to buy freestanding, ready-made or ready-to-assemble furniture—often from a coordinated line to ensure that all the pieces are the same style and finish—and to arrange it within the available space. This can save money, but it is often difficult to make optimum use of floor space in this way.

The second alternative is to commission a carpenter or firm to make

A professional painter added just enough texture to these walls to make them warm and inviting. They complement the furniture and other furnishings recommended by an interior designer.

Ample storage space has been provided with these custom-built units. Wooden flooring was installed around the carpet to make a feature of the units. Ceiling spotlights provide plenty of light in the room.

separate padding or solid wood or natural veneer floor coverings are what you need, although they are usually more expensive (see pp. 40–41). This, coupled with the fact that living rooms are generally larger than the other rooms in the house, means that the project is likely to be an expensive one. Professional installation will ensure that the work is done correctly, prolonging the life of the floor covering, and it will ensure that expensive materials are not wasted.

When work starts

If your living room is being given a complete makeover, you can expect it to be out of commission for a week or more. The work will proceed more quickly if the existing furniture and soft furnishings can be moved out. The walls, ceilings, and woodwork can then be stripped and the floor coverings removed more easily, and it will also minimize the risk of damage to your possessions.

The contractors will tackle the redecorating first; then they will install any built-in furniture (there is little point in wasting expensive floor coverings under storage units, which will in any case stand level and square better on a solid floor). After the new floor coverings are laid, curtains and other window treatments will be hung and finishing touches, such as new door hardware and electrical accessories, will be installed to complete the job.

custom-built units that can make better use of corners and can be tailored to your precise requirements. Custom built-ins also make it possible to hide the wiring that is an unavoidable part of today's electronic entertainment equipment.

Display units can feature integral lighting to show off your treasures to their best advantage. A mix of low and high-level cabinets and shelves will make the best use of available floor space. Turning to professional suppliers will ensure an efficient use of the space.

New floor coverings

When it comes to choosing floor coverings for living rooms an important consideration is coping with the high level of through traffic such rooms get. The materials must be capable of withstanding heavy wear. Poor-quality foam-backed carpet or printed and laminated wood flooring will simply not last. Sturdy cloth- or jute-backed carpet with

Furnishings

Providing new curtains, blinds, and other window decorations can be expensive in living rooms, especially where at least one window may be large, such as a bay, bow, or picture window, or at patio doors. Here, a professional can help you select suitable materials and styles, pick the correct types of track or rod, and achieve an overall effect that only the most experienced do-it-yourselfer could aspire to. The designer will also help you coordinate the new window treatments with any carpets, sofas, and other room decoration.

One of the most pressing demands in many homes is for extra bedroom space, usually thanks to a new addition to the family or to the need to give growing children space of their own—or you may want a larger bedroom to gain privacy for yourself.

Short of moving to a larger house, there are many ways of getting more bedroom space. You could convert your attic (see pp. 84–87) or, if you have planning permission, build an addition (see pp. 98–103). All of these can be potentially expensive options, and if none of them is feasible, your only alternative is to work creatively with the floor space you already have.

Partitioning rooms

If you live in an older house with large bedrooms, you may be able to divide one room into two to create an extra bedroom. Although such an alteration may sound simple, careful planning and sound execution are crucial if the project is to be completed successfully.

You can get professional help in the planning from an architect. Creating the partition is usually a job for a carpenter, but if electrical and heating services are needed—which is likely—or exterior work, such as masonry, painting, or certain kinds of siding, is necessary, you're better off with a general contractor who specializes in standard home remodeling.

The professional you hire will be able to find solutions to the two main problems in partitioning a room: providing access to both rooms and ensuring that each room has adequate natural light and ventilation.

An interior designer will not only help you decide on the layout for the bedroom but also assist in coordinating fabrics and patterns.

It is rarely satisfactory to provide access to one room through another, so if you cannot position a door to open onto an already existing corridor, some form of hallway or area may be needed between the existing room door and the entrance to the new room. This will eat up valuable floor space; however, the planning skill of an expert will help keep this to a minimum.

Ask yourself ?

- Has adding a new member to the family created a need for another bedroom? Or are older siblings constantly in dispute over their shared bedroom? Consider finding room to create another bedroom.

- Would you like to escape to your room for privacy but find it too small to do much other than reading? Think about changing the layout of your floor plan.

Light and ventilation requirements can pose problems. If the existing room has only one window, this cannot be shared. Each room must have an operable window large enough to serve as an emergency exit for fire safety reasons; so a new window opening will have to be created or the existing window will have to be replaced by two individual windows, with the framing, and, possibly, the exterior wall finish between them coinciding with the position of the new partition wall.

Other considerations

Any professional you hire will also have to consider changes needed to the existing room's heating, lighting, and electrical outlets and will have

to provide these services in the new room. In addition, he or she must ensure that the proposed changes will meet the requirements of all the building codes in your area, obtain any necessary permits, and arrange for all required inspections.

Extra work may be involved to strengthen the floor if the wall is to run parallel with the room's floor joists (see pp. 142–143), since all the load would otherwise be carried by just one or two joists not designed to take the weight. Again a professional can advise you on the best solution to this problem if it arises. There are generally no problems building a partition wall at right angles to the joist direction.

Changing the layout

More radical than dividing a large room in two, redesigning an entire floor plan by knocking down the interior walls and putting up new ones is an option. You'll want an architect's help, both to divide the available space as skillfully as possible and to determine which partition walls are load-bearing and which are not. Load-bearing walls are more difficult to move or alter than so-called curtain walls, which bear none of the building's weight, but coping with them is seldom altogether impossible. The real danger lies in tearing out partition walls before you know whether they are load-bearing or not, and in most

cases only an architect or other skilled professional, such as a structural engineer, building inspector, or experienced builder, can identify the two with certainty.

Such massive remodels as changing a floor layout are potentially disruptive for the occupants, especially if the bathroom is part of it. The best advice is to plan on staying at a motel or going on vacation while the work is in progress.

Alternative choices

Another source of bedroom space is converting a room designed for another purpose—for example, a little-used dining room or parlor in an older house, or a downstairs den in a newer split-level. This is viable only if you really can spare the space and if the location of the room truly enables it to function as a bedroom, with access to a bathroom and with a certain amount of privacy. Beware of converting below-ground basement areas into sleeping quarters; even if windows are present, such spaces may not be permissible for use as bedrooms by the terms of your local building codes.

Rooms to spare

If you have more bedrooms than you need, there is little point in furnishing them all as bedrooms unless you have guests who stay on a regular basis. Instead, you can turn one of the bedrooms into a hobby room or workroom or a photographic darkroom; or, if you work at home, an extra bedroom can make an ideal home office (see pp. 60–61).

Another possibility is to combine two adjacent bedrooms to form a spacious master bedroom suite. The additional space can can be used for a separate dressing area or exercise room, and, sometimes, even a luxurious bathroom/spa, while creating more room in the sleeping area as well.

Creating and improving closets

Built-in shelves, racks, and other features make the best use of storage space in the bedroom closet, especially in the typical small bedrooms of new homes. In larger bedrooms, you can install freestanding units or extend the size of the closet.

Stores specializing in closet organizer systems will usually have in-house design consultants to assist their customers; alternatively, you can hire a professional closet designer. Both can provide sound solutions to bedroom and other storage problems based on a wealth of experience and a knowledge of the full range of options.

Assessing your needs

Your present collection of clothes will give you an approximate idea of the amount of storage space you need. The first priority is hanging space, and if you have conventional built-in closets, you already know how much space is wasted when there is just one hanging rod (perhaps with a storage shelf above it). This rod is fine for full-length apparel, such as coats and dresses; however, shorter items, such as jackets and trousers, would be better hung on a lower rod.

Divide your clothes into two groups, long and short, and measure how much rod space each of these groups requires. Be generous: clothes become creased if they are crammed close together. In addition, if you are going to the expense of remodeling your closets, make allowances for new items to be added in the future.

Next, look at what you currently store in drawers or on shelves. A handy way of measuring how much you have is to stack up clothes in piles of approximately 18 inches square (46 cm sq) and total their height. This will give a consultant or designer a guideline to use when suggesting closet compartments and

storage racks. Finally, don't forget accessory items such as shoes, boots, hats, ties, and belts. All will need to be given storage space within the new units.

Built-in closets

Existing built-in closets can be outfitted with organizing components. This is a straightforward job, and the store in which you made your purchase may offer installation services or recommend someone to install them. Make sure you remove items in the closet before the installer arrives.

Another possibility is to have the closet enlarged, which may involve removing wall sections before add-

Dividing and organizing clothing and other articles by size makes the best use of closet space, especially in closets built in confined areas.

When to inspect !

- You won't be able to inspect the job until it is finished. When it is, check every surface for any signs of damage.

- Make sure that all fittings and hinges are secure and that drawers, sliding baskets, and doors operate smoothly.

- If you find any faults or defects, you should notify the installer immediately so they can be fixed promptly.

Freestanding wardrobe units lend themselves to being repositioned if you become bored with the current arrangement of the furniture in the bedroom or if you want to make room for new furniture.

open shelves and pull-out baskets will make up a sizable part of the arrangement. Closet stores and designers also have other interior fittings available.

When work starts

If wardrobe units are to be installed, or if the closet is to be enlarged, workers will want to clear the bedroom of as much furniture as possible, perhaps including the bed, before starting the job. Find out in advance if they will do this. They will also need as much floor space as possible for the assembly of new walls or wardrobe units. In addition, carpets may need trimming to allow new walls or wardrobe units to stand directly on the floorboards.

Each wardrobe unit will be put together, set in place after any necessary trimming to fit around baseboards (in many cases, baseboards will be removed where they run behind units), and secured against the wall with brackets. Units are also fastened together side-by-side for maximum stability. The frames of the walls will be assembled before being secured in place and covered with wallboard (see pp. 136–137).

Once the run of units or new walls are completed, the various interior fittings will be installed and their operation checked. Molding and trim are added next to match new walls with existing ones and to give the units a built-in appearance; then the doors will be fitted and aligned to complete the installation.

ing new ones. Additional doors will also have to be installed; if you cannot match existing doors, you may want to consider replacing the original ones to keep the style consistent. If you extend your closet, you may want to add a light, which would mean calling in an electrician.

Freestanding units

If you don't want to enlarge the closet, wardrobe units are an increasingly popular option. Most are based on a modular design—units in a range of standard widths and heights that are mixed and matched to give you the storage space you need. Custom-built units are available from cabinetmakers, but these are usually expensive compared to what you can find in stores and will take longer to obtain. However, in

an awkward-shaped room this may be the best solution.

Depending on the size and layout of your bedroom, you may want wardrobe units along just one wall or prefer them running around a corner. If the only available wall has the bed against it, a designer may suggest a row or two of units over the bed, but this may be difficult to reach unless space in these units is reserved for little-used items such as hats or winter woolens. Freestanding units look best if they reach ceiling height; in addition, you are then making full use of all the available space and are avoiding dust traps on top of the units.

What goes into each unit will depend on your individual storage needs. Hanging space at different levels is the main component, but

Saving floor space

Most closets and wardrobe units along a wall have hinged doors to each section. If floor space is tight, installing bifold or sliding doors may be a sensible way to gain more room. It's a simple procedure for a carpenter to replace the doors.

Working from home is a way of life for more people as telecommuting becomes more common. You will have to create space that allows you to work uninterrupted and that has room for all the furniture, storage, and equipment you'll need.

Depending on the size and layout of your house, there are several options for creating an office. The obvious one is to use a spare or underused room—perhaps a bedroom or a dining room—unless the house already has a study. The dining room option will be possible only if part of the kitchen can be used for eating or if there is room for a table in the living room. The office can still function as a dining room on special occasions if the table is kept as a work surface that can be easily cleared.

Converting space

Unused attic space is the next option, and this has the advantage that it does not encroach on the existing living area (unless you need to install a staircase). Attic conversions almost always require professional help (see pp. 84–87). Apart from creating access, the job will probably involve installing windows or skylights that can do double duty as a fire escape, putting in a floor, insulating and finishing the underside of the roof, and possibly strengthening ceiling joists. You will also need electrical service, telephone lines, and perhaps baseboard heating units extended to the area, and, of course, you'll need a building permit and inspections.

Another option is to convert an integral or attached garage. Creating access to an existing garage is usually no problem, and often electrical and heating services are already installed and need only modification. Again, professional help will ensure a speedy, efficient and code-compliant conversion (see pp. 92–93). It will usually start with moistureproofing, insulating and covering the garage floor, replacing the door with windows or a sliding glass door, and installing an insulated ceiling below the rafters.

You can also consider converting a detached garage for office use, but

19" maximum
(475 mm)

28"
(700 mm)

When working at the computer, your arms should be held at a 90° angle and your back should be straight, with your feet resting flat on the floor.

2

A home office is best located in a secluded part of the house, where other family members are less likely to interrupt.

Ask yourself

- Will you be working at home part-time or full-time? A part-time office can be tucked into a corner; a full-time office should be secluded.

- Does the area you have chosen for your home office have good lighting to work in and enough electrical outlets for telecommunication equipment? You may need to hire an electrician to upgrade the wiring.

- Will your home office have room for office equipment, such as computers and telephones, for work resources, such as files and books, and for stationery and other office supplies?

the building will need weatherization, and extending electricity and heating services may be complicated.

New construction

If you have no space suitable for converting to an office, consider building an addition (see pp. 98–103) or an outbuilding (see pp. 106–107). While you may want to hire an architect to plan an unusual project, many general contractors specialize in standard additions and can be less expensive. A professional can see to it not only that any addition you plan is structurally sound, efficient, and appealing, but also that it conforms to your budget and to local codes, zoning, and tax laws.

An outbuilding may be a satisfying home office, but it may be problematic to construct unless you have a large property or live in an area where building regulations are reasonably nonrestrictive. Most building codes and zoning laws regulate where buildings can be put up on the property and what percentage of it can be covered with construction. In addition, certain features in an outbuilding can qualify it as a second home, which will add to your tax bill. Hiring an architect is the best way to avoid expensive problems.

Furnishing an office

Home-office design firms can supply built-in and modular work surfaces, filing and other storage, and lighting, power, and telecommunications services. Always opt for a business phone line separate from your residence line for tax purposes, and add a second business line if you use a computer that links to other computers or to the Internet, so phone and fax messages are not blocked when the computer is on line.

Creating a laundry room

If your house has a basement, the washer and dryer will probably be located there. In a house without a basement, the utility room often doubles as a laundry room. However, the laundry room is gaining in popularity.

Most homes built since the 1950s include some provision for laundry equipment. In the oldest of these, the provision usually consists of plumbing hookups in the basement, if there is one, or in the utility room, which may also house the furnace, water heater, and electricity service panel that are normally located in a basement. Newer homes may have a laundry alcove or a larger space, often near the kitchen. In some houses and apartments, the kitchen is built to accommodate laundry appliances along with the traditional kitchen equipment.

Reasons for change

There are plenty of houses with basements that could benefit from a laundry room upstairs, and there are plenty of homes with utility rooms that are too small for laundry appliances or that could benefit from a separate laundry area. Relocating a washer and dryer from the basement to a room of their own on the first floor, for instance, adds convenience and may even brighten the task of doing laundry by eliminating trips to a gloomy basement. If it is large enough, a laundry room can as function as general-purpose

utility room offering a convenient space for ironing and folding the family's clothes, storing bulky items (perhaps even a freezer), and, if located by an entrance door, a place for taking off and putting on boots and outerwear during rainy weather or in the winter.

Options for change

Whether you can create a laundry room depends on the layout and facilities you have. If you have a large kitchen, for example, it may be possible to partition off an area, at least one large enough for your laundry equipment. Such an area may need to be no more than a few square feet (meters) if you invest in a stacked washer and dryer to replace side-by-side appliances.

If you have a separate pantry (a common feature in prewar homes), you may be able to convert it. If the

By keeping the washing machine and dryer side by side, you'll have room for storage space above the appliances. A laundry area doesn't have to be in a separate room—for example, you can partition it off a large kitchen.

Rules & regulations

You will need a building permit to make alterations to the plumbing and electrical systems. In some cases you may also need a permit for the new laundry room space—for example, if it is located in a garage. You should have your contractor (or each tradesperson if you hire them yourself) obtain the necessary permits and arrange for any required inspections. If you take out a permit in your name, you—not the professional you've hired—are responsible for following building codes.

You can use sliding or bifold doors to hide a washing machine and dryer. Stacking the machines allows you to utilize a confined space.

space is small, you will have to stack the laundry appliances, but the arrangement will at least enable you to concentrate your laundry activities in one compact space.

A third option is to convert part of an integral or attached garage to act as a laundry and storage area. If you can afford to sacrifice a minimum of 3 square feet (915 sq mm) at the back of the garage and extend plumbing and electricity to this area, this option has the benefit of not taking up any space within the house itself.

Upstairs laundry

One more possibility you could consider is creating an upstairs laundry room. As with the first-floor options already mentioned, you do not need a large area for the appliances, and you may be able to partition off part of a large bathroom or of a bedroom next to it to create the space you require. The convenience of an upstairs laundry cannot be underestimated in a house where all the bedrooms are also upstairs. The only drawbacks are the possibility

of noise from the appliances during operation and water damage to the ceiling below due to an overflowing or malfunctioning washer. Noise can be lessened to some extent by placing the laundry equipment on vibration-damping rubber blocks and by closing off the area with solid sliding doors. The risk of an overflow can be addressed by installing the washer on a plastic tray sold specifically for the purpose; it has a built-in drain that connects to the household plumbing.

Nevertheless, you probably won't want to do laundry late at night if children are sleeping upstairs, nor will you want to run the appliances when you are entertaining downstairs in a room below the laundry.

Plumbing and electricity

Extending supply and drain pipes to a laundry room is usually less of a problem the closer the room is to the kitchen or to a bathroom from which the plumbing runs can be extended (see pp. 152–153). The biggest problem will probably be venting the washer's drain pipe (see pp. 154–155), which is called a standpipe; the vent must either connect in a code-approved manner with an existing vent or run separately to the roof. In both cases several openings may need to be cut in various walls and in the roof to install it; however, in some situations a standpipe can run outdoors. Before considering any new laundry location that involves installing pipes, you should consult a plumbing contractor for advice or be sure your architect or general contractor does so.

A new laundry area will probably need power supplies for the appliances, such as wall outlets and lighting; however, extending your existing circuits shouldn't pose any problems. A new, dedicated circuit may have to be run from the service panel for the dryer; most require 240-volt

current instead of the ordinary current of 120 volts (see pp. 156–157).

The professional help you need for this job depends on which option you choose. You will need a carpenter to put up any partition walls, and a plumber and electrician (whom the carpenter will subcontract if he or she is also a licensed general contractor) to install the services. If you are simply converting a pantry, a plumber and an electrician can do whatever is necessary.

When work starts

Depending on the scale of the changes, the professionals' first job will be to make the laundry space ready, creating partition walls and a doorway, if necessary, or stripping out a pantry. Before any new wall framing is covered, plumbing and electricity alterations will be carried out and inspected by a code official. The walls will then be covered and painted or otherwise finished, and the electricity connections finished with outlets, switches, or lighting fixtures; a second electrical inspection may be necessary. Finally, the new appliances will be installed and connected, including running an exhaust duct for the dryer to the outside. A final plumbing inspection may also be necessary.

Improving staircases

A staircase is a complex structure, and in an older house it will probably have been tailor-made and assembled on site by a carpenter. These, as well as newer models, can often be improved with new decoration.

Houses that were been built after World War I are likely to have pre-fabricated staircases. These were made to match standard ceiling heights and dimensions that met building code requirements in effect at the time of construction.

Staircases seldom need replacing because of structural damage except in rare cases where they have been damaged by dry rot or wood-boring insects. However, they can eventually be damaged by everyday wear and tear. It is well worth keeping

stairs in good repair to prevent small problems from getting bigger—and, therefore, more dangerous and more expensive to fix.

Structural work

Repairing stairs is a job best left to an experienced carpenter with a good knowledge of staircase construction. Creaking is the most common problem. A stair's treads (the horizontal steps) and risers (the vertical boards between treads) fit in slots cut in the stringers (the sloping side parts that run the length of the staircase; see pp. 144–145). In better-quality construction the parts are held in place by thin wooden wedges. These can work loose over time, allowing the treads to move slightly as the staircase is used and to grate against the stringers, causing the creaks.

The treads may have been damaged, usually by careless hauling of furniture up and down the steps. This can result in cracks across the treads or even split nosings—the projections at the front of each tread. The treads should be repaired or replaced to ensure sound footing when using the staircase.

Another area where problems are common is the balustrade—the handrail and the decorative balusters that support it. The balustrade may have loose or broken parts. This is a serious safety problem, because it could give way if someone stumbles. A damaged balustrade should be given expert attention to fix it properly.

You may have a sound but old-fashioned balustrade that you want to replace with a modern design. This is a job for your carpenter.

A new staircase can be made a featured attraction in a hallway. The traditional style of this staircase was enhanced by designing it with curved steps and treads, which creates a flared effect.

The repair work

Making repairs to the treads and risers usually requires access to the underside. This is not a problem if there is a storage closet beneath the staircase, because the structure is often left exposed. However, if the underside has been covered with lath and plaster in an older home or wallboard in a newer one, the covering will have to be removed.

The carpenter's next job is to reglue all the wedges and to replace any loose or missing ones. He or she may also decide to glue and screw reinforcing blocks into the angles between each riser and the tread above it to prevent them from moving against each other and causing more creaks. If any damaged treads need replacing, freeing them may involve cutting through tongue-and-groove joints between the tread and the risers above and below it. Then the broken tread can be slid out from below the staircase and a replacement tread installed.

If exposing the underside of a staircase is not possible or desirable, a carpenter may be able to make repairs from above. This will require removing the stair carpet. The car-

New staircases

You may decide to replace a staircase because it looks old and dated and you want a new look, or because its structure has become so damaged by wood-boring insects, for example, that it would be dangerous to continue to use it. There are plenty of styles to choose from when it comes to prefabricated staircases. Alternatively, you could have a staircase custom-made, which may be your only choice if you have an old house that doesn't follow standard dimensions.

Before the new staircase is installed the old one will have to be removed, which will mean that you won't have access to any rooms on the floor above. You may want to stay elsewhere while the work takes place.

penter can then prevent creaking steps by driving screws down through each tread into the riser beneath and injecting woodworking adhesive into the seams between the treads and risers to bond them together.

A new balustrade

Modern replacement balustrade kits make replacing an old balustrade a relatively straightforward job for a carpenter to carry out. He or she will cut away the existing handrail and balusters, and the newel posts (the large posts, often at the bottom of the balustrade) if these are being changed too. Then new posts will be mounted on the newel post stubs, new handrails will be attached using special brackets, and new balusters will be installed between a capping on the stringer and the underside of the handrail to complete the job.

Stairwell decoration

The problem of gaining access to the upper walls and the ceiling of a stairwell makes decorating this area an ideal job to leave to a professional. He or she will have the appropriate equipment for reaching and working comfortably in the space, and will be experienced at handling rollers on extension poles or long lengths of wallpaper.

An interior decorator can advise you about choosing suitable materials and selecting matching colors

and patterns, and a professional painter or wallpaperer can complete the job in far less time than an amateur, thereby minimizing any household disruption caused when the staircase becomes temporarily out-of-bounds.

Once your painter or wallpaperer has put down drop cloths and set up scaffolding, he or she will strip old wallcoverings, wash all painted surfaces, and repair damaged wallboard, plaster, or wood surfaces. Next will come painting or papering the ceiling, then painting or papering the walls and painting, staining, or varnishing any woodwork.

Because this graceful, slim balustrade requires less room than a traditional balustrade, it's a good choice for a narrow staircase.

2 | Improving the services: Plumbing

Older homes may have plumbing systems that have been modified over the years in a ramshackle way; supply pipes may also have become constricted by mineral deposits. The plumbing can be replaced during a bathroom or kitchen remodeling.

With the exception of leaks and pipes located in areas that are vulnerable to freezing, it usually isn't practical to replace old plumbing that still functions. However, a major kitchen or bath overhaul offers an excellent excuse to do so, at least in the area where plumbing modifications will take place.

The first thing your plumber will do is to survey the existing system (see pp. 152–155) to see what services are required, and to suggest possible improvements that could be made to improve its efficiency and guarantee a long and trouble-free life.

Types of pipes

Galvanized pipe, which was standard until around 1950, may have become choked with rust or mineral deposits, especially in hard-water areas. Leaks and brownish-colored water from the faucet are signs it needs replacing.

Copper pipe became standard after 1950. It usually ages well, except in areas where the water supply contains unusually corrosive minerals or chemicals. Copper pipes are joined with solder, which contained

Extending pipes to the plumbing system was part of creating this stylish shower off a sauna room.

lead until it was outlawed for plumbing use in 1988. Lead in the solder is not considered a major health hazard by the Centers for Disease Control and is seldom a cause to replace plumbing in otherwise good working order. If you believe your water supply pipes contain lead solder, the Environmental Protection Agency (EPA) recommends running faucets for two or three minutes before using them the first time each day to flush out the water that has stood in the pipes overnight. Never use hot tap water from such pipes for drinking or cooking; hot water leaches lead from solder joints.

Plastic pipe has been used with increasing frequency since the 1970s. One type, polybutylene, has since lost the approval of the Uniform Plumbing Code (UPC) because of problems reported with fittings that developed leaks (see pp. 152–153). As with copper plumbing containing lead solder, there is no inherent reason to remove polybutylene plumbing that is in good working order. However, a number of class-action lawsuits have been won against manufacturers of polybutylene pipe and fittings, qualifying many homeowners for financial assistance to replace such plumbing if they wish or to compensate them for having done so in the past. If you believe you have polybutylene plumbing—the pipes and fittings are a characteristic gray color—contact your local building inspector's office for complete information.

Water heaters

Rust and mineral buildup can occur in water heaters, which do not have the typical life span of other plumbing components. Repairs are sometimes possible if the problem is simply lack of adequate heat, but if even the slightest leak is noticed underneath the tank, it should be inspected immediately by a plumber and most likely replaced within a day

or so. Waiting longer can result in a flood. Another reason to replace a water heater is the need for increased capacity—for example, if an extra full bathroom is added.

When work starts

There is no disguising the fact that replacing plumbing will massively disrupt your household routine. You will have no water or toilet facilities at least while work is going on, but most plumbers are organized enough to restore supplies at the end of each day. Much plumbing renovation can be done from the basement, but the plumber may have to open walls, ceilings, and floors to access old pipes or install new ones. All this adds up to a strong case for leaving the house during the day and allowing work to take place unimpeded.

Wiring and lighting

Today's homes use more electrical equipment than ever before, and even many new houses lack sufficient wiring and outlets to handle the load. With more activities occurring in the house, lighting often requires updating, too.

When you decide to renovate a room, take a look at how it currently supplies electricity for your needs. For example, do most of the outlets in the room contain adapters for plugging in several devices instead of the usual two? Or do extension cords snake along the walls? Both are signs that your house could use additional wiring circuits. How about lighting fixtures; do most rooms feature only an overhead bulb?

Inspecting and upgrading household electrical systems is definitely a job for a professional electrician, but it can be one of the most rewarding renovations you can make to a room or to the whole house, and it is well worth the cost and disruption.

Inspecting the system

Any electrical repair or upgrade is likely to start with a wiring inspection—for good reason. Ordinary building regulations do not require existing wiring to meet present code standards; generally, even obsolete wiring in poor condition can remain in use as long as it is not modified or

extended. An electrician can usually determine at a glance how much of an inspection is necessary.

In a new house built within the last 5 to 10 years, the electrician may only check the capacity of the service panel to accommodate additional circuits and the condition of any circuit wiring to be modified. In an older house, an inspection might begin with the condition of the supply wires entering the house and proceed to an examination of all the circuits, especially if different types of cables have been used. The electrician will look for any of a number of potential safety and fire hazards, from fraying insulation and wiring connections to the presence of aluminum wiring and the absence of continuous grounding. Aluminum wiring, installed in many homes

Rules & regulations

All the work your electrician carries out in your home must comply with the building code requirements that apply in your area. Most code requirements follow the guidelines recommended by the National Electric Code (NEC), which is updated every 3 years by the National Fire Protection Agency, a private nonprofit organization.

Downlights can provide extra light in work areas. To install new downlights in this kitchen, the electrician made holes in the ceiling to accept the fixtures and ran new wiring to a circuit.

The ever-increasing equipment found in today's home entertainment centers often requires installing extra outlets in the living room or den.

Home computers can be sensitive to electrical surges. You should dedicate an outlet for the sole use of your computer, and equip it with a surge protector.

during the 1960s, has been the cause of many fires. Although the wiring itself is safe, the original connectors may need to be replaced with a newer approved type to eliminate the hazard. Continuous grounding of an electricity system means that outlets on circuits are linked by a grounding wire that serves as an "emergency exit" for stray—possibly dangerous—current in the event of a short circuit or other malfunction (see pp. 156–157).

Wiring in older houses

Inspecting an older house will also include checking any suspicious outlets that may have been wired improperly. The electrician will also see if ground-fault circuit interrupters (to prevent shock injuries; see pp. 156–157) have been installed in the locations they are now required such as in any bathrooms. Sometimes, too, he or she will inspect particularly old wiring for signs of high-resistance faults—current leaking from wiring that seems sound but actually isn't, due mostly to deteriorating insulation.

During the course of an inspection, an electrician can also calculate your power needs and make determinations about which circuits should be extended, where and how many circuits should be added, and how much amperage.

When work starts

Electrical inspections are seldom disruptive except to expose connections within wall switches and outlets or in ceiling fixtures. For many years, electrical codes have required that all connections be easily accessible, so it is unlikely that any demolition will be necessary.

Extending and adding new circuits can often be quite a nuisance, as the process usually requires cutting holes in the walls, floors, and ceilings to draw, or "snake," wiring from one outlet to another and, in the case of new circuits, to the service panel. You should remember to address the issue of demolition and repair in the contract; electricians seldom patch the surfaces that they must open to run new wiring. For that, you will probably have to hire a drywall contractor, followed by a painter or wallpaperer.

Relatively minor jobs, such as upgrading outlets or installing lighting fixtures, may take only a day or so, but running several new circuits may take a week or more and may put individual rooms out of commission for a day at a time.

When to inspect !

- You will have relatively little opportunity to inspect the work, since much of it is hidden. In general, check that the outlets are located where agreed on in the contract and that all other terms are met.

- If the work involves installing new circuits or a new service panel or subpanel, make sure the electrician labels all the circuit breakers with the outlets each one controls.

- Most residential electrical modifications require at least two inspections by a municipal building code officer; one after any new wiring is run and the other after any new outlets or fixtures have been connected.

Central heating systems—namely furnaces—generally last for decades, and in normal circumstances it is seldom cost-effective to replace a working furnace. However, improvements can often be made to increase comfort and lower energy bills.

It is only necessary to replace a furnace if it develops a major malfunction or if it becomes so obsolete that it is impractical to continue using it. However, it is usually possible to make improvements to an aging or inadequate system.

You can also increase heating in a designated room, usually the living room, by having a zero-clearance fireplace (see pp. 132–133) installed. It will provide an inviting atmosphere that will be appreciated when coming inside on a cold winter's day.

Inspecting the system

Heating system repairs and alterations should be left to licensed heating professionals, because of their complexity and the interconnectedness of heating system components with each other and with a home's overall ventilation and airflow. Annual furnace inspections and repairs can be handled by a heating technician. Larger issues, such as resizing a heating system to accommodate a major remodel or replacing an obsolete furnace, are the province of a heating engineer.

Practically any licensed heating contractor or utility representative can inspect and diagnose problems specific to a furnace or to other heating system parts—for example, failure of the furnace to turn on, noises during operation, or cases of poor heating due to mechanical malfunctions. Besides making the necessary repairs, these professionals can advise you on the condition of the furnace and other system components and present you with options for upgrades and replacements.

Home energy audit

If your complaint is broad—general lack of heat or high heating bills, or if you know you need to renovate the system but don't know how to get maximum results on a limited budget—consider hiring a home energy auditor to assess your home's entire heating, insulation, and ventilation environment, the so-called thermal envelope.

A thorough home energy audit focuses on the heating system and also on the ability of the house to retain temperature-controlled indoor air. The audit will assess the amount and quality of the insulation, the condition of the weatherstripping, and the number and soundness of the windows and doors. The most accurate energy audits employ a device called a blower door, a calibrated fan used to pressurize a home's interior and gauge its airtightness.

In most cases the results of an energy audit will be an energy rating based on the five-point scale created by the federally funded Home Energy Rating System Council (HERSC), together with an estimate of the home's energy costs and a list of feasible options for improving the rating. It may turn out, for example, that increasing a home's insulation or replacing single-pane windows with new multi-pane thermal models will increase comfort and lower heating bills to the desired levels for much less money than replacing the furnace or augmenting the rest of the system.

Some modern fireplaces can be installed without the need of a chimney or the masonry work of an old-fashioned fireplace.

A seat around a fireplace is an inviting place to sit when coming inside from cold weather. The glass enclosure provides protection from hot flames.

Annual heating system maintenance and any necessary repairs do not require inspection by code officials. However, alterations to the system of any kind usually require a building permit and inspections similar to those required for plumbing and electrical work.

account a home's energy efficiency and utility bills when figuring allowable loan amounts.

System improvements

If your system is hydronic, zoned heating can be installed by replacing mechanical inlet valves with valves that are thermostatically controlled. A weather-responsive aquastat may be a worthwhile upgrade for hot-water systems. With the aquastat, water in the boiler is heated to a temperature that relates to the outdoor temperature; the colder it is outside, the hotter the water supplied to the radiators. Other improvements to hydronic systems include cleaning all parts, especially furnace components, radiators, boilers on steam systems, and expansion tanks on older hot water systems (newer tanks containing diaphragms don't need maintenance), and insulating any accessible pipes; servicing the circulating pump on hot-water systems; and upgrading older furnaces with parts based on newer technology, including flame-retention burners on oil furnaces and electronic ignition on gas furnaces.

If your furnace is over 15 years old and is suffering and if improvements cannot raise its efficiency to more than 70 percent, you should consider replacing your furnace with a new one. The latest generation of home furnaces, both oil and gas, can achieve anywhere from 80 to 99 percent efficiency.

Choosing an auditor

You may have to hunt for an energy auditor, because in many parts of the country, few businesses are devoted strictly to the service. Good sources include independent home inspectors who are members of the American Society of Home Inspectors (ASHI; see pp. 168–171), a non-profit organization, as well as inspectors referred by banks offering energy mortgages, which take into

Insulation performs two important functions in the home: thermal (heat) insulation keeps the house warm in winter and cool in summer; acoustic (sound) insulation blocks outdoor noise from entering your home.

Besides controlling the temperature in the house, thermal insulation also keeps hot water hot and prevents water in cold pipes from freezing. Acoustic insulation can stop noise only to some extent, but it can help reduce noise if you live in an environment where traffic, aircraft, heavy industry, or noisy neighbors are a problem. If your home is deficient of either type of insulation, the professionals could help put things right.

Thermal insulation

Your house loses heat to the outdoors through the roof, walls, windows, doors, and floors. In newly built houses, these areas are insulated to meet the Department of Energy standards at the time of construction, but many older homes are underinsulated. The best way to have the insulation in your house evaluated is to call in an independent home inspector, preferably one who does energy audits (see pp. 70–71). Hire an insulation contractor to have it installed.

The largest gains in comfort and the greatest reduction in energy bills come from adding insulation beneath unheated roofs, inside or against exterior walls, and beneath floors above unheated basements or crawl spaces (see pp. 148–149). If you have insulation in those locations, adding an extra layer can improve performance; but there is no point in exceeding DOE recommendations in some parts of the house if other parts are below the standards.

Attics

In attics beneath pitched roofs, where the space is used for storage, if at all, the usual method is to place narrow batts of fiberglass or mineral wool insulation between the ceiling joists. Wider blankets of the material can be laid over the top, or more batts can be used, laid perpendicular to the layer underneath. Older houses may have some type of loose-fill insulation, such as vermiculite, between the ceiling joists; there is no harm in laying fiberglass or mineral wool over it.

Where attic space must be insulated—for example, if the attic has been converted as a living space or is used as a home office or studio (see pp. 84–87)—insulation batts can be laid between the rafters, or solid foam insulation can be installed instead. To comply with fire safety regulations, wallboard or other paneling must cover both materials.

In some cases, especially with flat roofs (which normally have little space for insulation above the ceiling), the best strategy is to insulate the roof from above by laying insulation over the existing roof deck and then covering it with a new waterproof surface.

Walls

Existing frame walls built without insulation can be insulated by blowing in loose-fill insulation through holes strategically drilled in the siding. Afterward, the holes are plugged. If you have solid walls, one answer is to apply insulation to their exterior sides; they are usually finished off with a synthetic stucco or aluminum or vinyl siding. The alternative is to demolish the inner wall surfaces, add insulation batts between the studs, and put up new wallboard, plaster, or paneling.

Sound insulation

Insulating an existing house against outside noise, and even insulating rooms from one another, is almost always a challenge. Before undertaking a sound insulation project, it may be worth consulting an acoustics engineer or specialist who can pinpoint problem areas and recommend the best fix for each. Few realistic options are available for barring external noise. Double glazing, in the form of new windows or added storm sashes outside old windows, usually has the greatest effect, but often at great expense. Replacing hollow entry doors with solid or insulated doors will provide additional soundproofing, but only in combination with improving the windows.

Indoors, rooms can be insulated from each other by adding another layer of wallboard on one or both sides of dividing walls. The layers should be separated by a grid of resilient strips made of metal, which help prevent sound from being transmitted from one layer to the next. Preventing sound from traveling between floors is more difficult; the only truly effective method is to add insulating materials to the floor surface, which means adding a new finish floor above the original.

Windows

Old single-pane windows can be refurbished with new glazing, replacement sashes and channels, storm windows, and plenty of caulking to eliminate drafts. If you are on a tight budget, consider all of these improvements before deciding to upgrade to new windows—usually a very expensive proposition.

New high-tech windows achieve much greater energy efficiency than old-style windows ever can, regardless of how meticulously they are rebuilt. In addition, modern windows are easier to clean, as well as practically maintenance-free—and they are one of the home improvements that can add to an older home's resale value.

A window contractor is the best person to handle replacing windows, although most carpenters can also perform the task. The best replacement windows for most areas of the country have been double-glazed with low-e glass, which provides maximum insulating value. (For more details on windows, see pp. 112–113 and pp.138–139.)

Floors

Insulating floors above an unheated basement or crawl space can make them warmer underfoot and can have a favorable impact on energy bills, provided the insulation in the rest of the house is adequate. The insulation—usually fiberglass or mineral wool batts—should be installed under the floor, with the vapor-barrier side facing upward so it lies against the underside of the flooring. It is more convenient to install batts with the vapor-barrier side facing down, but doing so can allow condensation to form inside the insulation, ruining it and possibly damaging the floor.

Slab floors can also be insulated; however, the job involves attaching framing to the slab. Batt or solid foam insulation is then laid down and covered by new finish flooring. Insulating a slab floor means hiring a carpenter, or a carpenter and an insulation contractor, to install the insulation, then a flooring contractor to install the finish flooring.

DIY jargon !

Double-glazed A window containing two panes of glass; sometimes the space between the panes is filled with a gas.

Finish flooring The final top layer of flooring that provides a decorative finish. Examples include sheet vinyl and carpet.

Low-e glass A term that stands for low-emissivity, it refers to a coating on glass that reflects heat while allowing light to pass (see p. 112).

In an uninsulated house, the roof, floors, and walls are responsible for 31 percent of air leaks.

Vents and exhaust fans account for 4 percent of air leaks.

Another 14 percent of air leaks escape through the fireplace.

About 10 percent of air leaks occurs from windows; doors are responsible for 11 percent of leaks.

Where plumbing enters the house another 13 percent of air leaks occur; ducts are responsible for 15 percent.

Condensation and infestations

The two problems that may plague your house are condensation and infestations by insects, mice, or other unwelcome visitors. Both situations can cause damage to your house and affect your health.

If your home has condensation, it can ruin its decor, affect your health, and lead to long-term structural damage. A pest infestation can also cause structural damage, especially to roof framing and floors. Both situations can be complicated to address—and hazardous if pesticides are involved.

About condensation

Air always contains water vapor, and some activities in the home, such as cooking and bathing, create larger quantities of it. The warmer the air is, the more water vapor it can carry. But when warm moist air meets a cold surface, its temperature drops and it can no longer hold the vapor, so it deposits it on the surface as droplets of water, or condensation.

You will see condensation most often on windows in cold weather, but it forms on other surfaces, such as poorly insulated exterior walls and ceilings, causing damage to paint and wallpaper as mold patches thrive in the damp conditions. It can form within the structure of the building, reducing the effectiveness of insulation—and sometimes ruining it—and creating the conditions for rot to flourish, especially below floors and roof sheathing (see pp. 150–151).

If you see signs of dampness, hire a weatherization contractor to determine the causes and solutions. A main cause of condensation throughout a house, even under the roof, is a damp basement or crawl space, especially one with a dirt floor (see pp. 146–147). Sealing the basement or crawl space will be the priority, unless another source of moisture accounts for the symptoms. Beyond

that, alleviating the problem will involve improving ventilation, insulation, and heating.

Improving ventilation and insulation

Adequate ventilation deters moisture-laden air from accumulating. A contractor will check for built-in vents in the basement or crawl space and in the attic and for powered ventilation in bathrooms and the kitchen. Most building codes specify minimum capacities for each of these systems; however, many homes need greater airflow than builders are required to install. The contractor will also check exhaust fans, range hoods, and clothes dryers to ensure they vent to the outdoors, instead of to unoccupied spaces such as the attic. (Many kitchen range hoods do not vent cooking vapors at all; they simply remove odors.)

If built-in vents are inadequate, the contractor will recommend making them larger or installing more vents, in addition to installing new exhaust equipment if none exists. Exhaust fans in bathrooms can be linked to humidity detectors, which switch the fans on whenever the humidity level rises too much.

Better insulation can ensure that wall and ceiling surfaces are warmer and less likely to offer a cool surface for moisture to condense on. Proper installation is crucial to avoid trapping moisture within the insulation or between the insulation and the building materials. Caulking and weatherstripping are also important. By reducing air leakage into and out of a home they enhance the ability of the insulation to perform.

Termites

The most serious pests that can attack a home are termites—they are the only ones that actually eat wood. You should have a professional termite inspection every few years. The

---

Alternative choices

More controlled heating can contribute to solving condensation problems. Unheated rooms are more prone to condensation, so maintaining a constant level of background warmth is better than heating the room up and the letting it get cold. If you have rooms that lack registers or radiators, a contractor may recommend installing electric baseboard heaters with thermostatic controls to provide the necessary background heating on an economical basis.

Simple steps to reduce condensation include:
• Closing bathroom doors when bathing or showering.
• Keeping pans covered when boiling large quantities of water.
• Opening a window in steamy rooms.
• Avoiding drying clothes on radiators.
• Keeping few indoor houseplants if you have restricted living space.

To help reduce condensation in the kitchen, the contractor will inspect the range hood. If it is inadequate, he or she will recommend updating it to a model that is a larger size or offers proper venting.

Rules & regulations

Ventilation specifications for houses are written into all building codes, but the specifics vary between local codes. As a rule of thumb, bathroom air should be ventilated at a rate of at least 8 air changes per hour (ACH), kitchens at a rate of at least 15 ACH.

Real-estate transactions in most areas involve a termite inspection by a licensed inspector. Building codes in termite-prone areas may also require certain features, such as termite shields at the tops of foundation walls, to be included in new house construction.

most common termite variety lives underground, so you may not know of an infestation until you encounter damaged wood. By then you may have a serious, expensive problem.

The first sign of an infestation is shelter tubes built by termites to cross exposed surfaces on their way to sources of wood. The tubes are sand color, about ¼ inch (6 mm) in width (but several tubes can be built together, making the overall width up to 2 inches/50 mm), and are most often found snaking their way upward along foundation walls.

If you spot even one tube, call a licensed professional pest-control operator (PCO) immediately. The conventional way to deal with termites involves injecting a chemical into the soil around the house and through the foundation and base-

ment floor. The chemical repels termites (it doesn't kill them). A newer method involves sinking termite monitoring stations—or traps—around the outside of the house and, after the stations detect termite activity, baiting them with a growth-inhibiting chemical. Termites visiting the traps ingest the chemical and eventually spread it throughout the colony, where it disrupts the insects' molting cycle and eventually eradicates the population. With both methods, success depends on regular inspections; treating new infestations is covered in the contract.

Other pests

There are other wood-damaging insects that can invade homes, including carpenter ants and bees, borers, powder post beetles, and

furniture beetles. Carpenter ants are the most common of these. Besides seeing them (they are black or dark brown and ¼ to ½ inch/6 to 13 mm long), a sign of their presence is piles of coarse sawdust at the entrance to their tunnels, which lead to their nests inside the wood. Carpenter bees resemble bumblebees; they, too, leave piles of sawdust beneath their tunnels, which are about ½ inch (13 mm) in diameter. For all these pests, call a licensed professional pest-control operator as you would for termites.

The list of other pests and vermin that could infest your home, garage, and outbuildings is a long one. It includes bees, wasps, ants, fleas, cockroaches, mice, rats, squirrels, chipmunks, raccoons, skunks, bats, moles, and even birds. If you have a problem with any of these, contact your local health department or animal control office before calling a commercial exterminator. The former will assist with infestations that are judged to be a health hazard, such as cockroaches, mice, and rats; the latter can help trap a larger animal that might be dangerous, especially if it feels cornered.

The day you moved into your house, the functions of its various rooms probably seemed predetermined—living room, dining room, kitchen, bathroom, and bedrooms. However, there is no reason why you should not put rooms to different uses.

Depending on your needs, some changes may be simple and not difficult to accomplish on your own. However, complicated rearrangements may require professional help from a designer, architect, or contractor to ensure the best results.

Living spaces

Altering the way you use your "living" space is the first place to start. For example, if you have separate living and dining rooms, you could simply swap their functions. The shapes of the two rooms may suit certain pieces of furniture better than the existing arrangement. Perhaps one room has a long uninterrupted wall against which your three-seater sofa could be placed, while the other has a bay window that would take the dining table, allowing space for the sideboard you could not fit into the original dining room.

Trying this out will involve moving a lot of furniture around, so make sure you have enough help for the job. This changeover is also

worth experimenting with if you have a large combined-use room where one end has been the established sitting area and the other the dining zone. Changing ends may simply work better for you.

Another way of changing the living space is to turn the existing main room into a combined kitchen and dining area, and to reclaim the existing dining room and kitchen for other uses. One could be the home entertainment center, for example, with television and audio equipment for family use. The other could then become a quiet zone for reading, homework, and the like. Whether this change is possible will depend on how easy it is to provide services to the new kitchen site, especially plumbing. This, and the planning of the new kitchen, is a job you may prefer to leave to a professional kitchen designer or remodeling contractor (see pp. 44–49).

Underused spaces

If you are fortunate enough to have a sunroom, improving its heating and ventilation could allow you to use it as the dining room, or as a second living room to enable parents and children to have their own leisure spaces.

Another possibility is to redesign the existing kitchen to provide space for family meals, perhaps by removing some of the kitchen cabinets you do not really need and making better use of the storage areas that remain. Because separate dining rooms are often used less than an hour a day for meals—usually only dinner—reclaiming them for use as

alternative living space would make better use of the space. It could even become an extra bedroom, or equipped with a fold-out sofa or futon for combined use.

You should also consider the way you use the existing bedrooms. Parents traditionally take the biggest bedroom in the house but use it only for sleeping; however, children often spend far more time in their bedroom during the day, so it may make sense to change places. The larger room could then become a combined bedroom and homework area, as well as a retreat for entertaining friends, while the parents simply sleep in the smaller bedroom.

If you have a spare bedroom but you rarely if ever entertain overnight guests, you can get rid of the beds and turn the room into a children's playroom, a space for your hobbies, such as sewing or painting, or a home office (see pp. 60–61).

Another possibility—especially if family members are always waiting to use the bathroom—is to convert a small, underused bedroom into a bathroom (see pp. 52–55), provided the new plumbing can be routed to the room without too much effort. Calling in a plumber or a bathroom remodeler will give you the opportunity to get some professional advice and solve any problems of this nature.

Turning a large living room into a combination kitchen and dining room allows the homeowner to prepare food while entertaining his or her guests.

Rules & regulations

Changes that do not involve structural work, installing new electrical wiring, or adding new pipes to the plumbing do not require a building permit. If your plans do involve such changes, hiring professionals will smooth the process, because obtaining the necessary permits and inspections is part of the contractor's job.

Connecting rooms

In examining the way your home works and trying to make the best use of the space, you may come to the conclusion that its layout needs redesigning. One way to do this is to create fewer but larger rooms by removing one or more interior walls.

You will not gain any additional floor space by connecting rooms together; however, you are likely to end up with rooms that work better for you. If this sounds like the solution to your problems, it is well worth enlisting professional help, both in the planning and in the execution of the work. This will ensure not only that the alterations provide workable solutions from a practical point of view, but also that the building's structure is not compromised in any way.

Options for change

In theory you can enlarge a room anywhere in the house by removing the wall between adjacent rooms. The most popular enlargement is to combine the living room and dining room. Another popular arrange-ment—if the dining room and kitchen are adjacent to each other—is to combine those two rooms to create a spacious eat-in kitchen.

You could also remove the wall between a front hall or foyer and a living room to enlarge the latter, but this may not be a good idea unless you have an enclosed front porch with an outer door; otherwise, the front door will open directly into the living room.

Another popular type of room that is often a candidate for enlarg-ing is the bedroom. You can com-bine two bedrooms into one large master bedroom, creating space for a dressing area and possibly an attached bathroom.

There are two points to bear in mind when thinking about enlarging a room. The first is the resulting loss of wall space for furniture to stand against. This may be offset by the fact that a doorway will become redundant, and blocking this off may reinstate some wall space. The second is the need to redecorate the two rooms as one, and possibly to lay new flooring as well.

What type of wall?

By far the most important factor in enlarging a room is whether the wall you want to remove is load-bearing or not. The likelihood is that walls running perpendicular to floor and ceiling joists (which are visible from the basement and attic, respectively) will be load-bearing, while walls running parallel to joists will not (see pp. 136–137).

Identifying load-bearing and non-load-bearing walls is often much more complicated than it looks, and considering the consequences of making the wrong decision, deter-mining the type of wall involved is something best left to an architect, building inspector, or experienced contractor. If the wall is load-bearing, not only must the correct type and size of supporting beam be specified to substitute for the wall after it is removed, consideration must also be given to the effect on other walls in the house of removing what amounts to a transverse brace between them. Transferring the load of the floor or roof above via a beam to the side walls may also transmit extra loads down to the foundation, and it takes an expert to assess the effects correctly and recommend any strengthening that may become necessary.

Another important reason to hire a professional is that removing a load-bearing wall requires a build-ing permit, and in order to obtain the permit, accurately drawn plans must be submitted along with a written description of the work. An architect and even an experienced contractor can draw up building plans far more easily and accurately than a homeowner; and obtaining building permits is part of their job—along with assuming legal responsibility for carrying out the project according to any building code requirements.

When work starts

The first job, if an allocated wall to be removed is load-bearing, is to provide support for the floor above it by using props of one type or

DIY jargon !

Joist A length of lumber, often a 2 x 8 (50 mm x 200 mm), that helps to support the floor above it and/or the ceiling below. A number of joists are laid running in the same direction across the room.

Load-bearing wall An interior wall that helps support the weight of the framing of the house above it.

Transverse brace In the context of load-bearing walls, a wall that acts as a link between other framing elements and transfers weight to them.

After creating a large opening in a wall, the adjacent areas may require redecorating—for example, a new coat of paint and putting up new matching curtains.

Furniture and decorative elements from the two smaller rooms can be redistributed in the larger room to provide a balance in the style.

If the original flooring in the two rooms is different, you should consider replacing it with a continuous flooring material to help join the rooms visually.

Ask yourself

- Are there never enough seats in your living room? This is an indication that you could benefit from a larger living area.

- Do you like to talk to your guests at the same time that you prepare the meal? An adjacent dining room and kitchen would be ideal for you.

- Are you tired of battling with your children to get into the bathroom first thing in the morning? Consider changing the function of two bedrooms to create a master bedroom with an attached bathroom.

another—usually a beam supported by an arrangement of posts and braces. Once the structure has been secured, an opening is created in the wall. The wallboard is removed and any services, such as electrical cables, plumbing, and ductwork, inside the wall are disconnected and set aside for rerouting elsewhere. The wall studs are then cut through with a saw and pried away before the remaining plate at the top of the wall and the sill at the bottom can be cut through and removed.

Next, the posts that will support the ends of the new support beam are installed in the openings in the wall at each end of the room. The beam is then lifted against the ceiling and the posts driven into

place beneath it and fastened. Afterward, the temporary supports are removed and the walls, ceiling, and floor repaired. Often the new support beam is concealed by enclosing it with wallboard.

Removing a non-load-bearing wall is much simpler, and in many areas it does not even require a building permit (although you may need one for a project that also includes installing new wiring or plumbing). The project consists of simply removing the wallboard from the wall, disconnecting and rerouting any services inside, then removing the wall framing as already described, followed by making the necessary repairs to the end walls, ceiling, and floor.

2 Dividing rooms

The opposite of enlarging rooms is creating more but smaller rooms by installing new partition walls within existing large rooms. This is a relatively straightfoward job, but dividing the room may mean changes to the electricity, heating, or plumbing.

If the room provides electricity, plumbing, and heating, these may need repositioning, and new components may have to be installed. You may also have to provide an additional window. If you are planning anything more elaborate than a partition, you should enlist the help of an architect to achieve the best arrangement. Otherwise a building or remodeling contractor should be able to plan and carry out the work.

Options for change

The most popular reason for dividing a room is to gain an extra bedroom. You may be able to partition only one existing large room, but you may get a better result by removing an existing partition wall between two rooms, then dividing the floor space to create three rooms. A variation on this involves removing a wall and building another to form one larger and one smaller room—for example, to create a bedroom suite with an adjacent dressing room or bathroom. You could, of course, simply partition off part of a large bedroom to achieve the same goal.

Another possible conversion is the partitioning of a bathroom to separate the toilet from the shower or bath area. This is an ideal project if the bathroom is shared by several family members—it allows simultaneous occupancy by two people.

Elsewhere in the house, you may want to create a laundry room, using part of the kitchen (see pp. 62–63). Another possibility might be reversing an earlier enlargement by reinstalling a dividing wall that had been removed. This restores two separate

This high-tech bathroom—with a shower, basin, and toilet—was designed to make the best use of available space without detracting from the style. A space for it was carved out of the main bedroom.

Ask yourself ?

- Is the room that you are thinking about dividing large enough to comfortably accommodate two rooms?

- Are both rooms to be used as bedrooms? If so, you may have to add windows.

- If you are creating another bathroom, have you planned to provide adequate ventilation? (See pp. 150–151.)

- Have you thought about how to provide access to the room?

living spaces, which may suit your lifestyle better than a big open-plan space, and it adds back wall space in the two rooms, providing more options for positioning furniture.

If you are planning to divide a bedroom, each room needs its own door; one room leading into another is awkward from a privacy standpoint. This means that if a new door cannot be placed where it will lead to the main hall, part of the floor space between the two rooms will have to be taken up by a hall of some kind giving access to the door.

When work starts

After clearing furniture and lifting floor coverings, your builder will check the way the joists run above where the new wall is to go (see pp. 136–137). If the joists run perpendicular to the new wall, the builder

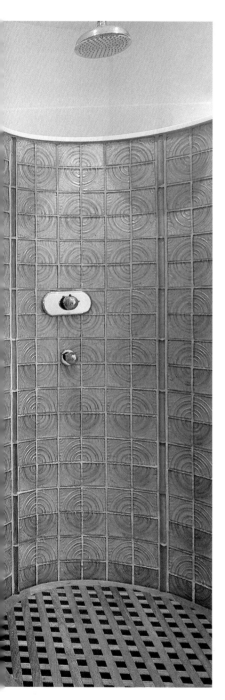

will mark their positions on the ceiling so that the top of the wall framing can be attached to them.

If the joists run parallel to the new wall, the builder must open the ceiling (unless there is access from the attic) to fasten 2 x 4 (50 x 100 mm) blocking at intervals between the pair of joists on either side of the new wall's location; this provides a nailing surface for anchoring the top of the wall. Many builders also attach a 1 x 6 (25 x 150 mm) board to the blocking, running between the joists to create a nailing surface. The walls at each end of the new partition's location will also be opened, and blocking installed for anchoring the new wall's ends.

Building the frame

If the room is large enough, most builders prefer to build a partition wall's framework on the floor, then tilt the assembly into place for fastening. To do this, a 2 x 4 (50 x 100 mm) is first nailed to the floor to mark the location of the new wall and to serve as the wall's sill. Measurements are then taken between the sill and the ceiling; these are used to cut and fasten together the wall's studs, plate, and a second sill that will rest on top of the first, making it easier to install the finished frame. If the plans specify, the framing may include a doorway or other opening.

When the frame is assembled, it will be lifted into position over the lower sill, then checked to ensure it is vertical. Shims will be inserted so the frame fits snugly between the ceiling and lower sill; then the plate will be fastened to the ceiling joists or blocking, the upper sill will be fastened to the lower sill, and the studs at the ends of the frame will be fastened to the end walls.

If no space is available to assemble the wall frame on the floor, it will be built in place, piece by piece, starting with the sill and plate. In both cases, after the framing is up, services will be installed, the sill will be cut away where it spans the doorway, if there is one, and the walls will be covered with wallboard. In some cases, insulation may be added for soundproofing. Finally, paint or wallpaper will be applied, moldings attached, and the door hung and radiators installed if specified.

Light and ventilation

Each new room must have adequate natural light and ventilation. This means providing an operable window in each room; and to satisfy most building codes, the window must be large enough to serve as an emergency exit. You may also find you need to shift the position of the existing window; for example, if the new partition wall divides it. (For more about windows, see pp. 112–113 and pp. 138–139.)

If the newly created room will be used as a kitchen, laundry room, bathroom, or half-bath, it need not have an operable window to satisfy code, but it must have adequate mechanical ventilation provided by an exhaust fan. If the room will contain a fuel-burning furnace, gas water heater, or gas clothes dryer, check with an installer to be sure the appliance will have adequate ventilation to run safely.

2 Conversions and additions

The opportunity to convert unused space into living space or to add on extra rooms—and at the same time control the quality of the building as it progresses—is one that cannot be had from buying an existing house. You can decide on the energy efficiency of the addition, and the levels of daylight, sound insulation, and sturdiness of construction that you want instead of settling for what builders have chosen for you (which may be the bare minimum required by building regulations). You can also decide on its layout and decoration to ensure that the changes suit your needs and tastes. In doing so and by taking a careful interest in how the work is planned and done, you will undoubtedly add value to your biggest asset—your home.

With the help of an imaginative architect, you can convert just about any room in your house; this individualistic bathroom (far left) was once an underused bedroom. An architect can also design an addition, such as this appealing kitchen (left).

Converting an attic can enhance your home by creating attractive and interesting living space. Because it, in effect, adds an extra habitable room, it will also add to your home's resale value if you plan to sell it at a later date.

Just because your unfinished attic seems cold, dreary, and uninhabitable, it does not mean it cannot be made into a comfortable living or work space. With help from an architect or experienced remodeling contractor, you'll most likely find that even a small attic can be modified by adding dormers, support walls, a staircase, or even raising the roof so that it conforms with building codes, as well as be more comfortable and practical.

Assessing your attic

The key to knowing whether adding a dormer or other serious remodeling feature will be necessary is to measure the ceiling height. A standard specification of most building codes is that at least half the floor area to be occupied must have an average ceiling height of 7½ feet (2,275 mm) or more. Measure from the tops of the floor joists to the collar ties that span the rafters near the ridge board to determine the

Rules & regulations

Most building codes set minimum standards for dimensions, such as ceiling height, the number and size of windows, and the size and location of entry doors, to ensure the safety of the occupants. It is essential that your architect and contractor start your attic conversion only after they have planned the remodel to meet local building codes.

attic's maximum height. To alter the proportion of the floor and ceiling areas so that the code specifications can be met, you should plan on having kneewalls installed along the sloping sides of the roof. Generally, kneewalls must be at least 4 feet (1,220 mm) high to influence the calculations satisfactorily.

Another key component to check is the size and condition of the attic floor joists. In most homes built since World War II, these will be made of 2 x 8s (50 x 200 mm—the exact measurements are closer to 1½ x 7½ inches/38 mm x 190 mm), spaced so their centers fall at intervals of 16 inches (405 mm). If the joists are smaller or are spaced at greater intervals, it will probably be necessary to strengthen the floor by adding supplementary joists, which can add to the cost of the project.

Inspecting the roof

Finally, and perhaps this should be the first area to consider, check whether the roof is supported by actual rafters, by purlins and diag-

A curved window was artfully fitted into a gable wall for this renovation. Allowing for natural light is an important factor in any attic conversion.

In this attic conversion, the rafters were left exposed as a design feature and the space in the peak of the roof was left accessible to store belongings.

Skylights

In comparison to dormers, skylights lie flush with the roof. They admit light if one or more are positioned strategically and can be opened for ventilation, but skylights do not add headroom. Nor are they usable as emergency exits, because of their height above the floor—they are usually near the peak of the roof.

Having a skylight installed may or may not require a building permit where you live. Although the job is not likely to approach the cost of adding a dormer, the success of the installation depends on the skill of the installer. A poorly installed skylight can be an ongoing source of leaks and other problems such as difficulty opening and closing the window, fogging, and admitting too much light. Before choosing a skylight, investigate the many special features available for them, including electronic controls and shades.

onal braces, or by trusses. Attic conversions are easiest where rafters are present. Although a conversion that involves a purlin-supported roof is more difficult, it is not too great a challenge. In general, kneewalls can substitute for the diagonal braces found on most roofs of this type, which can then be removed to create open space in the converted area.

A truss-supported roof, unfortunately, is problematic and will add greatly to the expense of your conversion. Strengthening the trusses to the extent that their inner braces can be removed to make space usually means replacing them with rafters, and the truss members that might serve as floor joists—usually 2 x 4s (50 x 100 mm)—will also have to be replaced. (For more on roof supports, see pp. 128–129.)

After doing all of this preparation work, you are ready to begin planning the project seriously with an architect or remodeling contractor.

Dormers

Unfinished attics don't normally have windows. Any attic conversion that will be used for living or work space will require natural lighting. One possible way to provide it is to have dormers installed. They extend an attic's full ceiling height outward and provide a place to install conventional windows that not only admit daylight but permit easy ventilation and emergency escape, if necessary, in case of fire.

However, adding one or more dormers to an attic almost always requires a building permit, and you may also need a professional evaluation of how the new structure will affect the stresses and loads already present in the existing house. Dormers have the least effect on houses with steep roofs; on houses with shallow roofs, extra bracing is often needed, both to support the dormer roof and to support the rafters on that side of the house.

DIY jargon !

Collar ties A part of the roof framing near the peak of the roof, they link together the rafters to prevent them from spreading outward.

Kneewall A short wall that runs between the sloping side of the roof and the floor. It blocks off the low space where the rafters meet the tops of the walls and the attic floor joists.

Purlin An additional horizontal support for long rafters.

Rafter The sloping parts of the roof frame that support the roof covering.

Ridge board The central horizontal support at the peak of the roof.

Trusses Prefabricated roof frames that replace rafters.

Design check

Unless you are planning to include dormers or a major roof alteration, make sure that you are comfortable with the amount of headroom in the attic—and that it meets any local code requirements—before going ahead with a renovation. Too low a ceiling or too little overall ceiling space can prove to be claustrophobic, and it can also turn overhead light fixtures into obstacles unless the fixtures are recessed.

Stairs

The stairway is also a consideration. Older prewar homes often have ordinary, although often steep, stairs leading to the attic, which is accessible through a normal doorway.

When to inspect !

- Check the work in progress each day after your builder has left.

- Check to make sure that the items called for in the plans and contract are correct and are located where the plans specify. If something seems to be wrong, tell the builder the next day so that he or she can correct it as soon as possible.

- If a building permit has been obtained, at least two formal inspections must be conducted by a building inspector. You should plan to attend these—they are usually instructive.

Newer homes feature ceiling trapdoors as a means of access—with or without pull-down stairs.

It pays to get professional advice from an architect or contractor who is experienced in staircase installation before deciding where and how to create an attic staircase, and what kind to install. For both privacy and easy exit in case of a fire, attic stairs should come up from a landing or hallway, not from within another room. Creating room for a staircase may mean taking space from two upstairs bedrooms or giving up one of them entirely. Codes usually require that headroom above a staircase landing be a minimum of 6 feet 8 inches (2030 mm) high.

Plumbing

If your attic is to contain a bathroom, plan to locate it above existing facilities on the floor below to simplify installing the necessary pipes. Supply pipes can also be extended from a lower floor by routing them inside a closet (see pp. 152–155).

In all likelihood, floor joists in the area will require strengthening to support the toilet and other fixtures, especially if a tub is installed. The usual method of strengthening joists is to "sister" them by fastening an additional joist against each one. Blocking between joists also adds strength by distributing otherwise concentrated loads and stresses across the grid (see pp. 142–143).

Insulation

Insulating your new room is essential, and it is easy enough to do by installing batts or a combination of batts and rigid foam insulation between the rafters and wall studs, and on exposed areas of the floor. However, experts consider it essential that an

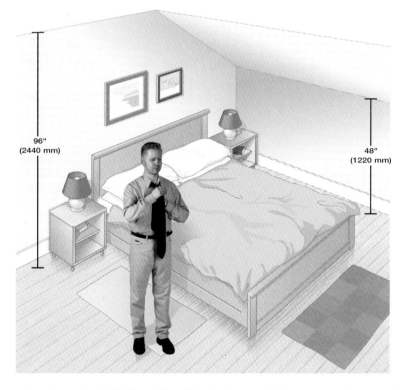

96"
(2440 mm)

48"
(1220 mm)

The ceiling of a gabled roof should be high enough for you to walk around without hitting your head; kneewalls set the boundaries.

air space be maintained for ventilation between the top of the insulation and the underside of the roof sheathing, or condensation trapped there can cause fungus and decay to thrive.

Normally, airflow is created by first installing U-shaped plastic or cardboard vent channels against the sheathing. The insulation is then installed, with care taken not to block the soffit vents located at the eaves. Gable vents, or else a continuous vent running along the ridge top, complete the system. (For more on condensation and ventilation, see pp. 74–75 and pp. 150–151. For more on insulation, see pp. 148–149.)

Floors and walls

After any wires, pipes, and ducts are run to provide electricity, water, and heating, the subfloor can be laid down if there isn't one. The finish flooring can be laid once the walls have been put up.

Although you probably wouldn't consider leaving it exposed, insulation in an attic (and in any other habitable area of a house) must be covered with wallboard or plaster at

An attic staircase with open treads (without risers) and a simple balustrade allows more light into a constricted hallway.

Rules & regulations

Usable attic space is almost always considered habitable by building codes; however, it must meet certain fire-safety requirements. (You will want to make sure the area is as safe as possible in case of a fire, regardless.) Chief of these is that the area contains a secondary exit in addition to the door. Generally, an operable window large enough to climb out of (or for a firefighter equipped with an airpack to climb into) will suffice; codes usually specify that the window must be more than 24 inches (610 mm) high as well as 20 inches (510 mm) wide; the bottom of the opening must be no more than 44 inches (1120 mm) from the floor.

least ½ inch (13 mm) thick. The gypsum in wallboard and plaster is fire-resistant. In the event of a fire, the code-specified material will shield the insulation—which is flammable and gives off toxic fumes—from igniting long enough for occupants in the attic to escape.

A conversion in an attic with a gable roof will require kneewalls to establish the living area. These are a special shorter form of partition walls (see pp. 80–81).

Fire safety

Installing one or more smoke detectors is important. If you have only one installed, the best place for it is on the ceiling above the stair opening. Choose a photoelectric model; they work best for detecting smoky, smoldering fires typical of the kind that start in bedrooms and other occupied areas. A battery-operated detector is okay to use, but a model that plugs into a wall outlet or is wired directly to a household circuit eliminates having to change the battery. Such models can be interconnected so that all the smoke detectors in the house will sound—even if only one is triggered. This is especially important in an attic, where an occupant might not hear a smoke alarm sounding on a lower floor, and vice versa.

2 | Converting basements

Basements can make ideal rooms in a house where an extra room is desired but all the available rooms are already claimed. Home offices, play or recreation rooms, bathrooms, and workshops are all suitable candidates for a basement conversion.

Basements are soundproofed from exterior noise and free from dramatic changes in temperature. Providing they are dry and you can introduce sufficient daylight and ventilation, underused or neglected basement space can become part of your home, offering opportunities for extended living space.

Assessing basements

Some basements are better candidates for remodeling than others. So-called buried basements, which are enclosed on all four sides, are the most challenging. On the one hand, because there are a number of specific code restrictions (see box above, right), many buried basements simply cannot be converted for occupancy without major alterations that may be too expensive to make the conversion worthwhile.

On the other hand, a buried basement with a bulkhead door leading to the outside, with adequate ceiling height, and with sufficient windows to furnish acceptable natural lighting and ventilation can be fairly easily converted to practically any use. Light in such basements (which, ironically, are often called daylight basements) is likely to be scarce by aboveground standards, so you should be prepared to devote a good part of your design and decorating budget to providing extensive artificial lighting.

Part of this buried basement has been converted into a bathroom, a quiet place to retreat to have a long soak in the tub.

Rules & regulations

Building codes typically specify that areas to be used for purposes other than simple storage and utility must have ample natural lighting (either 10 square feet/3,000 sq mm of window space or an amount equal to 10 percent of the floor area, whichever is greater), a minimum ceiling height of 7½ feet (2,275 mm) over at least half the floor area, and a minimum of two exits if the area is used for sleeping.

The easiest type of basement to convert is what is known as a walkout basement, which has at least one wall fully exposed above ground level. A walk-out basement is typically drier, better lit, and better ventilated than a buried basement, and it features either full-height sliding patio doors, standard-size windows, or both. Converting this type of basement is also more likely to recoup the most value if you sell the house in the future.

What's involved

No matter how you plan to use the basement, any dampness will have to be eradicated before finished floors, walls, and ceilings can be installed and the mechanicals can be enclosed. If the staircase is unsightly, you may want to make improvements to it (see pp. 64–65). You may need to add windows or improve ventilation. The basement will also require lighting and electrical outlets (see pp. 90–91). If the basement is to include a bathroom, it will require additional plumbing work.

Adding a bathroom

Installing a toilet and other plumbing fixtures in a basement is usually complicated but seldom impossible. The central issue is that the main household drain leading to the sewer or septic tank may be too high—and, therefore, too close to the fixtures, especially a toilet—to allow drainage by gravity. The best answer is to install a pumped drainage system, featuring a sealed collection basin, or sump, into which waste water drains and is then pumped upward to the main drain by an electrically powered ejector pump located inside the basin.

Installing the collection basin involves breaking through the basement floor and excavating a pit in the ground beneath. A separate, or dedicated, electric circuit to control the pump will be necessary (most

codes specify including a switchable light directly above the installation), and either the fixtures will have to be tied into the existing supply and vent plumbing or new supply pipes and vent stacks must be installed (see pp. 152–155). A bathroom must also be equipped with code-specified electrical circuitry (see pp. 156–157) and an approved exhaust fan or other mechanical ventilator (see pp. 150–151).

Hiding the mechanicals

Basements often house mechanicals: the furnace, water heater, and related heating, cooling, and ventilation equipment, and you will want to hide these. Fuel-burning furnaces and water heaters, and forced-air heating and cooling equipment, require air circulation to operate properly. For some equipment, codes also require a minimum distance away from combustible surfaces. Before planning to enclose mechanicals, obtain professional advice from an architect, heating systems engineer, or contractor, or the office of your local building inspector.

Ask yourself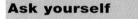

- Are there enough windows to provide adequate ventilation? If not, is it possible to add windows or ventilation?

- Once the floors and ceilings are installed, will there be enough headroom in the conversion?

- Is there a door to the outside? If not, the basement may not be suitable for a conversion. Remember, you need two exit doors for sleeping quarters.

- What is the condition of the staircase? It will have to take more strain than the occasional use many basements get.

Converting basements 89

Basement dampness

Before a basement is remodeled, the walls and floor must be dry. Achieving this may be as simple as investing in a portable dehumidifier to operate in the basement or coating the walls with moisture-resisting paint containing fine cement; or it may involve hiring a waterproofing contractor to install footing drains or exterior drainage materials (see pp. 146–147).

Initially, it may be a good idea to get an unbiased evaluation of your basement and advice on some likely courses of action by hiring an independent home inspector experienced in analyzing moisture problems. Only after you can be sure your basement will remain free of dampness year-round should you proceed with remodeling; otherwise, you run the risk of losing building and finish materials to mold and decay—and of creating an unpleasant, unhealthy space no one wants to be in.

Basement floors

Because most basement ceilings are low, it is important to consider floors that won't drastically reduce the space between floor and ceiling. In some basements, it is possible to "raise" the ceiling height by tearing up and excavating the floor a few

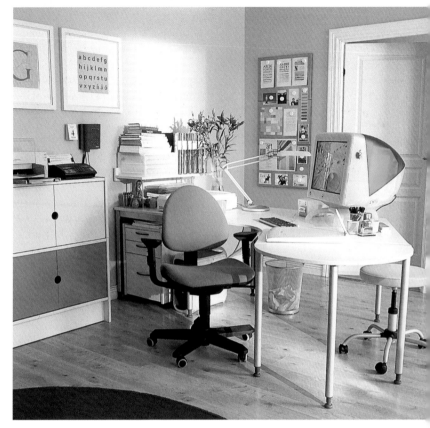

In a basement with little or no natural lighting, choose light colors to help the room appear brighter, and provide plenty of artificial lighting.

Rules & regulations

Electrical codes generally do not permit concealing junction boxes— covered metal boxes that contain spliced, or joined, circuit wires. Before deciding on a basement ceiling, you should consult a building inspector or an electrical contractor.

inches (cm). However, the digging must not expose the foundation footings or exceed their depth.

Types of flooring

The best solution is to cover the floor with a thin material such as asphalt or vinyl tile, sheet vinyl, foam-backed carpeting, or even linoleum, which has become trendy once again. You should also consider materials designed for commercial installations; office and similar buildings typically have concrete floors similar to the ones in basements. Laminated wood strip or

parquet flooring, with the pieces either glued to each other (called floating flooring) or embedded in mastic (called glue-down flooring) also is a possibility, provided the basement floor is level.

A conventional wood floor can also be installed if there is enough headroom for the level of the floor to be raised several inches (cm). Mastic or moisture-proof polyethylene sheeting is used to cover the concrete, on top of which are fastened pressure-treated (water- and decay-resistant) 2 x 4s (50 x 100 mm) laid on their sides. Called sleepers, these usually are embedded in mastic but sometimes are nailed to the concrete with fasteners "shot" into place with a tool that fires gunpowder cartridges. A layer of polyethylene sheeting is placed over the sleepers, followed by the floorboards. If you are installing conventional parquet tiles, plywood sheets must be nailed above the sleepers first, to create a subfloor for securing the tiles.

Leveling a floor

Leveling an uneven basement floor can often be achieved by floating a liquid filling compound over the surface. For a floor that is out of plane overall, the usual solution is to pour a fresh layer of concrete, about 2 inches (50 mm) thick, over it. This must be done by an experienced concrete contractor to avoid the new layer cracking or separating from the original material.

Walls

If appearance is the only concern, there is no reason why basement walls can't simply be painted to cover them inexpensively. Paint provides a finished surface that harbors less dust than bare concrete, is easier to keep clean, and can be of a color that is pleasing and reflects light. However, basement walls often are finished out with framed

Lighting

Overhead lighting—in particular, fluorescent fixtures—can be easily installed above acoustic ceilings and covered by translucent panels designed for the purpose. Wallboard ceilings can accommodate code-approved recessed fixtures, but these are harder to install; track lighting with surface wiring is easier, but it must be located so the fixtures are out of the way of people's heads.

walls, insulated, and covered with either wallboard or wood paneling.

One method involves attaching wood strips, called furring strips, to the walls to create a nailing surface for wallboard or wood panels. Rigid foam insulation is then cut and fastened to the basement walls in the spaces between the strips; afterward, polyethylene sheeting is attached to repel any indoor moisture, and this is followed by the wallboard or paneling.

Super-insulated walls

In cold climates, thicker fiberglass or mineral wool batt insulation can be installed by first erecting a standard wall frame made of 2 x 4 (50 x 100 mm) or 2 x 6 (50 x 150 mm) wood studs against the concrete wall. This type of an installation also allows for extending pipes and electrical circuits easily, just as in ordinary interior house walls. Insulation is fitted in the spaces between the wall studs. Polyethylene sheeting is then attached, followed by wallboard or paneling.

Ceilings

In basements, ceilings are used to cover unsightly joists, girders, pipes, and anything else beneath (and including) the subfloor; and some ceilings provide moderate sound-proofing between floors. However, while giving a finished look, basement ceilings often have the effect of making the headroom even less, so think carefully about whether you really need one before you invest in it. In a basement workshop, for example, you may decide against it.

Acoustic dropped ceilings are popular. These consist of a horizontal metal grid (suspended from short wires attached to the joists) into which are slid panels of sound-absorbing fiber material. Acoustic ceilings are inexpensive to install and are a feasible solution for covering pipes that are mounted to the

When to inspect !

- Check the work each day after the builder leaves, so that you won't interfere with his or her schedule. Inform the builder the next day of any problems so they may be addressed before fixing them becomes difficult.

- Pay particular attention to moistureproofing; don't allow remodeling to proceed until you are satisfied that the methods and quality of work meet the standards of the contract and will result in a permanently dry basement, barring an unforeseen catastrophe.

- If electrical and plumbing work are involved in the conversion, two formal inspections of each system is usually required. You should accompany the inspector during the inspections.

undersides of the joists; raising or rerouting these to accommodate an ordinary ceiling can be too costly to be worthwhile.

If pipes and wiring are not a problem in your basement, a better solution is to install an ordinary wallboard ceiling. It will look better and won't dramatically reduce the amount of headroom available. Usually a grid of furring strips is first attached perpendicular to the joists, with shims (thin strips of wood) strategically inserted above the furring strips to achieve a horizontal plane. The wallboard is then fastened with screws to the strips and finished.

Don't despair if your basement has a few problematic pipes or ducts but is otherwise a candidate for a wallboard ceiling. Pipes and ducts can often be separately "boxed," or enclosed with furring strips covered by wallboard, and when finished will blend with the rest of the ceiling.

2 Converting garages

Attached or built-in garages are usually economical to convert. Converted garages generally make spacious, well-lit living areas suitable for just about any use; they are well situated to become family rooms, dining rooms, and home offices.

Rules & regulations

You will need a building permit to convert a garage into a habitable space, because you will be changing its original use and probably adding services such as new electrical circuits, plumbing, and heating.

In a simple conversion, the only costs may be for interior finishing, adding a door and windows, and closing the original garage entry. An architect or designer can suggest ways to blend the conversion with the rest of your home and to customize it to your needs and taste. A new carport or other vehicle area may be built when the conversion takes place.

Evaluating a garage

Two important concerns are the floor (see box, below) and the ceiling. Unfinished garages may not have enough ceiling joists to support a finished ceiling; in older garages, the joists may be too small to meet code requirements. New or additional joists must be added, especially if you add a loft or second floor.

Most attached garages have an outside entry door and at least one window. You may wish to retain the existing door, but the window will be too small for your needs, even if it meets code requirements for size and location. Finally, you will want to have some landscaping done to remove all or part of the driveway.

The old door was removed and new windows and doors were installed, making this garage conversion a delightful, airy family room.

Subflooring

Preparing the subfloor is the first step, after moistureproofing and any foundation work is completed. One method is to fasten boards called sleepers in rows across the slab (see pp. 142–143). Insulation material—usually fiberglass or mineral wool batts—is then installed between the sleepers and a sheet of polyethylene is laid over the top as a moisture barrier. Sheets of ⅝-inch- (16-mm-) thick plywood are nailed to the sleepers to cover them.

If the ceiling height allows for it, another subflooring method is to fasten joists across the tops of the foundation walls, followed by insulation, a moisture barrier, and plywood. This raises what would be a sunken floor in the converted room to the same level as the floor in the house. With this method, you must add ventilation beneath the floor to stop condensation (see pp. 150–151).

For both subflooring methods, it is important to accommodate any under-floor plumbing. Pipes must be installed and inspected before the plywood sheets are attached.

Walls, ceiling, roof

Wall and ceiling framing (except as noted earlier) in the new area should already be in place and of adequate size. Insulation will be needed before

When to inspect !

- Inspect the progress at the end of each day—especially work that will be concealed such as wiring, heating, and plumbing.

- Once the floor is completed, inspect it to see if it is level.

- After the doors and windows have been installed, open and close them to ensure they operate smoothly.

covering the framing with wallboard or paneling; however, before this is done new electrical, plumbing, or mechanical services must be installed and inspected. The existing exterior wallcovering should be satisfactory; however, faded siding may have to be replaced, and walls that were modified to accommodate new windows and doors may need painting, so that all surfaces match.

Providing it is in good condition, the existing roof should be adequate. However, if insulation has been added to the interior, code-required venting must be installed to prevent condensation beneath it.

Windows and doors

The original garage door opening is a convenient location for sliding patio doors. However, there is no reason why windows similar to those used on the rest of the house cannot be installed in the conversion—preferably at the same height. You may also want windows installed on other walls or a skylight in the roof.

Fire codes stipulate that attached garages must be separated from the house by a fire-rated door, usually made of steel. Converting the garage to a living space will allow you to remove or replace this door, and to modify the doorway—for example, you may want an open archway without a door.

Garage floors

Several factors can influence the cost and design of a garage conversion. A major concern is the existing garage floor. Assuming the garage already has a concrete floor, installing finish flooring above it will first involve repairing and moisture-proofing the concrete surface, plugging any floor drains to prevent the release of sewer gas and odors, and carefully leveling the subfloor.

Garage floors usually slope toward the door opening to drain water dripping off vehicles. Sleepers or other framing on which the subfloor will rest must be tapered or set on strategically placed shims to compensate. In some cases masonry work may be involved to fill the gap across the door opening so it is level with the foundation walls supporting the rest of the garage. Foundation walls generally must rise 8 inches (200 mm) above grade (ground level) to satisfy building codes.

Adding new space: Sunrooms

Sunrooms, or sun porches, have always been a popular addition. They differ from so-called sun spaces, which are a concept from the 1970s and are designed to capture solar radiation for household heating—sunrooms are designed for livability.

Sunrooms can be any shape, but long shed-roof designs featuring vertical glazing and skylights are the most popular. They are easy to build, give plenty of headroom, and can be shaded with ordinary blinds and drapes. Hiring an architect or designer should pay off in a design that blends with the existing house.

Construction

Most sunrooms are built on a conventional concrete slab, 4 inches (100 mm) thick, supported by footings sunk below the frost line as required by local building codes. However, sunrooms can also be built on adequately supported decks, either at ground level or outside rooms on upper floors. To retain heat and release it slowly—thereby reducing daily temperature swings—ceramic tile finish flooring

Rules & regulations

You will need a building permit for a sunroom, because it is an addition to a house. Zoning and setback restrictions may also apply, so check with the office of your local building inspector before going too far with your plans. If the sunroom is attached to a bedroom in such a way that it eliminates a window or door designated by code as a secondary exit for use in an emergency, you will need to replace it by installing a door leading from the bedroom into the sunroom and an operable door or window in the sunroom that can serve as an emergency exit.

is often applied. (Localized intense sunlight in sunrooms can warp wood flooring and fade colored vinyl and other synthetic materials.)

Sunroom walls can be framed using 2 x 4 (50 x 100 mm) or 2 x 6 (50 x 150 mm) studs, sills, and plates, with insulation installed in areas not filled by glazing. Where one wall of a sunroom is an existing house wall, removing the siding and replacing it with wallboard, paneling, or another finish material is all that is needed. Insulation in the existing wall should be left in place.

Roofing can be standard. From a design standpoint, it is usually best to match the finish roofing with that of the rest of the house. A sunroom can be roofed simply by extending the line of the house roof so it overhangs the new construction.

All glazing should be double- or triple-glazed low-e glass (the term stands for low-emissivity) to give maximum insulation and reduce temperature swings (see pp. 112–113). Insulated shades may also be needed to limit heat loss during clear, cold nights and to prevent excess heat buildup during sunny days, in both summer and winter.

Orientation

To obtain sunlight during the winter months, sunroom glazing must face within 30 degrees east or west of true south (this is not magnetic south on a compass). In addition, the glazing must not be shaded by trees, an overhanging roof, or any other obstacles. An architect or designer experienced in sunroom construction can help you decide on the best location.

Ventilation

Adequate ventilation is crucial in a sunroom. In winter, natural ventilation can be induced by opening the sunroom to the rest of the house, with the benefit that solar-heated sunroom air will flow to the other rooms. However, much depends on opening and closing the sunroom at the right times. Because most sunrooms cool off quickly in the evening unless monitored, leaving a sunroom open too long can quickly lower temperatures in the entire house after the sun goes down.

In summer, excess heat can be vented from a sunroom by opening exterior doors and windows while keeping the openings to the rest of the house closed. In addition, operable vents can be installed during construction to take advantage of breezes. Such vents should be placed low on the sunroom wall facing the direction of prevailing winds—the windward side—and high on the opposite, or leeward, side. (Keep the vents closed during winter months.)

For year-round ventilation, install thermostatically controlled exhaust fans. These can be positioned to direct heated air into the house in winter and to expel it to the outdoors in summer. A heating and cooling contractor can determine the correct components needed.

A sunroom can have commanding views of the outdoors and offer a comfortable warm place to relax. This sunroom provides a sitting area—others may be used for dining.

The porch is a distinctly North American architectural feature, and it was popular from the 19th century through the 1940s. Although changing lifestyles (largely in favor of outdoor decks) have seen its demise, signs of a revival are appearing.

If you've inherited a house with a front porch, restoring and maintaining it will be worth the effort. There are also ways that you can convert a porch—for example, you can screen it in to keep out the insects in summer and wind in winter, or you can make it into another room. If your house doesn't have a porch, don't feel left out—it is possible to add one.

Restoring a porch

Water and attacks by pests are usually the chief elements causing a porch to slip into disrepair. Because of their shallow pitch, porch roofs are vulnerable to leakage and the effects of prolonged snow cover and wind-driven rain. An experienced roofing contractor is the person to hire to revive a failing roof. In most cases the job involves removing all the layers of the existing roof, followed by rebuilding it with new flashing and sheathing, as well as new shingles, gutters, and downspouts.

Porch flooring often decays due to moisture. Other vulnerable areas are the bottoms of posts or columns and the joints between rails and balusters. For these repairs, hire a carpenter experienced in porch repair. Restoring columns involves bracing the porch roof temporarily while the old columns are removed and either repaired or replaced. In some cases, creative repair of ornate columns is possible with skillful woodworking and the use of epoxy or other synthetic compounds. When replacing wooden components, moisture- and insect-repelling pressure-treated lumber should be used whenever possible, and careful attention should be paid to applying high-quality paint or another protective finish afterward.

Ventilation beneath porches is usually inadequate. As a result, rotting joists and other supports—particularly the ledger, which joins the porch to the house—are often the cause of major problems. Decayed framing must be replaced, even if the floorboards are still sound. A new ledger should be flashed (see pp. 146–147) to prevent moisture from seeping between it and the house.

It is important that porch joists slope away from the house slightly, so the floor will drain away rainwater. There should be a minimum vertical distance of 8 inches (200 mm) between the underside of the frame and the ground, both to allow ventilation and to discourage termites.

While an experienced carpenter is the best person to hire for frame repairs, as well as to replace lattice surrounding the base of a porch, a mason is best to repair brick, stone,

Screening in a porch

In many areas of the country, screening to keep out insects is the only way to make a porch habitable during the summer months. Where winters are fierce, glassing in a porch increases protection from wind, adds a measure of heat through solar gain, and provides an enclosed space for light utility use without having to go outdoors.

Unless the porch is large, a carpenter should be able to add framing to a porch to accept custom-made screen panels in summer and plastic or glass storm-window panels in winter. This involves attaching a framework around all the porch openings, then constructing individual panels to which screening material, acrylic glazing, or window glass is fastened. The panels are attached to the frame with bolts; the holes for these are drilled at uniform intervals so that the panels are interchangeable.

Rules & regulations

Because building a new porch is an addition, you will have to obtain a building permit before work can start. You may also have to address municipal zoning and setback issues in some areas.

If you want to enclose a porch to make a new living space, you will need a building permit.

Few outward aspects of a house spell charm, domestic tranquillity, and comfort more than a porch. This inviting addition provides a pleasant sitting area, and it supplies protection from the summer sun, from winter winds, and from rain.

Enclosing a porch

To obtain extra living space, your porch can be enclosed with solid walls in an easy and fairly inexpensive way. Provided the porch is in good repair, and unless you plan to install plumbing, you probably need to hire only a carpenter, a drywaller, and an electrician to do the main work, apart from finishing and adding new flooring. The basic procedure involves covering the porch floor with an adequate level subfloor (usually plywood), then erecting the walls—including any windows and doors—and ceiling. Siding is added; wiring is installed, followed by insulation; then wallboard is applied. Painting and finish flooring complete the job.

Adding a new porch

If you have a relatively new house without a porch, you can add one along one, two, or more sides of the house. A new porch can dramatically improve the house's appearance and add to its resale value. You should hire an architect or building designer to help with plans for a large porch. For a simple design, a general contractor who has completed similar projects is usually qualified, but beware—porch design is complicated, and a poor design may result in structural problems or an awkward appearance.

Building a porch is a major construction project. Footings must be poured (below frost level in areas where the ground freezes in winter) and piers or posts set on them to support the rest of the structure. Framing similar to that of a house floor or an outdoor deck must be installed, with flashing added and other steps taken to protect against moisture. A roof, also similar to that of a house, must be built. Porch decking (the floorboards), a ceiling, rails, and stairs must be added, along with gutters, trim, and a protective finish such as paint.

or concrete posts supporting the corners of a porch or running beneath it. In areas where the ground freezes in winter, porch posts must be set on footings sunk below the frost line to prevent heaving.

Finally, porch stairs often sag and fail with age and years of abuse. Hire a carpenter who will repair wooden parts using pressure-treated lumber (or have the entire staircase replaced with a manufactured one, provided the style is suitable). You

should take pains to ensure that the bottoms of the stair carriages (the slanting pieces on which the steps are built) have been fastened to galvanized anchors set in a concrete footing in a way that keeps their ends from touching the ground. They should not sit directly on the footing or on a flat stone, where they will eventually foster decay. (Stair footings, like porch support posts, should be sunk below the frost depth where appropriate.)

2 Additions

Adding rooms to your house provides extra space for living arrangements, activities, guests, and storage. Skillfully budgeted additions can also increase the resale value of your home and bring a healthy return on investment when you sell.

Like most other involved projects, careful thinking and good planning are the keys to success. Next to building an entire house, additions are the most complicated construction task that a homeowner can undertake. In most cases, hiring an architect or a building designer to help with the planning and to provide finished drawings will be money well spent (see pp. 12–13). Beforehand, however, you should ask yourself and your family some important questions to determine what you want from the addition.

What are your needs?

First of all, think about how you want to use the new space, whether it will be as another bedroom or as a larger kitchen or living room (if this makes the use of an existing room obsolete, you can modify that room to meet another use; see pp. 76–77). Write down the purpose or purposes of the addition and give the room a name—the new family room, for example, or the new study and guest room.

The next step is to make two lists: The first one should be of the things that you consider absolutely essential for the addition to include, such as increased counter space in a new kitchen, and the second list should feature what you'd like to include if you could—for example, expensive ceramic tiles as a backsplash behind the countertop. Think seriously about each item and on which list it belongs. Expect to move items back and forth between the lists many times before you settle on your final choices. This exercise will

Your house's potential

Before making a final decision on the type of addition you have in mind, make an inspection of your house to see how it may influence your choice.

- If there is enough extra property, you can build out; otherwise, you'll have to build up. (If up is your choice, you'll have to determine whether the foundation and framing of your present house are strong enough to support a second story.)

- Any jogs or ells in the existing house might be convenient locations for an addition to nestle into or spring from.

- Think about how an addition will be accessed from inside the house. For example, you may need further remodeling to create a hallway to it.

- If the addition will block natural lighting in another room, consider installing a new window or skylight to allow natural lighting into the affected room.

probably help you more than any other to define the goals of your project clearly and establish the basics of a working plan.

Is adding on a wise investment?

Consider the overall financial wisdom of going ahead with the project. An all-too-common mistake is pouring more money into an addition or remodeling than can be gained back when the house is sold. Naturally, the primary purpose of any home improvement is to increase comfort; but it also pays in the long run to be practical.

What is the fair market value of your house today? How much do you expect the addition to cost? Adding the two will give you the minimum price at which you should expect to be able to sell the house in the future and not lose money on your investment.

Another way to estimate how much you should consider spending on remodeling is to find the fair market value of houses in your neighborhood to which your house would compare in size and condition if the changes were made. Subtract the value of your house in its present condition from that figure; this will give you a conservative estimate of the amount you could reasonably spend. However, if the real-estate values in your area are on the rise, you can probably spend somewhat more.

Meeting the professionals

Having the fundamentals of your project firmly in mind and being able to present them clearly will make interviewing, selecting, and eventually working with a design professional or contractor much easier than if you approach the issue

A well-equipped kitchen with extra room for a breakfast table occupies this addition. The architect planned a change of ceiling height to help separate the preparation and dining areas.

Ask yourself

- What do you need from an addition? More living space? A larger kitchen? Additional sleeping space for guests or a growing family? A home office? The use of the space may affect the demands on the services, especially plumbing.

- What about the outward appearance of the house? Is there an architectural style you must incorporate in order for the addition to blend in unobtrusively with the existing house? Will landscaping or a new driveway be required?

with only a few vague notions. You will have an easier time gauging whether a candidate is the person you wish to hire, and he or she will have a clear idea of the type of designs that may best address your investigations. This includes not only the floor plan but also the types of architectural features or materials to be used in the addition—for example, a stretch of large windows along one wall.

In general, planning and building an addition follows the same pattern as that of house construction (see pp. 24–25) but on a smaller scale. However, there are a few distinct differences between the two: namely, building the addition without disturbing the existing house—or at least without disturbing it any longer than is necessary—and connecting the addition to the existing house and opening it for access.

Foundations

Any addition built on the ground will require a foundation. The choices are the same as for houses, the most common being either poured concrete or mortared concrete block. Both must be set on a continuous concrete footing located below the frost line. You will also need a footing drain. A crawl space foundation or a slab on grade (see pp. 142–143) usually makes the most sense, as excavation costs are less in both cases than for a full basement.

With a crawl space there is no need to pour a basement floor; and wiring, plumbing, air ducts, and insulation are easy to install and access beneath the first floor. With a slab, there is no need to construct a wood-framed first floor. However, services installed beneath a slab floor are difficult to access if repairs are needed. Also, slab floors rest lower than existing floors in a house with a basement or a crawl space foundation, and slab floors usually are harder and less comfortable underfoot than framed floors.

Once the foundation was laid for this living room, the framing for the walls—and windows—was next to be installed.

Upper floors

If your addition will be in the form of an upper story, you will have to make sure that the foundation and framing are sturdy enough to support the weight of the new construction, as well as the weight of the furnishings and occupants the room will eventually contain. A structural engineer is the right person to evaluate the strength of your present house. Although reinforcing a foundation can prove to be more of a task than is worthwhile, reinforcing framing is not too difficult.

Delivering materials

A major headache when foundation work is necessary is arranging for both excavating equipment and the delivery and pouring of concrete, even if only for the footing. Usually a relatively lightweight tractor equipped with a backhoe is used to excavate footing trenches. The soil is piled to one side of the trench and is later spread and graded against the finished foundation, a process called backfilling.

The concrete is virtually always delivered by a heavy truck. In order to unload, provision must be made for it to come within the distance of its chute—usually about 15 feet (4,575 mm)—from the trench. This often means preparing the area nearby by clearing shrubbery and laying down thick planks to support the truck's enormous weight, which is easily enough to create permanent ruts in driveways, tear up lawns, and destroy sidewalks. In addition, extra care is needed to make sure the truck does not come near buried pipes, a septic tank, drain tiles, or other items that could be damaged by compression.

Alternatively, concrete is sometimes loaded at curbside into wheelbarrows and brought to a site; but even that method requires a cleared path and a plank walkway. With all of these activities, count on needing some serious landscaping to restore your yard to its former condition after the addition is finished.

Framing and walls

After the foundation is finished, or if none is needed, the framing for the addition begins. For the homeowner, this event is often heralded by the arrival early one morning of a large flatbed truck delivering lumber and other building supplies. It is wise to have your contractor designate an area of your yard for storing building materials (unless they can be kept inside) and to have it clearly marked before the truck makes its entrance. If no specific instructions are given, many drivers will unload everything in the driveway or beside the curb.

To avoid storage problems, the contractor should plan for supplies to arrive in a succession of well-timed deliveries. Wallboard, for example, can be scheduled for delivery after the framing is finished so that the material can be stored indoors, out of the weather and close to where it will be installed.

Except in the case of dormers (see p. 25), additions are completely framed and closed in before access is created by cutting through the existing exterior wall of the house. An addition built from the ground up follows conventional house con-

struction, starting with floor framing and subflooring to cover the foundation (or the pouring of a slab floor), followed by the assembly of the exterior walls, intermediate floors, then the roof. Priority from that point is usually given to installing windows, doors, and siding; afterward come framing the interior walls, installing services, closing up the walls and ceilings, then installing built-ins, finish floors, appliances, and furnishings.

Joining the house

Access to the existing house is created during the interior framing stage, assuming the exterior of the addition has been closed in. The first step should be to install a protective plastic sheet around the indoor side of the wall that will be opened or removed. For walls that are to remain intact, siding and insulation are removed. Solid or veneer brick is

often cleaned, sealed with a clear masonry sealer and left exposed as a design feature of the addition's interior, or it may be sheathed over.

Windows are removed and their openings patched with framing, and doorway openings are cut and framed, which may involve rerouting services, especially wiring. Installing new doors follows covering the walls, which must be done on both sides if windows were removed.

Walls that are to be removed can be demolished after any windows and doors are taken out and any services are rerouted. However, the way in which a wall is demolished depends on whether or not it is load-bearing (see pp. 136–137). A non-load-bearing wall can be torn down. With a bearing wall, temporary bracing must be installed (see pp. 78–79), to be followed after the demolition by permanent bracing that is part of the finished remodeling.

You can turn your addition into a luxurious modern bathroom. If you want to emulate windows similar to those in the bathroom shown here, make sure the bathroom will be situated where it will have plenty of privacy.

Transitions at floors

The need to match first-floor levels often decides the type of foundation to build beneath an addition. Poured foundation walls can be raised to any height, and block walls can be adjusted by using bricks of different sizes and mortar joints of different thicknesses. Slab foundations result in a lower first floor than poured or block foundations covered with a framed floor (see pp. 100–101).

Transitions at walls

Matching inner and outer wall surfaces depends on precisely calculating the thicknesses of materials and on making use of filler strips, called shims. For example, with older houses having sheathing and framing whose dimensions are greater than standard building materials used today (see pp. 134–135), a common way to align wall surfaces is to offset the framing of the addition where it joins the framing of the existing house so that the exterior sheathing of both forms a smooth surface when butted together. (To disguise the joining of the addition to the house on the outside, new siding is applied to the entire wall.)

Indoors, vertical filler strips are fastened against the interior-facing edges of the wall studs so that wallboard attached across them will lie flush with the interior surface of the existing wall (see pp. 136–137). New wallboard should be joined to old with wallboard tape and joint compound. After painting or wallpapering both walls, the seam is invisible.

Joining wallboard to plaster is done in the same way; however, both surfaces may be given a skim coat of plaster to create a uniform texture before painting.

Additions that join the existing house at an angle are easier to match. There is no need to continue an existing surface, inside or out. Where new siding butts against the existing material, the seam can be covered by a vertical strip of molding (seams between different materials should be thoroughly caulked to keep out moisture and drafts).

Tying in walls of solid brick or block or veneer brick involves removing some of the existing masonry so that the new materials can be interlaced with the old. The new bricks or blocks must be similar in size and character to those that make up the existing house. In addition, the mortar composition and thickness must be considered if the transition is to be unobtrusive.

Transition at the roof

Joining new roofing to an already existing roof is a job best left to the professionals. For one thing, ensuring that there is a leak-free transi-

tion requires skillful sheathing and flashing. Both must be slid beneath existing roofing—taking care not to damage it (existing shingles can be extremely brittle and may break in the process)—then new shingles must be applied that match those already on the roof.

Practically speaking, it is often a good idea to consider reroofing the entire house when a sizable addition is planned. That way, all the shingles will match and be the same age and type; also they will age at the same rate, making replacement less problematic when the time comes.

Alternative choices !

Having the same floor level in an addition as in the existing house isn't necessary. A step or two up or down is an inconsequential feature that may even be desirable at the entrance to some additions. The steps must be of significant height—at least 4 inches (100 mm)—so they make a definite design statement and can be clearly seen; otherwise people will trip over them, with possibly serious results.

Careful planning of an addition is necessary to ensure that the floor levels align and the wall surfaces match. Choosing materials carefully, such as continuous wood flooring and complementary bricks, helps tie in the new room with the existing house.

When to inspect !

2

- Inspect the progress at the end of each day, especially work that will be concealed such as wiring and plumbing.

- Once they are erected, inspect the walls, floors, and ceilings of the new addition to see if they tie in with the existing house. Any steps needed should be at a comfortable height.

- When the interior room(s) have been completed, inspect the decoration to ensure that there are no problems with the work.

- Finally, inspect the yard around the addition to ensure that it has been properly landscaped.

maintain a sufficient slope to prevent blocking. Vent pipes for new fixtures and appliances must also be connected to existing vents or run to the roof (see pp. 152–155). To supply increased demand from added bathrooms, it is often necessary to have a larger water heater installed.

Heating and air conditioning

Extending heating systems and air conditioning is usually not difficult, because most furnaces and central air conditioners are installed slightly oversize to handle eventual additions. In any case, a qualified heating and cooling engineer will be needed to make the assessment.

An alternative to extending the heating (and air conditioning) systems is to install electric baseboard heating units and a window air conditioner. Baseboard units typically operate on 240-volt current and are wired directly to "dedicated" circuits supplying no other outlets. Most window air conditioners operate on 120-volt current and can be plugged into any wall outlet.

Tying in electricity

Requirements for additional electrical circuits—and plumbing, heating, and air-conditioning services—need to be specified in the planning of the addition. The location and design of an addition are often based on the ability to extend services to it economically. Electrical circuits are the easiest to deal with. With a small addition, it may be feasible to extend nearby circuits.

New circuits are run from the service panel. Professional electricians make use of exposed basement and attic areas to run the wiring from the service panel to the addition, then route the wires into the wall framing before it is covered. If several circuits are needed, a supplementary service panel, called a subpanel, may be required. The subpanel is connected to the main service panel (see pp. 156–157).

Extending plumbing

Plumbing is extended by splicing new pipes into existing ones. The plumber should take care in joining pipes of dissimilar materials so they don't leak or corrode at the joints. Drainpipes must be routed so they

Creating a self-contained space

Finding self-contained space, or a family-member apartment, for elderly or disabled relatives or grown children living at home can be difficult under any circumstances, but in modern houses it is likely to be impossible without building on.

A single-story addition that includes all the essential amenities of a separate dwelling on a smaller scale can be suitable for a relative, but there are some basic issues to consider.

Choosing an architect

You should choose an architect experienced in the type of living space you wish to create. The job of designing a self-contained space for a family member includes finding solutions that address the needs and desires of the occupant but at the same time fall within the locally allowed specifications for single-family homes. Some common issues are whether or not the addition will have a kitchen, a private entrance, and metered services separate from those of the main house.

Deciding on the site

Locations for family-member apartments generally depend partly on the design of the existing house and partly on how closely connected to the rest of the household the apartment's occupant will want to be. For elderly and disabled occupants, first-floor locations usually are the best choice, because they eliminate the need for going up and down stairs. Depending on personal preferences, the apartment may be closer to or farther away from other bedrooms or living areas; some

family-member apartments may be separated from the main house by the kitchen or even a garage.

For persons with normal mobility, building above a garage often satisfies everyone's needs, including those of the zoning board. Approval

Rules & regulations

Converting space or adding on always requires a building permit and permission of local zoning and setback authorities (see pp. 14–15). Applying to build space that can be construed either as rental property or as a modification that converts a single-family dwelling to a multi-family one is usually full of pitfalls. You should consider hiring an architect to pave the way for you through the legal maze such remodeling typically involves.

A self-contained apartment for a member of the family may have unusual arrangements; however, they should be both practical and comfortable for the occupant.

to build an apartment that is completely detached from the main house usually is difficult to obtain; however, connecting it to the house via a breezeway may be permitted, provided that the apartment meets other criteria that will disqualify it as a possible rental unit—such as having no kitchen.

Planning and building

Designing a family-member apartment is no different than designing any addition (see pp. 98–103). The same considerations must be given to location, construction, and how

the apartment will blend with the rest of the house inside and out. However, designing space for elderly or disabled occupants does present unusual challenges.

Having a professional designer on hand to supervise construction is usually a boon. When it comes to designing a space for accessible living (see box at right), few contractors have experience with unconventional building practices such as widened hallways, raised electrical outlets, and threshold-free entry doors. Although they are willing to comply with a client's wishes, many contractors may unintentionally overlook important details of the plans—for example, installing braces for bathroom grab bars—and revert out of habit to the ordinary building practices with which they are more familiar. Few accessible-living construction features are covered by any of the permit-related required inspections, and, if not spotted in time, they may go unnoticed until it becomes expensive to correct them.

Services

New electrical circuits will be necessary to supply power to a family-member apartment, and a subpanel may be needed (see p. 103). You may want a separate electric meter, but installing one may jeopardize the status of the apartment; talk to your architect or designer, or to the local building authorities, before including a meter in your plans.

The same goes for the plumbing. In all likelihood you will be limited to extending your present system to accommodate the apartment if you want to keep its status as a non-rentable family-member unit. Getting a separate municipal hookup generally qualifies the structure as a separate building address.

Heating and central air conditioning can be supplied to a modest apartment from the main house by extending the radiator plumbing or

Adapting space for "accessible living"

2

Architects and designers are increasingly specializing in so-called accessible home design; that is, making living areas accessible to occupants with physical infirmities such as those caused by aging. Hiring such a professional is recommended if you need planning help of this kind. Not only are there often legal hurdles to pass simply to build the apartment, designing spaces for disabled or elderly occupants requires expert knowledge of many unfamiliar specifications and details—for example, the amount of room necessary to turn a wheelchair and the most convenient height for wall outlets and light switches.

Even if you don't need an architect or a full-scale building designer, hiring a qualified kitchen or bathroom designer for either of those areas will pay dividends. Their knowledge of how to arrange and furnish kitchens and bathrooms for occupants with special needs is invaluable. You will also be glad to have their expert opinions when it comes to choosing from among the growing array of fixtures, appliances, furnishings, and decorations for the disabled and infirm.

air ducts. In-floor radiant heating supplied by hot water from the main house is also often a possibility, but it may be more expensive and require more planning. If the present furnace is too small, electric baseboard heating is usually the best alternative, complemented by a window air conditioner (see p. 103). Thermostats controlling the room temperature should be separate between the apartment and the main house, just as they likely already are on separate floors and in other heating or cooling zones.

2 Creating an outbuilding

There are many reasons to add an outbuilding or two on your property—if space allows for them. An outbuilding can be a place for storage, a workshop or studio space, or a place to relax or play.

A well-built, secure shed is a perfect place to house bulky equipment such as a lawn mower, garden tiller, snow thrower, garden tools, and all the other items that usually clutter most garages. A workshop or studio space can provide a snug hideaway separate from the main house for pursuing hobbies such as woodworking, gardening, pottery, painting, or writing—or you can even use it as a home office. A gazebo nestled in an attractive spot toward the back of the yard is an irresistible resting place; and few childhood pleasures surpass the joy of escaping to a backyard playhouse.

Permissions

Because outbuildings of the type described here are not designed as dwellings, fewer building code restrictions will apply to their construction than, for example, an addition. However, zoning and set-back regulations do apply; before proceeding too far with your building plans, seek advice from your local building authority on the laws regarding issues such as how large an outbuilding can be (most zoning regulations specify the percentage of your total lot that can be covered by all construction), how tall you can build it, and how close to property lines and the street you can build.

Local restrictions

Depending on the neighborhood in which you live, you may have to obtain permission from a home-owners' association or other community group overseeing real-estate standards. You may or may not need a building permit. In some areas, no permit is required for buildings of less than 120 square feet (3.36 sq m); in others, a permit is required for all new construction.

Some local codes distinguish between structures that are built on permanent foundations—for example, poured footings or concrete slabs—and those that are built on lesser foundations such as piers or posts. Adding electricity, plumbing, and heat to an outbuilding to be used as a studio can also be a problem (the more a shed or other outbuilding begins to resemble a house, the more closely building authorities will want to scrutinize its construction, intended purpose, and tax status); specific permits for these services will probably be needed no matter where you live.

An outbuilding kit

For a simple outbuilding, many attractive models for a variety of uses are available in kit form from manufacturers, lumberyards, home and garden centers, and landscape design firms. These sources will frequently supply trained carpenters to erect the building as part of the purchase price, or you can hire your own carpenter.

Kits typically cost about the same as having a similar building custom-made; however, buildings from kits often are of higher quality than site-built structures because they are manufactured in a controlled factory environment.

Ask yourself ?

- How do you plan to use the outbuilding? Will it be intended for storage, or designated as a place to work or relax?

- Will you need electricity or heating in the outbuilding? If you intend to use the building for work, both of these should be considered. A building used for relaxing can be restricted to warm-weather use if you don't want to include heating.

Planning

Deciding on the location of an outbuilding will probably be partly governed by the local ordinances. Apart from those, you should choose a well-drained location that is close to the building's point of use—for example, near the garden if you are building a potting shed, or near the driveway if you are building storage facilities for a snow thrower or lawn tractor.

Be sure your proposed site does not obstruct access to the house in case firemen need to reach it in an emergency (ordinances will cover this); nor should the location create awkward traffic paths, crowd activity areas in the yard, or block sunlight to the house or garden.

Simple structures

Small outbuildings, including most storage sheds, gazebos, and play-houses, don't require the kinds of foundations necessary for houses.

An outbuilding can be as complicated yet relaxing as this work studio.
The interior provides a work area away from the main house, and the
attached deck offers a place to take a break in the sunshine.

Often, concrete or pressure-treated wood piers are sufficient, as for an outdoor deck (see pp. 122–123). Simple buildings are available in a kit (see box, opposite page).

Large structures

For a more substantial or customized outbuilding, such as a workshop or studio for year-round use, you may want to hire an architect or building designer to help with the plans—and you will certainly need a contractor to tackle the construction. Don't dismiss the idea of hiring an architect as too expensive; designing a small building such as a studio is often the type of job given to architectural interns working at a

firm prior to taking their licensing exam (see pp. 10–11). The fee charged by the firm for the services of an intern may be quite a bit less than the firm's normal rate.

Constructing a major outbuilding follows the same general procedures as constructing a house or addition (see pp. 98–103). You will need a poured footing set below the frost line and foundation walls built to the code-required height above grade, usually 8 inches (200 mm).

A concrete slab floor is usually economical and practical, especially if the building will house heavy equipment. For a workshop or studio where a softer surface is desirable underfoot, cushioned car-

peting, wood flooring, or another resilient flooring material can be installed on top of the slab.

Weatherproofing

Insulation and a well-built roof with gutters and downspouts will be appreciated, so don't skimp on them to cut costs. Windows and doors, too, are worth taking pains to select, both for their quality and thermal properties and for their design appeal. Regarding the latter, outbuildings afford a chance to express creativity—after all, resale value isn't really at stake (most outbuildings do not add substantially to property values). Besides custombuilt windows, doors, and trim, investigate salvaged materials that can be refurbished or possibly used as is. Local design professionals and contractors can often point you to unusual sources of supply.

2 Your house's exterior

The outside of your house deserves as much care and attention as the interior. Its main purpose is to keep the elements at bay, and if its condition deteriorates, the whole property can be affected, both physically and in resale value. A poorly maintained house will take longer to sell than one in top-notch shape, and it will go for less.

This section explains what professionals can offer when it comes to performing exterior maintenance, replacing windows and doors, improving security, and maintaining or replacing a roof. It also tells you how professionals can help with constructing patios, creating garden paths and steps, building boundary walls and fences, and adding outdoor decks. Knowing what each project involves will help you make informed choices, make it easier for you to keep an eye on the work, and allow you to avoid costly pitfalls.

A patio (far left) partially surrounded by walls provides an intimate setting for entertaining guests. Keeping the exterior of your house in good shape (left) will provide an inviting welcome whenever you return home.

Maintaining the house's exterior

The outside skin of your house is the building's defense against the elements. It must be kept in good condition, otherwise wind, rain, sun, and frost will eventually attack the various materials that make up its structure.

Initially, a house that has been neglected will simply look run-down. But as time goes by, minor areas of wear and tear that are not repaired will turn serious, and what would have been simple repairs will become complicated and expensive. An ounce of prevention is worth a pound of cure. To keep your home in top condition and to minimize maintenance costs, have it inspected and brought up to par at least annually—spring and fall are the best times—just as you do your car.

Home repair professionals

Seasonal home maintenance is a job regularly taken on by remodeling and repair contractors. However, for much the same reasons that you shouldn't simply drive your car to the first garage that catches your eye when you need vehicle maintenance, you should always look before you leap into hiring the first repair contractor you come across.

You should locate and choose a repair contractor just as you would any other building professional. Start by obtaining recommendations from family, friends, and neighbors, if possible; then thoroughly investigate and compare each of the candidates, verifying his or her business address, confirming the contractor's license and insurance coverage, and checking with former clients before you make a final choice (see pp. 16–17). You should insist on a clearly written, comprehensive contract for any work that you do undertake, and make sure you retain a signed copy (see pp. 20–21).

A well-maintained house will not only be a welcome sight each time you come home, it will also be a less expensive house to maintain. Repairs to a run-down house are often more expensive than the cost of maintaining it.

Inspecting your home

Before you have a contractor inspect your property and assess what needs to be done, have a look at it yourself as a precaution. All too often, contractors tempted by a homeowner's apparent ignorance will try to sign him or her up for unnecessary work, often with warnings of disaster if the job isn't done immediately.

Giving the exterior of your own home a thorough inspection is not difficult; and as a rule of thumb, few problems short of a leaking roof need immediate attention. Most flaws discovered during a spring inspection can wait until fall before requiring repair (most reputable contractors have a waiting list of at least a month in any case), and, even then, the only reason to rush is to get the job carried out before winter weather exacerbates the problem. Your house is not likely to collapse within a few months of spotting a problem that did not herald itself as potentially catastrophic from the outset such as a burst water pipe inside the house.

Conduct your inspection by working from the top of the house down to the foundation. The contractor will make a similar inspection. In all cases, note any faults you discover, so you can compare them with your contractor's assessment.

Roof level

Start by checking the condition of the roof, either by climbing to the eaves on a ladder or by using binoculars from ground level. Look for curled, cracked, and missing shingles and for lifted, torn, or stained flashing, especially at the chimney and around vent stacks. If you are able to climb onto the roof safely (and are comfortable doing so), check the chimney cap and masonry for cracks and crumbling mortar.

Finally, inspect the gutters to see if they contain excessive amounts of shingle granules, appear blocked with leaves, or fail to slope evenly toward the downspouts at the corners of the house. Look also to see if the gutters are securely fas-

When to inspect !

- It is a good idea to inspect jobs, especially painting, at the end of each working day to ensure that the results are what you expect and that no areas have been missed or poorly finished. Bring any defects you find to the contractor's attention promptly, so they can be rectified without delay.

- Check that the site is left clean and tidy at the end of each day, and that access equipment is taken down or secured to prevent a burglar taking advantage of easy access to the property.

tened to the eaves; in snow country especially, gutters can tear away from a roof, allowing water to run directly onto the ground, causing foundation leaks (see pp. 116–117).

Wall level

Next, give the house walls a close inspection. Look for peeling or blistered paint, warped or cracked siding, and evidence of decay. On sheltered surfaces look for dark, sooty areas indicating mold. With masonry surfaces, including stucco, look for cracks, broken bricks, and crumbling mortar. Inspect around windows and doors for missing caulking and other gaps that can let in moisture and drafts.

On older windows make sure the putty around the panes is sound. Check for similar problems on deck and porch surfaces, and examine all metal—especially stair railings—for rust or corrosion. Iron stair railings are vulnerable where they enter concrete steps. Prompt repair is necessary if a railing wobbles.

Ground level

Moving farther down to the house's foundation, look for cracks, debris-choked basement window wells, and evidence of termite tunnels (see pp. 74–75). All downspouts should empty onto splash blocks or other runoff devices directed away from the building. Shrubbery should not touch siding surfaces, and the ground around the foundation should slope away from the house and not contain depressions that might trap water.

When work starts

Different subcontractors will be required for different jobs—for example, one specialist may be hired for roof repairs and another for siding. Consult the following pages in this section to understand what to expect from each in the way of repairs. Ideally, work should pro-

Rules & regulations

2

Repainting siding is more complicated than it used to be, owing to increased awareness of health hazards from lead in paint. If your house contains paint applied before 1978, it should be tested by an approved method or else considered to contain lead.

When choosing a painting contractor, ask to see proof of training in removing leaded paint, and ask questions about how extensive the cleanup will be, how workers are protected, and how the contractor plans to remove the leaded paint and prepare the surface for repainting. Sanding, dry scraping, and torching off leaded paint are not only hazardous, sending clouds of toxic dust or fumes into the air, they are also illegal in many areas.

For further advice, call your local health department or lead abatement office, or the nearest office of the Environmental Protection Agency (EPA). All are located in the government pages of the phone book. These organizations can furnish you with a list of approved lead-abatement contractors in your area and possible sources of financial aid for reducing lead hazards. Another information source is the National Lead Information Clearinghouse (see pp. 168–171).

ceed from the top of the building down—for example, to prevent the mess created by roofers from soiling the work of painters. In all cases, structural repairs must be made before any decorative work is done.

Most exterior repairs involve working from scaffolding and ladders. Be sure contractors exercise reasonable care not to ruin your plantings, shrubs, and lawn, and that protective drop cloths are used to catch and haul away any debris.

Because of rising energy costs, replacing drafty single-pane windows and ill-fitting doors is one of the fastest growing sectors of the home improvement business—and replacing windows and the front door is one way to make a house more attractive.

If you use a company that specializes in windows and/or doors, make your choice with care; it is better to pick a good local firm that can give references of satisfied customers in your area, than to take the cheapest quote from an unknown company.

Choosing the installer

The alternative approach is to call in a contractor or carpenter with the right experience. This route may be less expensive than a package deal, especially if you need to replace only a few windows. With a contractor, you can schedule a large window-replacement project over a longer period of time to suit your finances.

Windows and doors are often sold prehung—already mounted in their frames. These are much easier

Low-e glass

Insulated windows are available with invisible metal coatings that make the glass more energy efficient. Low-e glass (the term stands for low-emissivity) blocks elements of sunlight, such as infrared rays, which carry heat, and ultraviolet rays, which can damage interior decorations such as upholstery, carpeting, and paintings. Low-e coatings can be applied to any of the surfaces of a multipane window; consult with a supplier or window contractor to determine which configuration best suits your needs. A source of free information on energy-efficient windows is the Efficient Windows Collaborative (see pp. 168–171).

and less expensive to install than individual window sashes and doors, which require custom-fitting. However, should you want custom service, for example, to replace an architecturally significant window or front door, most contractors and carpenters can provide it (most package-deal companies cannot).

Window frames

The most popular replacement windows are vinyl, chiefly because they are the least expensive and require no upkeep. Replacement windows also are manufactured of solid, vinyl-clad, and aluminum-clad wood. Wood enhances the insulating qualities of windows. Solid wood windows are intended for painting and must be maintained like any wood surface exposed to the elements. Clad-wood windows require less maintenance or none at all. While metal-frame windows are available, they usually are not the best choice, being both more expensive and less insulating than vinyl.

Windowpanes

Choosing the right glass is essential. From the standpoint of energy efficiency, there simply is no point in obtaining new windows with old-fashioned single-pane glazing. In fact, you may even have trouble finding them. Nowadays, new windows contain double- or triple-pane glazing, referred to as insulated or thermal glass. The panes are assembled in sealed units with air- or gas-filled spaces between the layers, which provide insulation. Argon, an inert gas, insulates better than air and is a

When to inspect !

- As soon as the work is completed (unless you are advised otherwise—caulking compound around finished installations often needs time to harden), check that all operating parts of windows and doors work to your satisfaction. Inspect all hardware for a good fit and unmarred finish.

- Check for gaps in sealing materials inside and out, and make sure the frames and glass are clean and free of fingerprints and smudges. Be alert to leaks, which are fairly common. Your contract should require the installer to fix leaks promptly, free of charge, for six months to a year or more.

step up in quality. While triple-pane windows offer slightly more insulation than double-pane units, their chief advantage is increased sound insulation. In all cases, the multipane units are set into gasket-lined grooves cut into the frames. On new windows, putty is a thing of the past.

Window styles

You should choose a window style that suits the architecture of your house. The appearance of many otherwise attractive homes has been ruined by windows of an inappropriate style or size. Small windows near a door are appealing, but they could pose a security risk if the right steps aren't taken (see pp. 114–115).

When choosing a new door and windows, make sure the style is in character with the rest of the house. Installing small windows around a door enhances the entrance and provides natural light indoors.

pany that also does windows or using a local builder. The former will be the most convenient if you are having your windows replaced; the company will be able to supply front and back doors, patio doors, and any others you require—even garage doors—in a style and material that matches the new windows. If you just want to replace a front or back door, a builder or carpenter will offer you faster, cheaper services, and may also be able to order a wider range of styles and hardware.

Hardware can add considerably to the price of an entry door, so weigh the options carefully when shopping; standard hardware on doors is often of poor quality. If you want to use your old door hardware, make this clear before agreeing on a price.

When work starts

Always have the window company representative or contractor measure your windows and doors. That way they, not you, will be responsible if the wrong size is ordered. As with any contract, you will have to pay a deposit at this stage, but for your own safety, never pay the full amount in advance (see pp. 22–23).

It is up to you to take down curtains and blinds and to move any furniture out of the way and cover it with drop cloths. The installers should protect floors and other surfaces. The old windows and doors will be stripped of moldings and trim, if necessary, then carefully removed, and the new ones installed in their place. Any interior gaps should be packed with insulation or filled with expanding foam. Caulking should be applied outside and beneath thresholds. If appropriate, old trim may be reused; it is just as common to install new trim. In all cases there should be minimal damage to walls, and any that does occur should be repaired. Weatherstripping, if necessary (many units have built-in seals), is part of the job.

Replacing doors

Wood entry doors are standard, but insulated steel and fiberglass doors have become increasingly popular. Both offer more insulating qualities, need less maintenance, and cost less than wood doors—and neither material warps, as wood is inclined to do. Steel doors provide a measure of security and fire safety not matched by wood or fiberglass. (Steel doors are required by code between a new house and an attached garage.)

If you want to replace all your exterior doors, you have the options of contracting a replacement com-

Replacing windows and doors 113

Most burglars are amateurs and opportunists. They look for a property that is easy to break into, easy to get out of, and not visible to neighbors. By eliminating these characteristics from your house, chances are any burglars will go elsewhere.

More break-ins occur on first floors than upper stories. Doors and windows are primary targets, especially those at the back of the house, obscured by shrubs, corners of the building, and other barriers to view.

You can get advice on how to improve your home's security from your local police. There are basic ways to strengthen entry points and deter prowlers that you can have performed by a locksmith or an ordinary contractor. There are also some tips on acquiring alarms and home security systems.

Securing doors

Every entrance door should have a deadbolt lock. The surface-mounting type is easiest to install and offers the most security. It is recommended even if the doorknob contains a built-in cylinder deadbolt. Normally, you should choose a single-cylinder deadbolt having a thumb-turn on the inside. This ensures easy escape from the house in case of fire. Double-cylinder deadbolts require a key inside and out. They are a good choice for doors with glass panels that a burglar might break to reach in and operate a latch, but they are illegal in some areas because of the difficulty of opening them from the inside in an emergency.

Doorknobs and some deadbolts can be strengthened by installing reinforced strike plates (the sockets that contain the latch) in the door frame, using long screws that enter the wall studs to which the frame is attached. Accompanied by a brass or steel wraparound plate mounted on the door to protect the knob area, these provide protection against the door being kicked in or pried away from the frame with a crowbar. Additional protection from prying is possible by replacing the hinge screws with longer ones. Rounding out door security should be a peephole viewer and chain limiter to allow you to view visitors before opening the door to let them in.

Securing windows

Windows can be fitted with keyed locks or pins to prevent them from being opened from the outside. In vulnerable locations, and where insulated windows aren't essential, you might also consider replacing ordinary window glass with tougher polycarbonate plastic glazing. While this material scratches easily, making it unsuitable for most windows, it is practically impossible to smash, even with a hammer. Window bars are unsightly and may be illegal in your area. It is best to install them only if you have no other option.

Special locks are available for sliding patio doors and French doors. Both doors are easy to force open and are often located advantageously for burglars, so you should secure them as strongly as possible.

Alarms

Elementary but effective protection from prowlers is possible by installing motion-detecting floodlights in strategic locations—for example, high on the corners of your house, aimed at potential break-in points. When the sensors (which operate by infrared technology) detect movement, the lights switch on automatically, as if someone inside has seen the intruder. After a preset interval, the lights shut off automatically.

Conventional models will connect directly to the household electrical circuit and can be installed by an electrician. Other models are battery-powered and send a radio signal to the light switch without the need for wiring. Motion-detecting floodlights can be linked to indoor house lights, to audible alarms, and

Electronic systems

Alarm systems increasingly offer extended capabilities by detecting emergencies and monitoring and controlling household systems. They incorporate smoke detectors and sensors for gas leaks and basement flooding. In case of fire, some systems turn on lights to enable exit in the dark and turn off air circulation equipment to prevent smoke from spreading throughout the house.

Some systems can also function as a speaker phone, allowing you to listen for noises in your house or to broadcast your voice through a speaker. Home systems can also operate lights and thermostats, not only to give an empty home a "lived-in" look but to save energy by regulating temperatures.

to telephone connections that will automatically alert the local authorities if there is an intrusion.

Whole-house systems

Have a full-scale alarm system installed by a licensed security technician employed by a company that is approved by your state's burglar and fire alarm association or the National Burglar & Fire Alarm Association (see pp. 168–171). Interview several candidates and check their qualifications and background before making a selection (see pp. 16–17); review all contracts before signing (see pp. 22–23).

A good alarm system will suit your family's makeup and habits and any valuables requiring special protection. Consider the latter real-

istically before meeting with sales representatives to avoid being sold a system more elaborate than you need.

Alarm systems may be wired or wireless. Common features of professionally installed systems are a central control panel (normally hidden in a closet or cabinet), indoor and outdoor sound and motion detectors, electromagnetic contacts on doors and windows (these activate an alarm when the door or window is opened), and wired contacts that signal when glass is broken or a window screen is torn or removed. Bedside "panic buttons" that can be pressed to activate the alarm and other functions, such as lights, are also included. The key to all full-scale systems is a link to a central monitoring station or the police.

A low roof can be climbed onto from a nearby tree or fence. If either is near your house, make sure you keep the upstairs windows secured. Always keep first-floor windows secured, especially those at the back of the house.

Windows near a front door may be smashed to reach the lock. Replace ordinary glass with a stronger version such as one that has wire mesh embedded in it or one of polycarbonate plastic glazing.

A garage door may be forced open to gain entry through a door that connects the house to the garage. When upgrading your home's security, make sure you include any garage doors.

The roof is the most important part of the house structure when it comes to keeping the building weatherproof. Any roof should give decades of good service with little maintenance. However, most roofs do wear out over time and require replacement.

The one area of home maintenance that is best left to professionals is repairing and replacing a roof. They are experienced in working at heights, and they also have the necessary tools, equipment, and technical knowledge to ensure success.

Making repairs

Minor repairs can be made to a roof for years before replacement is needed. Inspecting your roof once or twice a year should ensure that small problems don't turn into large ones (see pp. 110–111). Depending on the type of roof you have, minor repairs include replacing broken, curled, and lifted asphalt shingles, refastening or replacing loose and broken tiles and slates, replacing broken and decayed wood shingles (and regularly removing moss), and

(see pp. 110–111)

mending or regularly coating metal and so-called built-up roofing.

Torn or loose flashing can be repaired and sealed with roofing cement; even small areas of structural decay, often found at the eaves, can be repaired without having to replace the entire roof covering.

When to replace

When repairs become frequent and the roof covering is worn over large areas, it is time to replace it. Asphalt shingle roofs, by far the most popular in the United States, can need replacing in as little as 10 years, but they often last 20 years or more. Most other roofing, if maintained, lasts 30 years or more (but poor-quality wood shingles may last only 15 years); tile and slate roofs can and usually do last centuries. One sign that asphalt roofing needs replacing is that the coating of protective granules disappears from the surface. They protect the shingles from ultraviolet rays, which degrade asphalt.

Choosing materials

If reroofing is called for, it is best to replace the old roofing with a similar material unless it has proved unsatisfactory. Opting for cement or ceramic tiles or wood shingles in place of asphalt involves strengthening the roof's frame or rebuilding it.

Do some research before selecting new roofing. Asphalt shingles, for example, come in several weights, with heavier shingles costing more and lasting longer than lighter versions. Consider how long you plan to live in your present house before deciding on heavier shingles.

A wood shingle or slate roof may be a more appropriate choice for an older traditional home.

If you choose asphalt or wood shingles, you have two choices for reroofing, referred to by roofers as tear-off and re-cover (see box, facing page). Most shingle roofs can support the weight of two re-covers (three shingle layers in all). However, if you have already had one re-cover, consult a building inspector. Many local codes allow no more than one re-cover before a complete tear-off is necessary.

Warranties

Roofing warranties do not guarantee against leaks except under strict terms. These are negated by such actions as failing to have the roof inspected as detailed by the manufacturer and by transferring owner-

(see box, facing page)

When to inspect !

- After workers leave for the day, if you're willing to use a ladder or scaffolding, check that the shingle courses are uniform and horizontal, and that all shingles match in color if they are supposed to, and that the flashing is orderly and neatly sealed where edges are to remain visible. Unfinished parts of the roof should be covered with tarpaulins in case of rain.

- At the end of the job, be sure the gutters are clear of debris before the scaffolding is taken down and that the area around the house is cleaned up.

ship of the house. In any case, manufacturers' warranties provide only that the manufacturer will replace defective materials; labor costs are not included. Warranty information can be misleading, too, especially with newly introduced materials, where there is no evidence that the materials will last as long as their warranties declare.

Roofing professionals

Locate and choose a roofing contractor as you would any building professional. Obtain referrals from friends or reputable professionals if possible; check all the candidates' identifications, licensing qualifications, and insurance coverage, and follow up with former clients. Insist on a written proposal containing a complete description of the work, materials to be used, approximate start and end dates, and payment procedures before negotiating a formal contract (see pp. 20–21).

Reroofing costs vary widely, depending on variables besides materials. It is best to get three or four proposals from contractors in your area before making a final decision to hire one of them (see pp. 16–17). Keep in mind that price is only one element of a reroofing job; the quality of the materials and workmanship are more important.

This new asphalt shingle roof uses shingles of different hues but in the same color range; the irregular pattern helps break up the large area of roof.

Free information and help obtaining qualified roofing professionals is available by contacting the National Roofing Contractors Association (see pp. 168–171).

When work starts

The vagaries of the weather force roofers to work quickly. Before work begins, clear your yard of obstacles that might interfere with scaffolding and ladders. Where old roofing will be removed, the contractor will want to deposit a refuse container or drive a dump truck onto your property so that the old roofing can be discarded directly into it.

In the case of an asphalt shingle roof, stripping off the old shingles will be the first step unless the job is a re-cover. Following that, sheathing and other repairs will be carried out, then new metal drip-edge material will be fastened along the eaves to conduct rainwater into gutters and stop it from running under the roofing. In snow country, it should be supplemented by a strip of neoprene to prevent ice dams. Afterward, overlapping strips of roofing felt are laid over the sheathing (see pp. 128–129).

Beginning again at the eaves, or as the first step in re-covering a roof, a double layer of shingles is applied; then overlapping rows, or courses, of shingles are applied horizontally up to the ridge. At intersections, such as chimneys, flashing is installed beneath the shingles and sealed with roofing cement. The ridge is capped with cut shingles or with a ridge vent open to the attic below.

During working hours, stay away from the area to avoid being struck by falling debris. At the end of the job, conscientious contractors will walk the area with a magnet to pick up stray roofing nails.

DIY jargon !

Built-up roofing This is "flat" roofing consisting of layers of asphalt and roofing felts.

Re-cover A less expensive roofing approach that involves simply installing a layer of new shingles over the existing layer.

Tear-off Where builders strip off the existing roof covering down to the sheathing before installing new roofing materials.

Coping with subsidence

Settling of the foundation, or subsidence, is one of the most serious problems that can affect a house. Settling in older houses is common; however, provided the condition has stabilized, corrective action is usually not warranted.

Evidence of settling may show up in your house in a number of ways, including foundation cracks, zigzag cracks in brickwork, rippled siding, and dipping rooflines. Sticking doors and windows, an indication that their frames are out of square, are also a frequent clue.

Most older houses will show signs of having settled but then stabilized. However, if you notice any new symptoms or if signs of settling occur in a new house, call in an experienced building inspector or a residential structural engineer to find the cause of the problem and recommend a solution.

Causes of settling

The footings and foundation (see pp. 142–143) support the weight of the house and transmit the load evenly to the subsoil beneath it. If they fail to do this properly, the house will move, and, being a rigid structure, something must give. Frequent causes of settling are:

• Loose soils, which are prone to compaction from the weight of the house. One example is soil beneath the basement floor of a new house that was initially dug too deep, then backfilled to the correct depth.

• Expansive soils, such as clay, which expand and contract significantly, depending on the moisture content. When saturated, clay soil swells, or heaves, raising the footings or distorting foundation walls by pressing against them. When dry, clay soil shrinks, allowing foundations to sink.

• Tree roots, which can affect the moisture content of soil. A large tree extracts a lot of water, leading to soil shrinkage. Felling such a tree can then cause the soil to heave as it regains its natural moisture.

• Underground streams, which can wash away the subsoil from underneath footings.

• Slope influence, when a high mound of soil exerts steady pressure against a foundation—it can even move the entire house if the soil begins to slowly slide downhill. During a heavy rain, excessive pressure can develop suddenly, with serious consequences. Houses built on sloping lots also run a higher risk of having been built on partially disturbed soil, created when earth cut from the side of the slope was used to extend and level the building site.

• Absent, undersized, and damaged footings. Of these, absent footings are uncommon but may occur in old rural houses and structures not originally intended for permanent habitation such as summer cottages. Undersized footings are more common. These can reflect poor building design or can result from adding substantial weight to the original house, usually in the form of a second or third story or a brick fireplace. Footings can be damaged by deterioration—for example, if the concrete was mixed or cured incorrectly—or by exterior forces such as tree roots. Foundation walls can also be damaged by improper backfilling during construction.

• An outside basement stairwell that was added to or included in the basement construction; it effectively lowers the frost depth around it. Unless the footing beneath the stairwell is dug to a corresponding depth, frost heaving is likely, which can crack the foundation.

Remedies

Unless settling has been sudden and catastrophic—for example, due to flooding rains—most inspectors and engineers will first analyze the evi-

---

When to inspect ❗

• It will be beyond your ability to judge the quality of settlement repairs to foundation work. Let your architect or engineer and the municipal building inspector handle it. After the final permit-required inspection is completed, make sure you are given a certificate of occupancy (see pp. 14–15).

• Your contractor should leave the site clean and the ground level; it will be up to you to replant the yard.

Testing methods

The two most common tests for analyzing settling include gluing thin strips of glass or other material across foundation cracks, or simply marking across cracks with an indelible pen. Any substantial movement will affect the materials. It is often necessary to monitor a building for months or even years to learn whether a problem warrants repair.

Any large trees growing within 5 feet (1,525 mm) of a house can potentially contribute toward settling. Before having the tree removed, consult a subsidence specialist to determine the best way to handle the situation.

dence to determine whether the settling is continuing or the situation has stabilized.

Correcting settlement damage is expensive. The most common procedure is called underpinning, which consists of excavating beneath the footings, a small amount at a time— 4 feet (1,220 mm) in length—from inside the house, then pouring concrete into the space to deepen and widen the existing footings. Buckled or cracked foundation walls can be buttressed by pouring concrete against them on the outside.

Where a floor slab has subsided it may be possible to pump consolidating material beneath it, but in severe cases the slab will have to be removed and a new one poured. After all belowground repairs have been made, repairs can proceed on other damaged areas of the house. In some cases this may involve jacking the house off the foundation and placing shims and new framing underneath it, so the structure sits level when set back down.

Whom to hire

Repairing subsidence damage is a job for expert concrete and restoration contractors who specialize in such work. Consider hiring an architect or a structural engineer to oversee the project. Obtain referrals from other professionals or from people you know who have had

Rules & regulations

If you recently purchased the house or if it is less than 10 years old but it requires work due to settling, you may want to consult an attorney about recovering damages from the seller or builder. It is also possible that repair costs may be covered by your homeowner's insurance policy.

similar work performed. There are usually only a few qualified foundation and settlement specialists to choose from in any community, and you may have to search to find one. As when hiring any professional (see pp. 16–17), carefully check references and insurance coverage, talk with former clients, obtain preliminary estimates, and negotiate a comprehensive contract (see pp. 20–21).

Outdoor landscaping

Home improvements do not have to be confined solely to the house. Patios, decks (see pp. 122–123), and walkways—in addition to gardens, special plantings, and landscaping—all enhance the beauty, comfort, and value of a property.

Some people prefer to do landscaping themselves, while others will want to call in a professional. Large projects involving major construction or handling heavy materials will usually require professional help—at least for site preparation, which may call for a lot of digging.

Whom to hire

Given a large enough budget, skilled landscape architects and garden designers can perform miracles with practically any property. Their skills and expertise qualify them to solve such design problems as unifying discordant natural elements, focusing attention onto the house—or causing a house to nestle among its surroundings—and expressing a client's aesthetic and artistic interests.

Developing plans for your yard will involve several visits to your property by the designer, unless you are only interested in a small project such as a patio. If your wants are simple, you can hire a professional to help you come up with ideas for your property and to draw up the plans, which can then be handed to a landscaping contractor or individual subcontractors.

Patios and walkways

Most patios—basically a paved outdoor area—are situated at the back of a house, but they can be built off a side, fitted between additions, or located in a pleasant area away from the house. Determining where to build a patio depends on the size requirements, available sunlight, easy access, outdoor views, and other related criteria. You don't need to

Many homeowners want a patio where they can eat al fresco meals and entertain friends. A garden that has had time to mature around a patio is a particularly relaxing place to sit.

think of a patio as being only square or rectangular; curving, irregular shapes often suit their settings well.

Walkways or paths can serve a dual purpose. They are usually intended to link different areas of a property—for example, a vegetable garden with a storage shed. However, if interestingly designed and constructed, they can also serve as attractions on their own. They can run straight, follow flower borders, or meander through trees and along contours of the yard in a natural, haphazard way, leading anywhere or nowhere in particular.

Terracing

Varying ground levels by creating terraces brings a third dimension to landscape design. This worthwhile improvement may eliminate soil erosion and basement flooding. Terracing sloping ground can transform otherwise unusable property into level areas for gardens and lawns, and add interest as well. Like patios, terraces need not be square or rectangular but can weave and curve, following the natural contours of the property.

Planning the work

After the planning stage is completed, choosing materials is the next consideration. Patios and paths

are hard-surfaced. The simplest construction involves setting bricks or stones, such as flagstone or slate—or a combination of bricks and stone—in a bed of sand, using the dry-laid masonry technique. This is bordered with treated lumber or railroad ties set firmly into the ground to contain it. Or the area can be bordered with bricks set vertically into the ground.

A more elaborate method for creating patios and paths is to bed the bricks or stone in mortar made of sand and cement mixed with water. If done skillfully, this can produce a natural appearance similar to that of dry-laid masonry but of greater durability.

Concrete patios

The most elaborate way to create a patio or pathway is by pouring concrete in a temporary frame. It can be surfaced in a number of decorative ways or left bare. Methods for decorating concrete surfaces include coloring the concrete mix with pigments, tooling or stamping it so that the surface resembles brickwork or flagstones, and embedding it with marble or other colorful stone chips (this is called terrazzo). Concrete can also be transformed by covering it completely with bricks, stone, or ceramic tiles, arranged uniformly or in mosaic patterns.

Retaining walls

Walls that hold soil in place are known as retaining walls. They are used at the leading edges of terraces or bordering patios, and they are usually of brick, stone, or treated lumber stacked and spiked together. Adequate concrete footings and below-grade foundations are a must for retaining walls, and construction must counteract the pressure of the ground against the entire wall. Walls surrounding patios also require footings, but usually do not need to be built to resist sideways pressure.

When work begins

After choosing a contractor (see pp. 16–17) and negotiating a contract (see pp. 20–21), the first steps will be to lay out the construction site with string and to excavate the area, if necessary. Basic recontouring of the site may be done at this time as well; the object will be to prepare the site for construction and to get it to a stage where heavy equipment, such as a bulldozer, doesn't need to be driven onto the yard.

Next, materials will be delivered and building will commence. Paving materials are laid in place in a bed of sand or mortar. Pouring concrete proceeds in the same way as for a slab-on-grade floor (see pp. 100–101), except that the concrete may be mixed on site, eliminating a visit by a concrete-delivery truck. Masonry walls are built starting at the corners and working toward the middle.

Once all construction is finished, the final work consists of replanting trees and shrubs (or planting new ones), establishing and planting gardens and ground covers, then grading the remaining soil, usually by hand with rakes. Afterward, the new lawn is planted or turf is laid.

2 | Outdoor decks

Wooden outdoor decks for seating and entertaining have become enormously popular alternatives to traditional paved patios. Unlike masonry, decks can be framed to rest at any height on posts or piers set into the ground, so a level site is not essential.

The simplest deck is a level planked platform supported by a frame of joists resting on short posts of pressure-treated lumber or concrete piers—in effect, a wooden patio. Steps can be added for easy access and railings can be added for security, to support built-in benches, and to give the deck a feeling of being separate from the rest of the yard. A single-level deck is usually built so its floor surface is at the same height as the indoor room to which it provides a natural addition.

Pressure-treated softwoods—fir and pine—are popular lumber choices, because of their low price and long life. Redwood and cedar are expensive, but they are naturally decay- and insect-resistant. Redwood retains a reddish brown color as it weathers; cedar weathers to a silver-gray. It is common to use pressure-treated lumber for the posts and framework of a deck and redwood or cedar for the planking and railings, but decks are also built entirely of pressure-treated lumber.

Planning the deck

Complete deck kits are available, as are published plans that can be modified to suit individual sites and preferences. You can also hire a designer to create a custom deck that is unique. When planning a deck, keep in mind not only your needs—entertaining and relaxing—but also the size and style of your house and the natural aspects of the site.

You will want the deck to add to your home's overall appeal. A deck that is too large in relation to the rest of the house can make the house seem small and less significant, but a deck that is too small looks tacked-on and extraneous. You can divide a large deck into smaller connected platforms on different levels.

Existing elements

Incorporating architectural elements of your house and natural elements of the setting will help a deck blend in. For instance, design a deck with simple platforms if your house itself displays simple, unadorned geometry. The more elaborate your house, the more elaborate you can make the deck without it overwhelming the parent structure. Conversely, a plain deck attached to an ornate house will result in the deck looking

Decks can be built in almost any shape or size. Decks that are constructed on sloping ground allow for more variation in design.

Planking patterns

The way a deck is planked adds to its visual appeal and creates deliberate effects. Planks laid parallel to the house can make a wide deck seem narrow. Angling planks away from the house can make the deck seem larger and can lead the eye to attractive views or areas of intended focus such as gardens or trees.

Planking can be arranged in herringbone or parquet patterns. Varying patterns can make a single-level deck more interesting; but overusing this technique can spoil the effect.

When to inspect !

- Decks go up fast. Still, check during construction that trimmed ends of pressure-treated lumber are treated with a preservative.

- Check that bolts are installed with their heads facing outward. This results in a neater finish and eliminates the possibility of threaded bolt ends catching clothes or flesh.

- To prevent tripping accidents, the planking ends must not protrude upward and all fasteners must be sunk well below the deck surface. Steps, railings, handrails, and other construction must be firmly attached and smooth.

- Check freshly sealed areas for any missed spots.

This deck was built on several levels, with the top platform level with the room it leads to on the second floor.

unfinished. Site the deck and plan its shape to take advantage of the view and the sunlight and to incorporate features such as rocks and trees.

Trellising or a grid of beams over a deck can add shade and a feeling of enclosure while also helping the deck seem more "connected" to the rest of the house. Be careful not to create more shade than you want or to obscure views. The style of overhead construction should relate to that of the house.

Deck professionals

Although most decks appear simple in construction, expert deck builders use techniques and materials that ensure quality. It is usually best to hire a reputable deck-building firm or a carpenter with extensive deck-building experience. An experienced two- or three-man crew can erect a single-level deck in two days. An elaborate one may take only a week.

Checking references and following up with former clients is important. Interview owners whose decks were built at least 5 years ago. Ask questions about how well the structure has resisted decay and warping, whether squeaks or looseness has developed, and whether settling has occurred. Any contract you negotiate should provide for replacing warped boards and tightening bolts without charge for a year until the deck has seasoned.

When work starts

You will probably need a building permit before work starts. Building a basic deck close to the ground will begin with clearing the site of vegetation and covering it with a layer of weedproof plastic sheeting, topped with gravel to retard new growth. If the deck adjoins the house, the next step will be to attach a horizontal board called a ledger (to support one end of the joists) to the wall. It must be accurately and securely anchored, and the area where it contacts the wall must be protected from moisture by flashing.

The ledger also provides a reference for installing the posts. Usually, concrete piers are sunk into the ground and posts are anchored to brackets embedded in the piers. The main framing is then assembled and the planking attached. Planking fasteners should be stainless steel or galvanized to prevent rust stains. Planks should be separated by ⅛ inch (3 mm) to allow drainage, but wider gaps trap debris, which fosters decay.

Railings and other trim complete the construction. Sealer can be applied immediately to untreated lumber; pressure-treated lumber must season for several weeks or longer before it can absorb a finish.

Fences and walls

Fences or walls marking the boundaries of your property help keep intruders out and guarantee you a degree of privacy in your yard. They can also serve as an attractive frame to the property, especially if thoughtfully designed and constructed.

Installing new fences or walls, or replacing existing ones, is difficult work, and special experience is required to design and build fencing for sloping ground. It is worthwhile to hire a fence company or a fencing contractor to carry out the project.

Fence options

If security or keeping dogs and children from straying is the primary consideration, you may want to install a tall chain-link fence. Vinyl coated fencing (usually dark green) softens the characteristically severe appearance of galvanized fencing without compromising rust resistance. Other advantages are its relatively low price and the absence of maintenance requirements.

However, practically any wood fencing is better looking, especially in residential surroundings. A low fence will define the boundaries of a property. For greater privacy and security, consider a solid fence of tall, vertically placed boards, called a stockade fence. Solid-panel fences are a possibility, but they may not stand up to wind in exposed areas.

Other alternatives are customized wooden fences with distinct designs such as vertical boards that overlap each other—or that alternate on opposite sides of the horizontal support rails (called stringers) that connect the posts—basket-woven strips, and open lattice.

Cedar, which is naturally decay-resistant, is a good choice for wood fences that you want to remain natural-looking. Coating it with clear sealer will bring out the wood's color and provide increased protection from moisture. Almost any wood can be used for a fence that will be painted or stained. Pressure-treated lumber or lumber that has been soaked in preservative is best for posts that will be set into the ground.

Options for walls

Boundary walls can be built high for security and privacy, or low as property markers. Brick is the most widely used material for high walls; other choices are decorative concrete block, stuccoed concrete block, and—if artfully done—poured concrete. Stone walls, dry or mortared, are reserved for waist-high or lower walls. Masonry walls of any kind are massive structures and require solid footings and skillful construction to ensure they don't collapse.

A traditional picket fence is an inviting, friendly way to establish the boundaries of the property. It suits an older-style house.

Rules & regulations

You may need a building permit to erect fences or walls. Restrictions may apply to height, especially near roads, and to how close to property lines and easements (areas of your property, often near curbs, that are open to municipal use without your permission) you can build. In some areas you may have to get approval from a neighborhood organization.

Check with utility companies for buried lines where you plan to sink fence posts. You must stay at least 18 inches (460 mm) away.

fences, installing all the posts comes first. In some cases it may take a week for the concrete surrounding them to cure; when the posts are secure, horizontal stringers and the fencing are attached. Sealer, stain, or paint is applied as the last step.

Building walls

For a wall, the original foundation may be reusable, but your builder should first expose its full width and depth to make sure. If the new wall will be thicker or higher than the original one, the old foundation will need strengthening or replacing.

Masonry and stone walls will take from several days to several months to build, depending on their size. Masonry walls can be built only a few courses at a time, or freshly applied mortar will be squeezed out of the joints in the lower courses.

A stockade fence provides privacy in a residential area in an urban setting.
The top edge of the boards is staggered to provide a customized look.

Building fences

An old fence must first be removed. This usually involves breaking it down section by section and removing the old posts, plus any concrete used to secure them. However, sometimes the old posts can be sawed off flush with the ground and the stumps left in the ground.

Fence posts are set in concrete. They should be set into the ground a distance equal to one-quarter of their length; but in areas where frost heaving occurs, the depth of fence posts must be below the frost level. Concrete surrounding fence posts should be smoothed at an angle at the surface so water runs away from the posts. Thick posts, such as those used for rail fences, are simply set on a bed of gravel and surrounded by stones and tamped earth.

Rail fences must be constructed all at once in order to insert the ends of the rails into the slots in the posts. Once the posts are set in place, the rails cannot be removed without displacing the posts. With other types of

When to inspect !

- Confirm the route of the wall or fence when it is marked out, before construction begins.

- For a wood fence, make sure the concrete surrounding the posts is properly sloped at the surface. Check that all wooden parts are aligned and evenly spaced. The posts should be plumb—vertical on all sides. Fasteners should be galvanized to avoid rust stains. Make sure they are sunk flush with or below surfaces so they don't snag clothes or skin.

- Chain-link fencing should be stretched taut along the lengths of the posts, and the top edge should be horizontal.

- Footings for walls must be the correct size; confirm their dimensions before they are poured and inspect them immediately afterward. Walls should not have excess mortar.

3

How your house works

One of the most important things you can do before working with the professionals is to learn how your house works. Your new knowledge may help you avoid problems during the planning stage—for example, you will understand why a load-bearing wall cannot be knocked down or why an electrician cannot add an outlet to an overcrowded circuit. It may also provide you with ideas of how you can improve your home, or confirm ideas that you have been considering.

There are many components to a house, from its roof and siding on the outside to its floors, plumbing, and electricity inside the house.

3 Roofs

House roofs look relatively simple from the outside, but the shingles conceal complex framing that supports the roof's weight and the extra loads that wind or snow can impose on it.

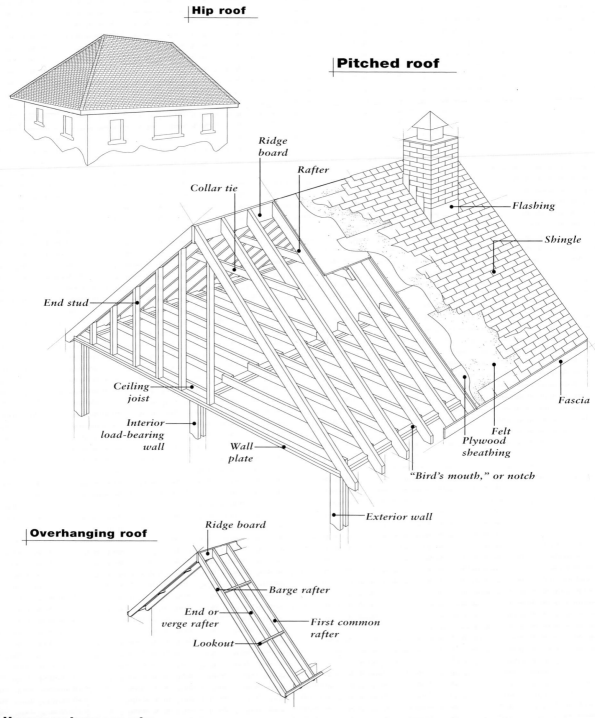

Hip roof

Pitched roof

Ridge board

Rafter

Collar tie

Flashing

Shingle

End stud

Ceiling joist

Interior load-bearing wall

Wall plate

Fascia

Felt

Plywood sheathing

"Bird's mouth," or notch

Exterior wall

Overhanging roof

Ridge board

Barge rafter

End or verge rafter

First common rafter

Lookout

Watertight covering

A well-constructed roof will last for decades as long as attention is paid to the condition of the individual components that keep it weather-proof, especially the shingles, tiles, sheet materials, or slates that cover it and the flashing that waterproofs the junctions with chimneys and adjoining walls (see pp. 146–147).

Traditional pitched roofs

In its simplest form, called a gable roof, a pitched roof consists of two slopes meeting at a central ridge. The rafters that support the roof covering rest on wall plates and are nailed to the ridge board. The rafters are linked at eaves level by ceiling joists, and often nearer the ridge by collar ties. These essential framing members prevent the rafters from spreading outward.

Additional support for long rafters may be supplied by purlins, horizontal members parallel to the ridge and eaves and midway between the two. A central load-bearing wall inside the house provides support for angled struts to be fitted between the purlins and the wall, transferring the roof load down to

Trussed-rafter roof

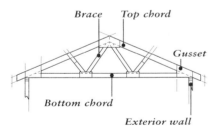

Brace *Top chord*
Gusset
Bottom chord
Exterior wall

that wall. Smaller joists span the spaces between the exterior walls and the interior walls.

A hipped roof has one or two sloping ends instead of vertical gables. These roof slopes run down to the building's end walls, inter-secting with the main roof slopes at an angle called a hip. If the house has a floor plan in an L- or T-shape, two or more roof slopes will inter-sect, with a sloping valley formed between the two.

Trussed-rafter roofs

Traditional stick-framed roofs are built on site by carpenters, but the process is slow and expensive. Most builders today use prefabricated roof trusses that span the width of the building with no need for interior load-bearing walls; they are quick to erect and cover. The main triangle of the truss is divided up by braces into a series of smaller triangles, which give the resulting frame great strength despite its lighter-weight components.

Trusses for the main part of the roof are symmetrical A-shapes; they are secured to the wall plates on top of the exterior walls. Smaller trusses are added to form hips, and they are also used to create roofs on lean-to structures such as attached garages. Trussed-rafter roofs do not require a ridge board. Instead the trusses are kept in position by lateral braces that are nailed across their bottom horizontal members, called chords, and by the sheathing applied over their surfaces.

Eaves details

The rafters of both stick-framed and trussed-rafter roofs may project beyond the face of the exterior wall or may finish flush with it. In either case the rafter ends are covered with a vertical fascia board, and if the eaves project, a horizontal soffit board bridges the gap between the wall and the lower edge of the fascia. At gable walls, the roof ends are finished with a sloping fascia called a rake. When an overhang at the roof ends is specified, barge rafters supported by lookouts create the extension.

Sheathing and shingles

Rafters and roof trusses are covered with sheathing, which braces them further and provides a fastening surface for the shingles or other roof covering. Sheathing is usually plywood, particleboard, or waferboard. On older houses and when the roof covering consists of wood shingles or shakes, tiles, or slates, the sheathing consists of individual boards spaced apart to allow ventilation underneath. In most cases, the sheathing is covered by a felt underlayment. It prevents direct contact between the sheathing and asphalt or fiberglass shingles (which can be damaged by wood resins in the sheathing) and protects against wind-driven rain, which can penetrate beneath finish roof coverings.

Most roofs are covered with asphalt shingles. These are made of asphalt-saturated felt or fiberglass coated with mineral granules (which protect the asphalt from the deteriorating effects of sunlight). Asphalt shingles are available in many styles and weights (the heavier the shingle, the more durable and long-lasting it is), but the most common are two-tab and three-tab strips.

Flat roofs

Although flat roofs are not often used in house construction, they are popular for extensions. Despite the name, they are not perfectly flat; if they were, rainwater would collect on them. Instead they have a slight slope running toward the eaves where gutters collect the runoff. The roof is supported on parallel joists spanning the width of the building and resting on a wall plate at each side. Ordinary sheathing is applied and covered with built-up roofing—alternating layers of felt saturated with asphalt and coats of hot tar, finished by a layer of gravel—or with one of the newer single-ply membranes or polymerizing liquid coatings.

Rainwater running off roofs is collected in gutters along the eaves of the building. They angle downward slightly so that the water drains along them into a downspout, which carries it to ground level for discharge in one of a number of systems.

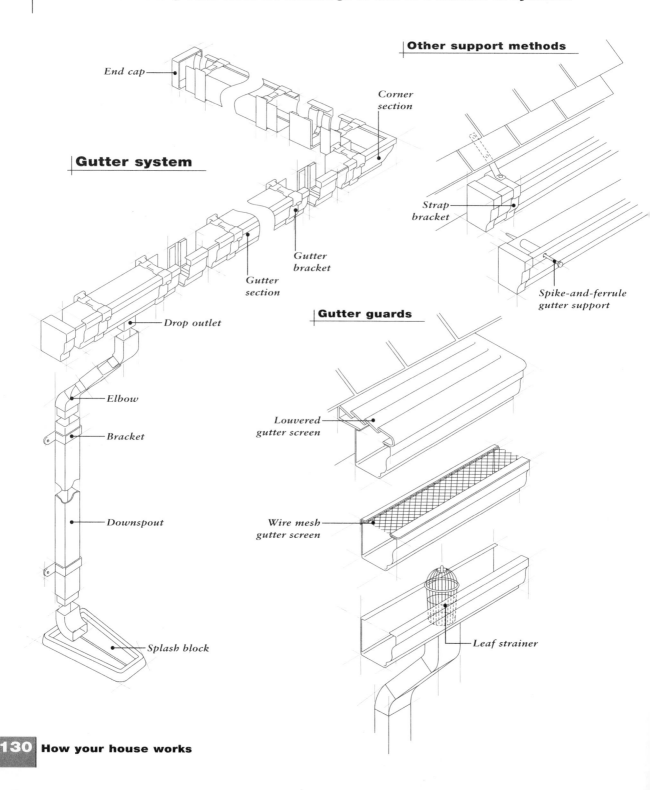

Other support methods

Gutter system

End cap

Corner section

Strap bracket

Spike-and-ferrule gutter support

Gutter bracket

Gutter section

Drop outlet

Gutter guards

Elbow

Louvered gutter screen

Bracket

Downspout

Wire mesh gutter screen

Splash block

Leaf strainer

Old gutter systems

Houses built before the 1960s featured galvanized and solid wood gutters. Most original gutters of this type have been replaced by more durable plastic and aluminum systems. Copper gutters are common on pricier homes. Although more expensive in materials and installation costs, they don't corrode under normal circumstances and often last the life of a house; however, their soldered seams may require repair.

Downspouts on older houses were metal, either galvanized or copper, to match gutters of the same material, or in rare cases cast iron. Downspouts require less maintenance than gutters because they are not subject to standing water. Downspouts that direct runoff onto the surface of the ground should empty onto a splash block of stone, concrete, or vinyl to divert the water away from the foundation.

Plastic systems

The most widespread material used for gutters and downspouts is PVC (polyvinyl chloride). It has many advantages over earlier materials and aluminum. It is light in weight, so it can be made in longer lengths that require fewer joints and can be supported on slim brackets. It is easy to cut to length and simple to install using connectors with flexible seals. Most important of all, it needs no painting and little maintenance apart from the removal of any debris that collects inside the gutter.

PVC gutters come in half-round, square, and ogee shapes and are made in white, gray, black, and brown colors to match the house's color scheme. Separate matching sections take the gutters around corners and angled bays and from outlets to the downspouts below. Downspouts are available in round and square cross-sections. They interlock with the gutters and are attached to the wall with brackets.

Aluminum gutters

Aluminum is used as a replacement for many worn-out original systems on older properties. Like the newer PVC, aluminum can be formed easily to shape and is lightweight, easy to handle and install, and practically maintenance-free. The gutters are available plain or painted. Paint is for decorative purposes only; aluminum does not rust, so even plain aluminum withstands exposure to the elements. It is formed into cross-sections that match the traditional cast-iron shapes, but since it is much lighter it is easier to handle and install.

Aluminum gutters can be cold-formed on site from flat aluminum strips by using a special machine. The resulting continuous runs avoid the need for joints, except at corners and outlets.

Sizing and siting

Gutters must be able to carry away all the rain and snowmelt running off the roof without overflowing, so their cross-sectional size and the number of downspouts must be matched to the roof area. In general, it is better to have a downspout in the center of each gutter section, instead of at the end, because this halves the volume of water each section has to carry. If this is not possible, the gutter should slope down from its mid-point, and there should be a downspout at each end of the run.

There is another reason for keeping gutter runs short. There is an optimum gap between the edge of the roof slope and the lip of the gutter to ensure that water runs cleanly from one into the other without overflowing or trickling back between the two and down the house wall. Because each length of gutter must have a slope, this gap will be too great toward the lower end of a long run and water will spill out as a result.

Gutters come in 4- and 5-inch (10- and 13-cm) widths. You should use the wider size for larger areas or if your house sits beneath trees whose leaves are likely to cause clogs. Even with larger gutters, install gutter guards to prevent leaf clogs in downspouts.

Water discharge

Downspouts emptying at ground level may open onto a splash block, as described, or may be attached to flexible soaker hoses that unroll as they fill and allow the water to trickle onto the grass. They may also be attached via short sections of PVC pipe to buried drainpipes that carry the water downslope to a surface opening elsewhere. Conducting the water to a dry well (an underground area of gravel that allows water to seep slowly into the surrounding soil) is no longer recommended; dry wells easily clog with silt and are overwhelmed during heavy rains.

In new houses, downspouts connect to footing drains underground. These may connect to municipal storm drains. The drains have an access point for clearing blockages easily. Before connecting a new downspout to a storm drain, consult your local building authority to learn of any regulations that apply.

Routine checks !

- Remove leaves and debris from gutters, downspouts, screens, and leaf strainers in the fall.

- Every two years, treat a wood gutter system with a water-repellent preservative.

- Anually flush aluminum gutters and downspouts with a hose to check for leaks; if any appear, recaulk the leaking joint.

- Paint galvanized steel parts on a regular basis to prevent rust.

The fireplace was once the only source of heat, but central heating systems have replaced this inefficient method of heating. However, the fireplace is still used to add warmth to a room—and the modern styles give off heat more efficiently.

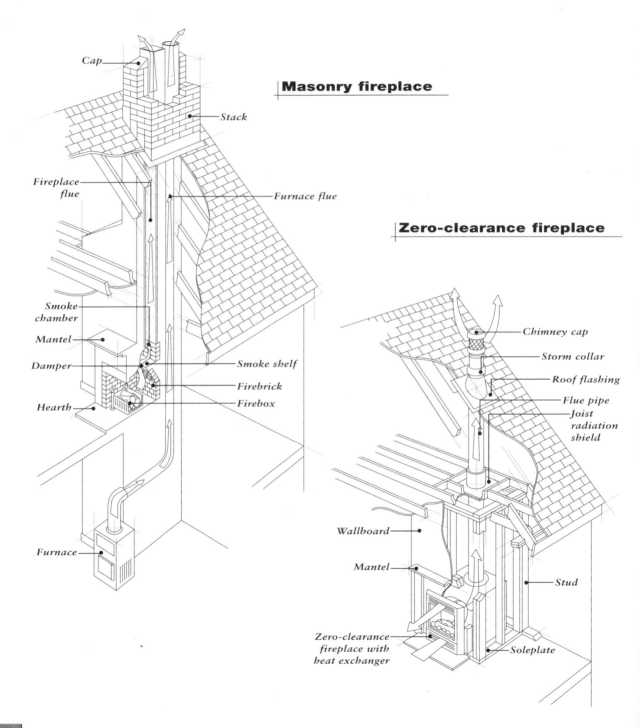

Masonry fireplace

Cap

Stack

Fireplace flue

Furnace flue

Zero-clearance fireplace

Smoke chamber

Mantel

Damper

Hearth

Smoke shelf

Firebrick

Firebox

Chimney cap

Storm collar

Roof flashing

Flue pipe

Joist radiation shield

Furnace

Wallboard

Mantel

Stud

Zero-clearance fireplace with heat exchanger

Soleplate

Masonry fireplaces

Traditional masonry fireplaces are made of bricks or stone atop a footing and foundation that is the same material as the house foundation. The floor of the fireplace, the hearth, consists of a concrete layer (4 inches/ 100 mm thick) covered by a layer of firebrick inside the firebox (the cavity in which the fire is lit) and a durable, decorative layer of brick, stone, or tile outside. Well-built fireplaces in older homes contain an ash dump. This is a trap door in the hearth that allows ashes to be raked into a pit below the fireplace. The pit is emptied through a door in the basement or on the outside wall.

The inner walls of fireboxes are lined with firebrick, using refractory mortar that withstands high heat. Joints between firebricks are as thin as possible. The opening at the top of a fireplace, called the throat, is separated from the chimney above by a damper, usually a hinged plate of cast iron the same width as the firebox. The damper can be opened or closed to control the rate the air is drawn upward, thereby controlling the rate of the fire. A damper can be closed entirely when the fireplace is not being used to prevent heat loss and drafts.

The damper is set at the front of a slab called a smoke shelf, which lies beneath the chimney opening. Its purpose is to deflect rain, snow, and downdrafts from outside. The masonry rising above the damper slopes inward and toward the rear to direct smoke from the fireplace to the chimney. This funnel-shaped cavity is called the smoke chamber.

Modern fireplaces

Prefabricated insulated, or zero-clearance, fireplaces have been used in homes since the 1970s. These consist of a metal firebox lined with firebrick or another heat-resisting material, and they usually feature a ventilation system that draws combustion air from outdoors and heats indoor air with an integral heat exchanger—often U-shape tubes or a chamber that wraps around the fireplace. Openings at the bottom of the unit draw in room air, which is heated as it flows along and up the rear of the fireplace to openings at the top, where it is expelled back into the room. The system is usually aided by a small electric blower.

Zero-clearance fireplaces do not need foundations and are placed where they have access to a chimney and can be isolated from combustible materials, as specified by building code. Some gas-burning models that vent exhaust directly outdoors do not need a chimney (see pp. 70–71).

Chimneys and flues

Traditional chimneys are made of brick or stone. Unlined chimneys were standard in homes built before the 20th century. Since the 1950s, new chimneys have included either rectangular fire-clay liners or, for gas-burning equipment, round vitrified (glazed) tile or stainless steel lining. Fire-clay lining comes in 2-foot (600-mm) lengths and is joined with refractory cement. Vitrified tile has a bell joint, allowing sections to fit together without mortar. Stainless steel lining can be continuous, or its sections are joined by forcing one end into another. Traditional chimneys may be built with concrete flue blocks. These contain holes in the center to fit standard flue liners.

A traditional chimney may contain more than one flue. A common combination is a flue for a fireplace and one for a furnace. Codes may allow connecting multiple combustion sources to the same flue if they produce the same exhaust gases. They also specify the space needed between individual flues in a chimney— 4 inches (100 mm)—to avoid exhaust from one flue being drawn down another. How well a chimney draws is influenced by its height relative to the location of the roof ridge, which affects air currents around the flue opening. Most codes specify that chimneys within 10 feet (3,050 mm) of the roof ridge should rise 24 inches (610 mm) higher than the ridge and must be 36 inches (915 mm) taller than the highest part of the roof next to the chimney. For chimneys farther than 10 feet (3,050 mm) from the ridge, the top of the chimney must be 24 inches (610 mm) higher than the highest point on the roof within a 10-foot (3,050-mm) radius.

Lightweight insulating concrete may be used to line new chimneys, but it is used more often as relining or to upgrade an unlined chimney. Relining a chimney involves first lowering a flexible liner down the flue, then pumping the concrete into the space between the liner and the flue walls. When the concrete has set, the flexible liner is withdrawn, leaving a smoothly lined flue.

Steel chimneys

Insulated steel chimneys are used in many new homes or as chimneys for zero-clearance fireplaces and woodstoves. Double- or triple-wall tubular sections are joined together to form a long pipe. The top section can be left exposed or can be enclosed in a wood chimney. Wood chimneys are built of conventional wall studs covered with sheathing (plywood or particleboard) and siding. The top is capped to keep out rain and snow.

Routine checks

- Check the flue for creosote buildup, and have the chimney inspected and cleaned annually.

- When the fireplace is not in use, check the damper to ensure that it is closed tightly.

- Before starting a fire, check that the damper is open.

3 Exterior walls

Wood-framed houses are the norm in most of North America. The earliest American homes, built in the 17th and 18th centuries, were post-and-beam construction, but most methods used today had their start in the 1830s, with framing from sawed lumber.

Platform framing

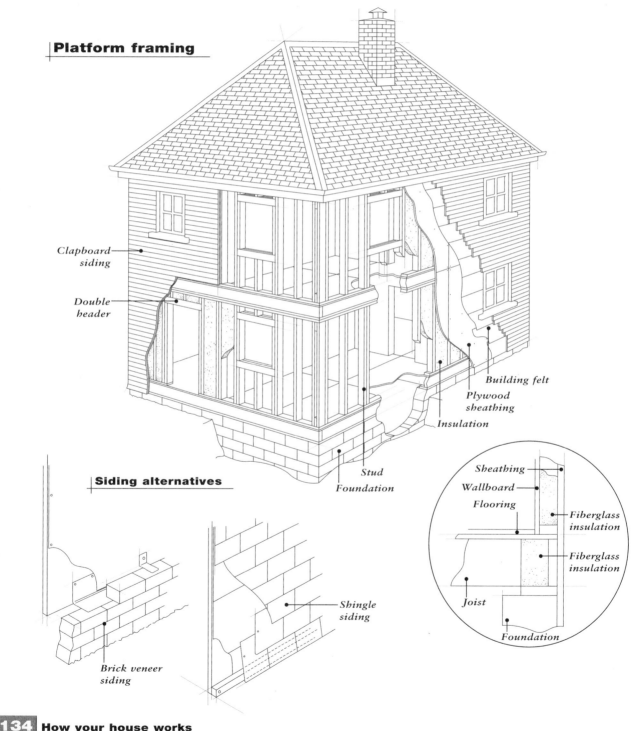

Clapboard siding

Double header

Building felt

Plywood sheathing

Insulation

Stud

Foundation

Sheathing

Wallboard

Flooring

Fiberglass insulation

Fiberglass insulation

Joist

Foundation

Siding alternatives

Brick veneer siding

Shingle siding

Post-and-beam house construction

This type of house was made with massive hand-hewn timbers that were smoothed and skillfully joined together without nails to form a rigid frame, which was sheathed on the outside with clapboards and on the inside with solid wood paneling or with plaster applied over wooden strips called lath. Post-and-beam construction survived long into the 19th century and is enjoying a modest revival among homeowners desiring craftsmanship and an alternative to standard houses.

Wood-framed houses

Sawed lumber framing, often called wood framing or stick building, is a product of industrialization, particularly the sawmill and foundry, which yielded inexpensive dimensioned lumber and affordable nails. Instead of wrestling heavy timbers into place, joining them meticulously, and relying on their size to lend strength to a house frame, builders using the new method were able to quickly and without much skill erect a framework of numerous uniformly-sized lighter members (none over 2 inches/50 mm thick), each of which gained strength from its neighbors and from the sheathing covering the frame.

Balloon framing was the earliest wood-framing style and typifies homes built into the 1930s. Its chief characteristic are long, vertical members, called studs, that reach from the foundation to the eaves and are continuous between floors.

The current standard features shorter studs and is called platform framing. Walls rest on top of sub-floors (platforms), each of which provides a foundation for the wall above in multistory construction. Platform framing is labor-efficient, allows using less expensive lumber, and is more fire-resistant than balloon framing (the long channels

between studs in a balloon-framed structure act as chimneys in a house fire, spreading flames rapidly).

With both methods, walls consist of 2 x 4s (610 x 1,220 mm) that are spaced 16 inches (405 mm) between their centers. Floor and ceiling members, called joists, are wider—up to 10 inches (255 mm)—but the spacing between the boards is the same.

In homes built during the end of the 20th century, wall studs may be 2 x 6s (50 x 150 mm) that are spaced 24 inches (610 mm) apart between centers. This economizes on lumber and creates thicker walls with more room for insulation. Rising lumber prices also have fueled an interest in lightweight steel framing, assembled with screws.

The layers of a wall

Exterior walls of wood-framed houses are sheathed on the outside for support and protection. Homes built prior to World War II feature individual boards, sometimes applied diagonally, such as sheathing. More recent homes have plywood sheathing, which is both stronger and less expensive than individual boards; and the newest homes sport synthetic sheathing such as oriented-strand board (OSB). Plywood sheathing may be installed at corners for strength, with less expensive sheathing panels installed along walls where only protection is needed.

Siding—common ones are shingles, clapboards (wood, aluminum, or vinyl), paneling, stucco, and brick veneer—is applied over the sheathing. However, on newer homes a layer of rigid foam insulation and a covering of windproof plastic film may come between the two. On older homes, thin building felt was applied over the sheathing to separate it from the siding and to provide further protection for the sheathing and the indoors from drafts and moisture.

Soft fiberglass or mineral-wool insulation is packed into the

exterior wall framing during construction, after the sheathing has been applied. Polyethylene sheeting is stapled across the studs to retard indoor moisture passing through the walls and into the insulation (moisture inside the walls can damage insulation and cause decay in wood framing). Gypsum wallboard, in almost all cases, is applied to cover the framework completely.

Brick walls

Brick construction is an alternative to wood. Many newer homes that appear to be brick are wood-framed structures with brick cladding added for appearance. However, true brick construction can be found in older homes. Their exterior walls feature cavity construction: A double wall of bricks with a 2-inch (50-mm) air space between them. The cavity prevents moisture entering the outside bricks from penetrating to the interior of the house and creates a column of dead air that provides some insulation. To strengthen the walls, metal links called wall ties are placed at intervals in the mortar between bricks; they span the cavity, tying the inner and outer walls together.

Routine checks !

- With the exception of damaged asbestos-cement shingle—which should be treated by an abatement contractor—scrub the siding with a mixture of 1 cup of nonabrasive household detergent in 1 gallon of warm water twice a year. As you clean the siding, look for missing or damaged shingles; have them replaced.

- Every 3 to 5 years, reseal or restain wood-base sidings (such as shingles and shakes) and clapboards; alternatively, repaint them every 7 years.

3 | Interior walls and ceilings

The walls of newer houses are "stick-built," using studs and horizontal members called plates, and are covered with wallboard panels. Ceilings use the same principles, with panels attached to the floor joists. Older homes may have plaster walls and ceilings.

Stick-built walls

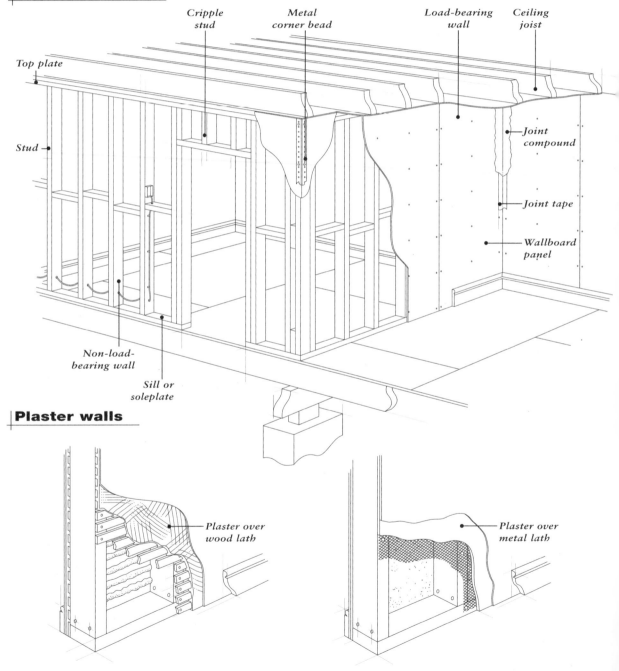

Cripple stud

Metal corner bead

Load-bearing wall

Ceiling joist

Top plate

Stud

Joint compound

Joint tape

Wallboard panel

Non-load-bearing wall

Sill or soleplate

Plaster walls

Plaster over wood lath

Plaster over metal lath

Stick-built walls

Wallboard is also known as drywall, plasterboard, gypsum board, and Sheetrock. Wallboard consists of gypsum plaster layered between two thicknesses of heavy paper. Panels come 4 feet (1,200 mm) wide and in 8, 10, 12, and 14 feet (2,400, 3,000, 3,600, and 4,200 mm) lengths. Thicknesses range from ¼ to ⅝ inch (6 to 16 mm). Most walls are finished with ⅝-inch (15-mm) wallboard to comply with fire codes. Half-inch wallboard is the most popular size for surfaces to which the codes do not apply such as closets. Quarter-inch wallboard is used as a veneer to restore a smooth finish to damaged walls in lieu of repairing them; the thin panels can also be laminated to create curved surfaces.

Wallboard is installed by nailing or screwing the panels against the framing, or wall studs. Spacing between studs is 16 inches (400 mm) on center, with some newer homes having studs at 24-inch (600-mm) intervals. Covering the fasteners and seams are special tape and plaster-like joint compound. Several layers of compound are applied, each wider than the other, to achieve a smooth surface. The wallboard is then painted with primer prior to finishing with wall paint or wallpaper.

Special wallboard with moisture-resistant paper is used in kitchens, bathrooms, and other damp areas. Moisture-resistant wallboard can serve as backing for ceramic wall tiles and prefabricated shower inserts.

Plaster

Prior to World War II, interior walls were covered with plaster. The earliest plaster, found in homes until the late 19th century, contained lime (calcium oxide). Although lime plaster is still used to achieve a smooth surface, modern plaster uses gypsum (calcium sulfate).

Plaster requires a backing, or lath, to support it, except on brick walls, to which plaster sticks directly. Colonial and late-18th-century lath either was woven of twigs or straw or consisted of irregular strips of wood split by hand. During the 19th century, sawed lath, uniform in width and thickness, replaced the hand-split variety. In the early 20th century, metal lath resembling screen was introduced; and since the 1940s metal lath has been replaced by a wallboard called gypsum lath.

Plastering is time-consuming and involves applying two or three coats of material, each with a different mix of ingredients. Plasterers must be highly skilled to achieve strong, smooth surfaces. As a result, true plastering today is expensive, and experienced plasterers are hard to find except in large, historic cities.

Load-bearing walls

Before making alterations inside the house, you need to know whether the wall is load-bearing or not. A load-bearing wall supports part of the house structure—a wall in the story above or the floor and ceiling joists spanning the rooms. It cannot be removed or have an opening made or enlarged in it without steps being taken to carry its load.

One way to identify a load-bearing wall is to examine the way the floor or ceiling joists run relative to it. If the joists are parallel to the wall (with the floorboards at right angles to it), the wall is not load-bearing and can be removed or altered. If joists are at right angles to the wall, it is probably load-bearing. You can be sure it is if, in the basement, you find foundation supports (columns or a girder) beneath the wall, transferring the load to the ground.

Don't take chances with walls that are perpendicular to joists but lack foundation support—they may not seem to be load-bearing, but they may be so. In such cases, seek advice from a building inspector or experienced carpenter. Load-bearing walls can be removed or altered but the process is complicated and subject to building code restrictions.

Ceilings

Between stories, the floor joists of the room above act as framing for the ceiling of the room below. A ceiling may simply consist of wallboard fastened directly to the undersides of the joists. Or a grid of narrow boards, called furring strips, or strapping may be fastened to the joists, and the wallboard panels are fastened to the those. Furring strips provide a level backing surface, especially in older houses, where settling and warping may cause joists to sag; shims are often sandwiched between the joists and the strips to create an even surface. Furring strips also allow wallboards panels to be installed with their long edges parallel to the joists. In restored houses, furring strips and wallboard may be installed to cover deteriorating plaster.

Wallboard ceilings with an attic above are applied over a layer of polyethylene sheeting to prevent moisture from rising into the attic, creating condensation. The cavities between joists are filled with insulation from above, either before the flooring is laid or by removing it in renovations (see pp. 148–149).

(see pp. 148–149)

Routine checks !

- In the spring inspect walls and ceilings for dark stains, bulges, and peeling paint; you should seek advice from a qualified house inspector if any exist.

- Periodically look for cracks in the walls and ceilings.

- If you have a wallcovering, occasionally inspect its seams to see if they are lifting at the edges. If so, adhesive should be applied to reseal them.

Single- and double-hung windows are common in most American homes. However, during the last quarter of the 20th century, casement windows have gained nearly as much in popularity.

Double-hung window

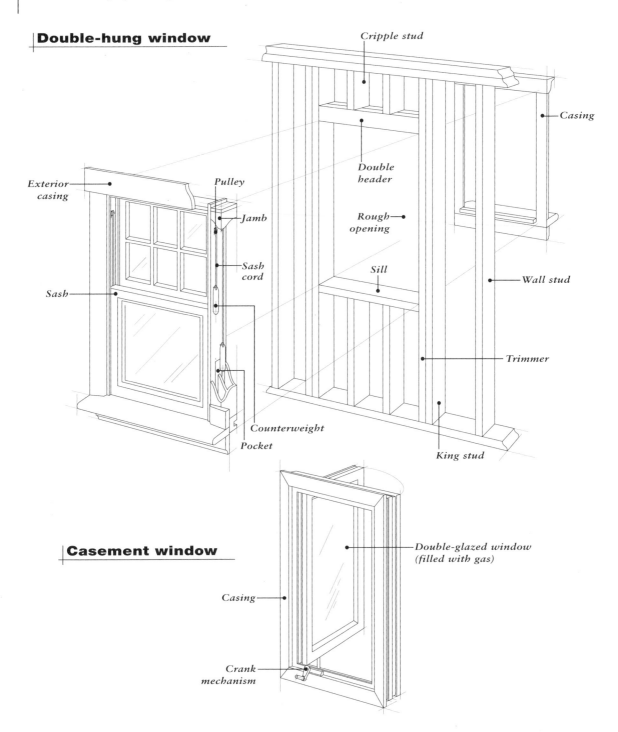

Cripple stud

Casing

Double header

Rough opening

Sill

Wall stud

Trimmer

King stud

Exterior casing

Pulley

Jamb

Sash cord

Sash

Counterweight

Pocket

Casement window

Double-glazed window (filled with gas)

Casing

Crank mechanism

Sash windows

Single- and double-hung windows consist of two sashes that contain glass; they slide past each other on vertical tracks set into the sides of the window opening. In single-hung windows, the upper sash is fixed in place and does not move. Both sashes move in double-hung windows.

The sashes in older windows are raised or lowered by sash cords or chains running over pulleys and attached to counterweights. Pockets near the bottom of a compartment on each side enable the weights to be removed to replace a broken cord.

In modern versions of these windows, springs and spiral balances at sides of the frame replace the weights on many varieties; the latest models rely solely on friction. Besides being lighter in weight, easier to install, and maintenance-free, modern single- and double-hung windows eliminate the drafty space occupied by the counterweight compartments.

Casement windows

The sashes on casement windows are hinged vertically and swing open and shut like doors. Casements offer 100 percent ventilation, and they can be screened on the inside. Having fewer parts, they are easier to seal and weatherproof.

Older casement windows have an adjustable extension arm to control the distance the sash opens and to lock it in a desired position. Since the 1960s, newer casements have crank mechanisms that make the sashes easier to open. Casement windows come in many different combinations of single, multiple, fixed, and hinged sashes.

Other window types

Houses often contain more than one window type. Other popular styles are fixed windows, such as picture windows, which are panes of glass mounted in a stationary sash or frame; horizontal sliding windows, which consist of one or two sashes that slide past each other horizontally; awning windows, which operate like casements but are hinged across the top so the sash swings outward from the bottom; hopper windows, where the sash is hinged at the bottom and opens inward at the top; and jalousie windows, which have rows of small glass panes, much like the slats in a venetian blind, set into a frame.

Window openings

Openings for windows in wood-framed walls are specified by building codes, but differences in construction style do occur. A frame is constructed around the opening to provide support, compensating for the missing wall studs. The dimensions of the opening, called the rough opening, match the outer dimensions of the window, plus a slight amount to make installation easier. After the framing is installed, building paper or another waterproof material is attached to sheathe the opening against moisture.

Modern windows are installed by placing them into the rough opening and leveling them with thin wooden wedges called shims. These are hammered between the window frame and the sides of the opening and trimmed flush with the wall surface. The window is fastened by nailing it through flanges in the frame to the pieces that make up the opening. Molding, or casing, is applied to cover the flanges and surround the window, followed by caulking compound to seal out drafts.

In houses built prior to World War II—especially brick houses, featuring cavity-wall construction—windows lack unitized construction and flanges. In wood-framed houses, they were nailed through their frames to the pieces of the opening. In brick homes, window frames are built into the walls and either fastened to wood blocks or metal flanges embedded in the courses. Removing window frames in old houses means sawing through nails or removing frame parts. Removing a window sill in a brick house means knocking out a row of bricks on the inside. Installing new windows of a different size than the originals is easy in a wood-framed wall, but in a brick wall extensive masonry work may be required, especially if the new windows are larger than the old ones.

Glass and glazing

In older windows a single thickness of glass is set into a notch in the sash and held in place by small metal pins called glazier's points. The edge of the glass is then covered by a layer of putty. Since the 1970s, most windows contain double or triple panes, often coated with high-tech insulating and reflecting films and separated by spaces filled with a gas, such as argon, to enhance their energy efficiency. Single-thickness windows are easy and inexpensive to repair when broken, but they constitute a major source of drafts and heat loss. Multi-thickness panes, while all but eliminating energy loss and other drawbacks of single-thickness windows, are impossible to repair without replacing the sash.

Routine checks

- Have new caulking applied around windows, if necessary, in the spring and fall.

- Lubricate movable hardware, such as hinges and casement operators, in the spring and fall.

- Have any cracked window glass replaced and loose windows reputtied as needed.

- For wooden window parts, you should have peeling paint removed and the parts repainted before rot sets in.

Most houses have a number of wooden doors—manufactured of solid wood, plywood, or a composite material—both for the front door (and any other exterior doors) and for interior doors to rooms.

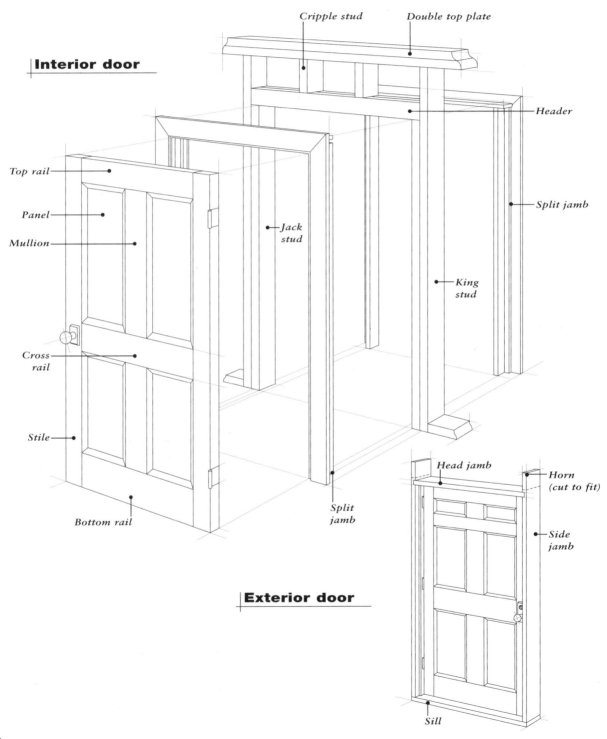

Interior door

Cripple stud

Double top plate

Header

Top rail

Panel

Mullion

Jack stud

King stud

Split jamb

Cross rail

Stile

Split jamb

Bottom rail

Exterior door

Head jamb

Horn (cut to fit)

Side jamb

Sill

Door basics

An exterior door provides security and weather resistance, while an interior door creates privacy and becomes a decorative feature of the rooms it separates. Interior doors may have to offer fire resistance, as in the case of doors separating the house from an attached garage.

Besides wooden doors, there are metal panel doors, made of steel, and doors made of molded fiberglass, which are becoming popular. Almost all doors are sold prehung in door frames. Exterior door frames include head and side jambs, the sill, and the casing. Interior doors include head and side jambs only.

Exterior door openings

Openings for exterior doors are framed in the same way as window openings (see pp. 138–139), but they extend all the way to the floor framing. Metal doors incorporating sills rest on top of the finish flooring. Wood sills are notched at the rear and require cutting away the flooring and subfloor so they rest directly on the rim joist or on a subsill attached to it. On older doors, the rim joist and any floor joists attached to it may have been sloped to accept the sill, a tedious step that is not needed with modern frames. Doorsills are sealed with caulking compound to prevent leaks. Flashing is used beneath sills that rest on a rim joist or subsill.

Installing a prehung exterior door involves setting it into place, leveling it by driving shims (small wooden wedges) between the jambs and the rough-opening frame pieces, then nailing through the jambs and shims into the rough framing. For extra strength and to prevent burglars from prying apart the door components, long screws are used for the jambs and the door hardware; they penetrate the side pieces of the rough opening and the wall studs.

Interior door openings

Interior doors rarely have a sill or threshold and do not need long fasteners. The frames often have split jambs to accept walls of different thicknesses. Split jambs are made of halves that slide together by means of a tongue-and-groove joint. To install one, the frame is separated and the half with the door is secured in the doorway. Working from the other side, the remaining half of the frame is slid against it and fastened. Casing is then applied on both sides to cover the seams between the wall and the door frame.

Types of exterior doors

Exterior doors need strength to be secure. The most common type consists of a frame of solid hardwood into which is set thinner panels made of wood or another material such as glass. The side members of a panel door frame are called stiles; the top and bottom members are rails. The central vertical member found on most panel doors is called a muntin, and any additional horizontal members are cross rails. All frame members are joined with mortise-and-tenon joints.

Panels are installed when the door's frame is assembled. Grooves in the edges of the frame members enclose them; by not using glue or fasteners, the panels are free to expand and contract with changes in humidity, which reduces the likelihood of their cracking. Glass panels are set into rabbets (one-sided grooves) and secured with removable molding so that broken panes can be replaced. Glass window panels should be toughened or laminated for extra security (acrylic plastic, which is almost smashproof, is a better choice than glass), and the panels should be small and away from the door's lock.

Flush doors are also used as exterior doors, often at the side or rear of a house. They consist of a skin (plywood, metal, or fiberglass) surrounding a solid core, which is often rigid foam insulation. Steel reinforcing components surround the hardware locations, and some doors have support struts for extra strength. Metal and fiberglass doors resembling panel doors are of flush-door construction; their skins are stamped or molded to the desired shape.

Types of interior doors

Interior doors, which don't need to be strong, are lighter than exterior doors. The difference between the two is their thickness; interior doors are 1⅜ inches (35 mm) thick; exterior doors, 1 or 2 inches (25 or 50 mm) thick. Interior doors may be flush or paneled. Flush ones feature a lightweight plywood or vinyl skin over a core of solid particleboard or a hollow cardboard honeycomb. Wood blocks are inserted at the side edges for installing handles and latches.

Paneled doors may be made in the same way as exterior types, in softwood or hardwood, or may be a flush door with facings that have been made of medium-density fiberboard (MDF) or another man-made material. Where privacy is not an issue, some or all of the panels may contain glass to allow light through.

Flush interior doors

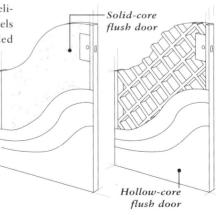

Solid-core flush door

Hollow-core flush door

3 Floors

In most houses floors consist of wooden joists covered by floorboards. In homes built since the 1940s, finish floorboards or other flooring are laid over subflooring—either floorboards, plywood, or composite panels such as oriented-strand board (OSB).

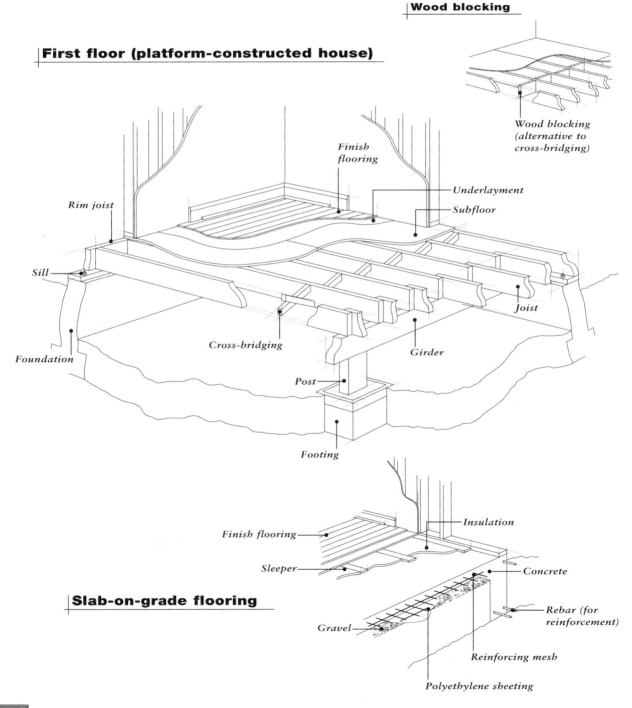

Wood blocking

Wood blocking (alternative to cross-bridging)

First floor (platform-constructed house)

Finish flooring

Underlayment

Subfloor

Rim joist

Sill

Joist

Cross-bridging

Girder

Foundation

Post

Footing

Insulation

Finish flooring

Sleeper

Concrete

Rebar (for reinforcement)

Slab-on-grade flooring

Gravel

Reinforcing mesh

Polyethylene sheeting

First floors

In a house with platform framing (see pp. 134–135), the first-floor joists rest on single or doubled sills (2 x 4s/50 x 100 mm or 2 x 6s/50 x 150 mm) laid flat and bolted to the top of the foundation walls. The ends of the joists are nailed to the rim joists from the outside or are suspended from them by metal straps, or joist hangers. Floor joists and rim joists vary in size from 2 x 8 (50 x 200 mm) to 2 x 12 (50 x 305 mm), depending on the span and wood species; building codes give precise specifications.

In balloon-frame houses the floor joists are fastened to the wall studs. Sills in brick homes rest on a ledge created by foundation walls that are wider than the brick courses rising from them. In older construction they are notched into the bricks.

Joist spacing may be on 16- or 24-inch (405- or 610-mm) centers. To span wide areas, pairs of joists are lap-joined and supported by a girder. (Girders are built of several layers of lumber nailed together or consist of a steel I-beam; they are suspended from notches in the foundation walls and are supported by posts set on concrete footings.) Solid wood blocking or X-shaped cross-bridging is nailed at intervals between the joists to distribute loads from above and to prevent the joists from warping sideways.

Subflooring, which covers the joists and add additional strength to the structure, consists of ¾-inch- (19-mm-) thick plywood panels; composite panels rated for subfloors are common in newer homes; in prewar homes subflooring consists of 1-inch- (25-mm-) thick boards—often tongue and grooved or shiplapped to stop drafts from below—laid perpendicular or diagonal to the joists. Older subflooring is fastened with nails to the joists. Newer installations use a combination of adhesive and nails or screws, which reduces squeaks.

Upper floors

Floors on upper stories in platform-constructed houses have joists resting on the doubled wall plates of the first floor (which have the same function as the sills on the foundation) and are end-nailed to the rim joists or hung from joist hangers. Subflooring is fastened across the joists; the wall framing for the story rests on the subfloor.

In balloon-framed houses, the upper floor joists rest on a ledger notched into the wall studs. In old brick houses, the joists are supported by notches in the masonry; metal joist hangers are used in new brick houses.

Concrete floors

Solid concrete is ubiquitous for basement floors (floors in older basements may be dirt; gravel is often used in crawl spaces). In newer homes, a 4- to 6-inch (100- to 150-mm) layer of gravel is spread over the area, followed by polyethylene sheeting to bar moisture rising from below; then concrete is spread to a 4-inch (100-mm) thickness. Concrete basement floors often slope toward a drain.

Houses without a basement or crawl space have solid concrete floors, called slab-on-grade floors, poured at ground level. In cold areas, they are poured separately from the foundation walls, which are installed first and extend into the ground with their footings below frost level. In warm climates, where frost risk is minimal, slab-on-grade floors often function as both floor and foundation by being formed with edges thicker than the rest of their surface. A typical slab-on-grade floor measures 12 inches (305 mm) thick around the perimeter and inward for a distance of 8 inches (200 mm). The remainder of the floor usually has a thickness of 4 inches (100 mm).

To prepare the ground for the slab, a trench is dug for the rim and the remaining area is spread with a 4- to 6-inch (100- to 150-mm) layer of gravel and covered with polyethylene sheeting. Preparation of the site may include laying air ducts and plumbing pipes. The floor may also contain a grid of steel reinforcing mesh for extra strength and to reduce the likelihood of cracking. The mesh is spread over the polyethylene and propped so it will be embedded in the middle of the concrete.

Finish flooring

Wood subfloors are covered with underlayment panels before the finish flooring is installed. It provides a smooth surface and support beneath heavy flooring. The panels are ¼- or ½-inch- (6- or 13-mm-) thick underlayment-grade plywood or particleboard; ¾-inch- (19-mm-) thick moisture-resistant cement board or plywood is installed under ceramic tile. To reduce squeaking, lightweight building felt is used as the underlayment beneath wood strip flooring.

Any flooring except solid wood strips can be applied over a concrete floor, preferably over an underlayment. To install a solid wood floor, sleeps made of 2 x 4s (50 x 100 mm) are attached to the concrete; narrow finish floorboards (up to 4 inches/ 100 mm wide) are nailed to the sleepers. For wider floorboards or greater support, underlayment panels are first installed over the sleepers.

Routine checks !

- Periodically check wooden floors for loose or split floorboards and for wear.

- If windows or doors stick, check the floor for sagging; if there is a sag, call in a home inspection engineer or contractor to inspect it.

- Periodically inspect floor tiles and vinyl flooring for cracks and other damage.

One of the most complex components in a house is the staircase. It provides access between floors and consist of two main parts—the stairs themselves and handrails or balustrades to guard against users falling while climbing or descending them.

L-shaped staircase

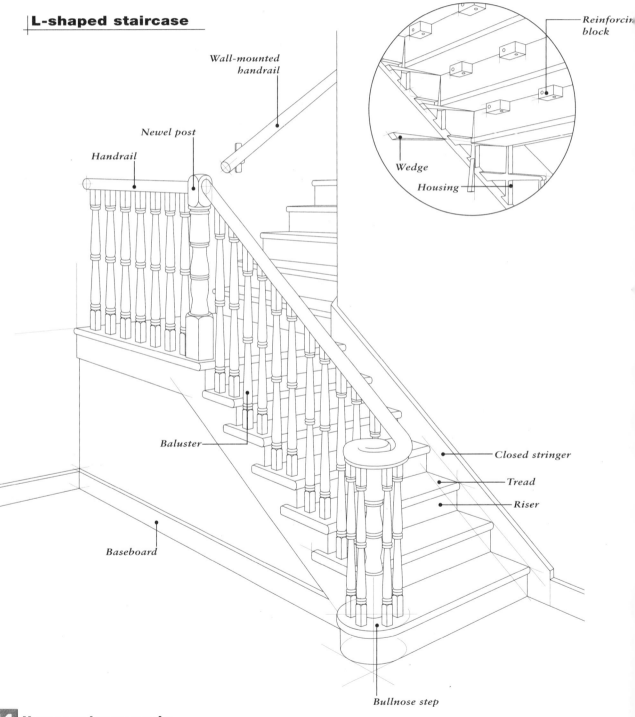

Reinforcing block

Wall-mounted handrail

Newel post

Handrail

Wedge

Housing

Baluster

Closed stringer

Tread

Riser

Baseboard

Bullnose step

Staircase configuration

The basic ingredients of a staircase are horizontal treads, vertical risers, and side members variously called strings, stringers, or carriages, which support the ends of the treads and risers. The simplest staircase is a straight flight that rises directly from one floor to the next.

Other staircase arrangements where the flight changes direction as it rises are common, because they make more economical use of floor space. The flight may be turned at a 90-degree angle, incorporating a square quarter-landing the same width as the flight. This type is usually called an L-shaped staircase. Alternatively, a stairway may turn at a 180-degree angle, with a half-landing twice as wide as the flight. This type is called a U-shape or dog-leg staircase. A dogleg staircase with a wider half-landing and clear space between the flights is known as an open-well staircase.

The staircase may also be constructed to turn through the use of a number of triangular steps called winders, or may even be a continuous spiral with wedge-shaped steps.

Staircase construction

Where one or both stringers are attached to side walls, the treads and risers fit into slots (housings) cut into their inner faces and are retained in their slots by long thin wooden wedges. This is a closed stringer. Where the staircase abuts just one wall, the inner stringer will be closed while the outer stringer may be closed or open. In the latter case, the top edge of the stringer is cut to form steps on which the treads rest.

On a traditionally built staircase, the back of each tread will fit in a slot cut across the face of the riser above it, while the top edge of the riser below will engage in a slot cut across the underside of the tread.

On a modern prefabricated staircase, these joints are often simply glued and nailed together. Reinforcing blocks may be added beneath the step, fitting in the right angle between tread and riser. Some wide staircases may have a stout central stringer fitted beneath the treads midway between the two stringers.

A common design feature found on many staircases is a projecting bottom step, with one or both sides having a rounded shape. This is known as a bullnose step.

A variation on the standard enclosed staircase is the open variety. Here the risers are omitted and the treads are either fitted between two stringers in the usual way or are supported on stringers placed closer together so that the treads project at one or both sides.

The underside of the staircase may be exposed, especially if the space beneath it is enclosed by an understairs storage closet. This allows easy access to the staircase structure if repairs are needed—for example, to cure squeaking caused by movement between treads and risers or to replace a damaged tread. In other situations the underside of the flight may be paneled in, with lath and plaster in older houses and with wallboard in newer ones. This will generally have to be removed if repairs are needed.

Balustrades

A staircase built against one wall has a balustrade along the open side. This runs between stout vertical posts called newel posts, which are bolted to the floor joists at the top and bottom of the flight. Extra newel posts are also fitted wherever the flight changes direction. The handrail is fitted between the newel posts, and the space between the handrail and the outer stringer is filled in with a series of closely spaced balusters or other open or solid material.

Where the staircase is fitted between two walls, a simple wall-mounted handrail will be installed at one or both sides. It may be screwed directly to the wall, or it may be fixed with brackets at intervals.

The top ends of the balusters may simply be toenailed to the underside of the handrail, or they may fit in a groove and be separated by nailed-on spacers. On a closed stringer, a grooved capping piece is usually fitted to the top edge of the stringer and the ends of the balusters fit into this, again separated by spacers. On an open stringer, the ends of the balusters are set in notches cut in the treads and are retained by a cover molding nailed to the outer end of the tread.

Altering staircases

Unless a staircase has suffered physical damage or has been affected by decay or pests, it will generally last the lifetime of the building. However, replacing the balustrade is a popular way of changing the look of the staircase, and kits of parts are widely available.

Routine checks !

- A squeak occurs when wood rubs against wood. It can be cured by attaching a support block to the underside of the step if the squeak is at the top of a riser and front of the step; or insert shims between the riser and tread if the squeak occurs at the rear of the tread.

- Look for loose balusters. These can be tightened by inserting a wood shim at the loose end or by toenailing the baluster to its support. A damaged baluster may need to be replaced.

- If the front of a tread becomes worn, the worn section or the whole tread may need replacing.

3 Moisture proofing

An essential part of any house is its ability to prevent water from getting into the structure. Moisture creates unhealthy living conditions, spoils decorations and furnishings, and encourages the spread of rot—a potentially serious problem.

Chimney cricket

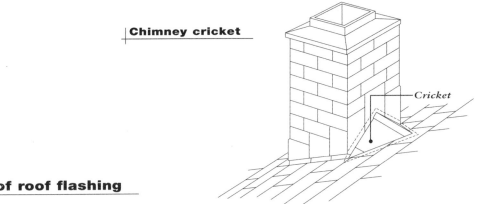

Cricket

Types of roof flashing

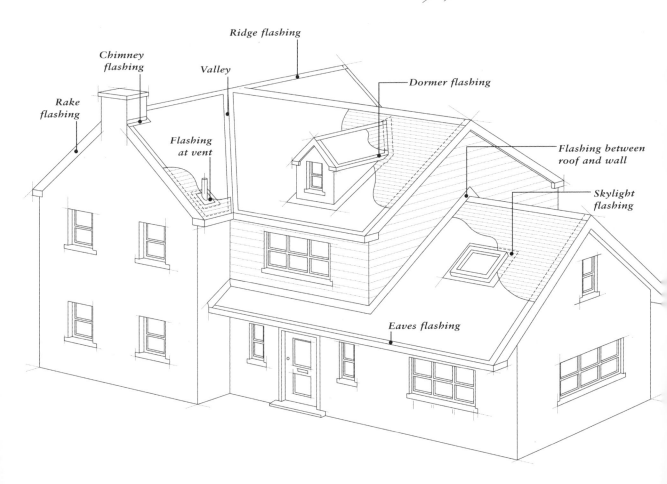

Ridge flashing

Chimney flashing

Valley

Dormer flashing

Rake flashing

Flashing at vent

Flashing between roof and wall

Skylight flashing

Eaves flashing

Moisture from above

The roof of a house is the building's first line of defense against moisture. Asphalt or metal flashing, which comes in the form of sheet material, prevents rainwater from penetrating the structure. They are used where roof slopes meet at ridges and hips, and at valleys—the V-shaped angles that form between two roof slopes. Valley flashing runs downhill to the eaves, where the collected rainwater is discharged into the gutters.

Chimneys

Where a chimney passes through the roof, any junctions between the two are waterproofed with specially shaped overlapping pieces of sheet metal or copper. In the best installations, two layers of flashing are used. After installing a piece of flashing called an apron against the downslope face of the chimney, the first layer of side, or step, flashing is placed under the ends of the shingles adjacent to the chimney and folded upward along the chimney sides. Then an upslope apron is installed by tucking it under the shingles above it and folding its ends so they overlap the highest pieces of the step flashing. The second layer of flashing, known as counterflashing, fits over the first layer and is installed by embedding the upper edges of each piece in the mortar joints of the chimney faces.

Some chimneys emerge 12 inches (300 mm) or more below the roof ridge. To divert the flow of runoff water against a chimney of this type, a triangular-sided miniature roof structure called a cricket is installed against its upslope face. Crickets are made by first cutting and folding flashing to the correct shape—pieces of wood may be used as stiffening beneath the metal—then by tucking their flanges under the shingles surrounding them. Counterflashing is then attached to the chimney.

Windows and doors

The openings in the exterior walls into which window and door frames fit are an obvious place where rainwater could penetrate the structure of the house. Older houses relied on little more than a good fit. In newer houses, weatherstripping, caulking compound, expandable foam, and weather-resisting housewrap keep out water and drafts.

Moisture from below

Another source of leaks, and often the most common one, is moisture penetrating the foundation. Crucial to avoiding basement moisture problems is adequate roof drainage. Gutters must be large enough and placed properly so they do not overflow (see pp. 130–131). Downspouts must direct runoff well away from the foundation: At least 6 feet (1.8 m), but 10 feet (30 m) or more is better. If this is not done, water collected on the roof will saturate the soil around the foundation and the added pressure against the walls will force water through the pores of the concrete, creating leaks, even without cracks or holes.

Other easy steps for reducing ground saturation are to grade the earth surrounding the foundation so the area slopes away from the house and to cover basement window wells with clear plastic "bubbles" that prevent water from accumulating in them. In lieu of covers, keep window wells free of leaves and other debris. Wells should contain a layer of gravel at the bottom to disperse water; the best have drains, which must be kept clear.

Foundations themselves often have perimeter drain systems—a ring of perforated or porous pipe (often called drain tile) installed at the time the footings are laid (see right). Footing drains collect moisture trickling down foundation walls and direct it to storm drains or elsewhere away from the building.

In new homes, footing drain systems can be elaborate, connecting to downspouts and basement floor drains and having aboveground extensions allowing cleanout by power equipment. In older homes they are usually minimal, clogged with silt or broken by tree roots, or nonexistent. Footing drains can be retrofitted—installed after a house is built—either by excavating around the outside of the building or, more economically, by breaking through the basement floor.

Other aids against foundation leakage include belowground wall coatings and "drainage fabrics." Older foundations were coated with some form of asphalt waterproofing, and today many still are. However, newer synthetic coatings and high-tech membranes work much better, provided they are correctly applied. Coating the insides of basement walls with special paint, usually containing fine cement, is touted as a cure for moisture seepage. While such paint can solve minor problems if meticulously applied according to the manufacturer's directions, exterior coatings combined with proper roof and footing drainage are the only proven fix for most conditions.

Foundation drainage

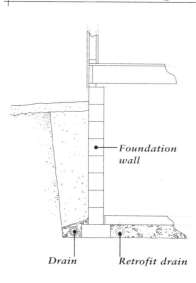

Foundation wall

Drain   *Retrofit drain*

3 | Insulation

A vital part in your house, insulation keeps the building warm in winter, reducing heating costs, and cool in summer. It stops heat loss from hot-water pipes, water heaters, and heating ducts, and it prevents cold-water supply pipes from freezing.

Insulation around a house

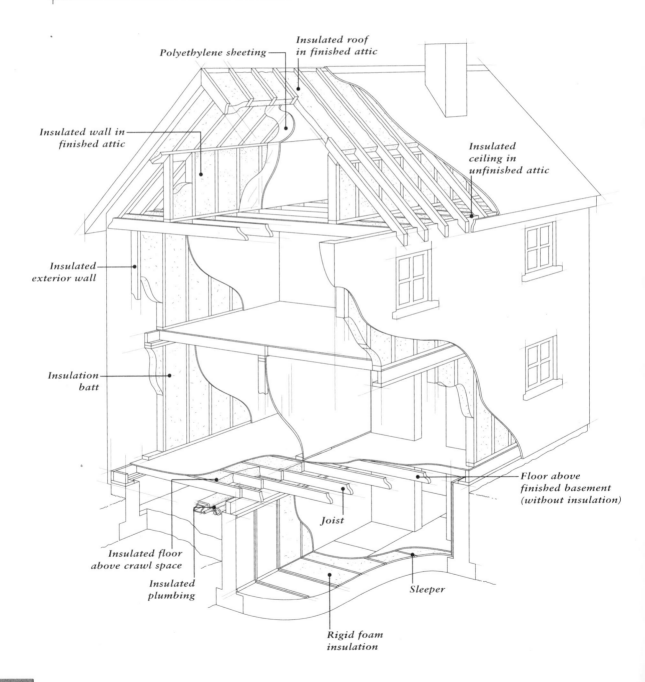

Polyethylene sheeting

Insulated roof in finished attic

Insulated wall in finished attic

Insulated ceiling in unfinished attic

Insulated exterior wall

Insulation batt

Floor above finished basement (without insulation)

Joist

Insulated floor above crawl space

Insulated plumbing

Sleeper

Rigid foam insulation

Attic insulation

Few homes built prior to the 1940s included insulation. As heating costs rose, homeowners became conscious of the need to insulate. Because heat rises, the attic is the first area insulated, keeping heat in the living areas.

Mineral wool and fiberglass are common materials in attic insulation. Both come in strips, called batts, that fit between joists. Batts may be faced with a moisture-retarding layer of foil or paper on one side, or they may be unfaced. Mineral wool and fiberglass are also available as loose fill.

Cellulose and vermiculite (only as loose fill) are also common, especially in old homes. Cellulose is shredded paper, treated to resist fire, moisture, rot, and pests (but it gradually absorbs water, which ruins it). Vermiculite is noncombustible and fireproof, but it is expensive and blows around in drafts.

All insulation works by trapping a layer of air and stopping it from rising, making the space above the attic floor colder than before. Moist air rising into the insulation from rooms below can result in condensation, which makes the insulation wet and useless. The condensation can also dampen roof framing if the attic is poorly ventilated, encouraging rot. This is why ceilings in new houses have a vapor barrier placed across the bottoms of the joists, before the ceiling panels are fastened to them. In older houses, polyethylene sheeting can be placed beneath the insulation to serve the same purpose.

If the attic is converted for use as habitable rooms, the underside of the roof slope must be insulated instead. Slabs of rigid foam insulation, such as expanded polystyrene, are usually used. They fit between the rafters and must be installed with a gap between them and the the roof to allow air to circulate. After the insulation is in place, wallboard or other paneling is attached across the rafters to conceal it.

Flat roofs

Older flat roofs rarely contain insulation and lose heat at a high rate. Insulating them is difficult. Installing batts from below means removing the ceiling and installing a new one. Loose-fill insulation may be blown in by drilling holes at the eaves, but this requires scientific equipment to monitor the job. Flat roofs can be insulated by building a new roof above the existing one and sandwiching rigid-foam insulation boards between the two.

Exterior walls

Walls are insulated by placing batts between the studs before attaching wallboard. Rigid foam panels may also be applied on the exterior side of the sheathing before the siding is added. In homes already built, insulating the walls involves drilling holes in the sheathing (after removing the siding) and blowing in loose fill.

Existing solid and cavity brick walls—which are poor insulators—are best insulated with batts or rigid foam insulation placed against the interior side. This means tearing down existing walls or building new ones after the insulation is applied. Cavity walls may be insulated with blown-in loose-fill or expanding polyurethane foam, but the effect is minimal; the space between bricks is inadequate to hold enough insulation for cold climates.

Floor insulation

Flooring over unheated basements and crawl spaces is usually insulated by installing batts between the joists from below. To prevent condensation from forming inside the insulation, dampening it and reducing its effectiveness (and fostering decay in the flooring above), it is crucial to install the batts with their vapor barrier facing against the underside of the flooring, not facing the basement or crawl-space floor. Batts can be secured with string or wire wrapped around nails driven into the lower edges of the joists; flexible fiberglass rods that can be inserted against the batts are also available.

Insulating plumbing

Water heaters contain some insulation. Exterior insulating jackets surround a heater with several inches (cm) of heat-trapping fiberglass. Hot-water supply pipes should be insulated with closed-cell foam pipe insulation, especially along long runs. Insulating cold-water pipes only reduces the condensation that forms on the pipes in the summer and contributes to basement humidity.

Hot- and cold-water pipes in unheated areas, such as crawl spaces, need protection. In mild areas, sheathing hot-water pipes with closed-cell foam is enough, but if there is a danger of freezing, use heat tape wrapped around the pipes.

Ways to insulate an attic

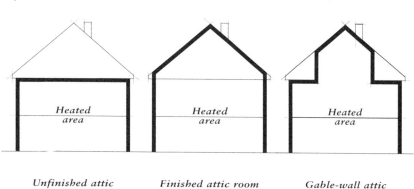

Unfinished attic   Finished attic room   Gable-wall attic

3 | Ventilation

Good ventilation ensures fresh air in the house and removes odors. It prevents condensation by allowing moist air to escape. It is vital for the safe operation of fuel-burning appliances; without it, dangerous levels of carbon monoxide can build up.

Types of roof ventilation

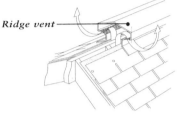

Ridge vent

Ridge vent

A ridge vent runs along the ridge of a roof. It is used in conjunction with soffit vents.

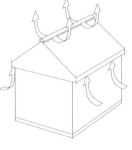

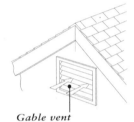

Gable vent

Gable vent

Rectangular-, triangular-, or semicircular-shaped gable vents are placed on either side of the house.

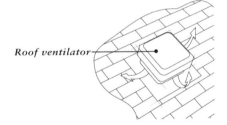

Roof ventilator

Roof ventilator

Mechanical roof ventilators work in conjunction with soffit vents.

Types of soffit vents

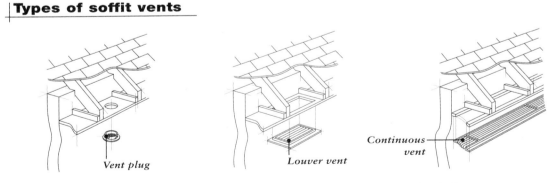

Vent plug

Louver vent

Continuous vent

Soffit vents must be used with other vents to promote air circulation.

Tight houses

Houses built before the 1950s were drafty. Air was continuously moving into and out of the house through unweatherstripped doors and windows with thin or no insulation and through gaps in floorboards over basements and crawl spaces.

Homes built since the early 1970s are well insulated and tightly sealed to reduce the exchange of air with the outside. Doors and windows fit well and have effective draftproofing. Subflooring panels below floorboards eliminate drafts from below. In fact, today's homes are too well sealed, resulting in indoor air pollution. Modern homes need carefully engineered natural ventilation, and often supplementary artificial ventilation to maintain healthy airflow.

Natural ventilation

Breezes through openings and air currents generated by rising warm air and falling cool air constitute the natural airflow through a house. In open rooms and living areas (barring tightly sealed conditions), such airflow is sufficient to provide healthy air and to remove excess moisture and other contaminants. However, such is not the case in closed basements, crawl spaces, and attics, especially if those spaces are insulated and cannot exchange air with better-ventilated parts of the house. For this reason, these areas contain vents. Their size is governed by building codes, such as the ones that specify the area of attic ventilation openings for the area of attic space. Attic vents are divided between soffit openings at the eaves and openings at or by the roof peak, an arrangement that fosters air movement to the outdoors.

Codes also specify the amount of vents needed for a basement or crawl space. In most cases, more vent space is needed to control condensation, except in dry regions. Vents in basements and crawl spaces are located at the tops of foundation walls. At least two vents are required, one at each end of the basement or crawl space, to induce a breeze.

Artificial ventilation

Kitchens and bathrooms can create large amounts of water vapor through cooking, washing, and bathing. This can cause condensation unless it is removed from the room. Smells also need dispersing if they are not to become stale and unpleasant. Opening a window is often not enough to do the job; what is needed is some type of mechanical ventilation. This is also essential in windowless rooms, such as bathrooms, where vapors or stale air can accumulate.

In general, artificial ventilation is provided by an electric exhaust fan, which draws air from the room and expels it to the outside. A wall-mounted fan can be fitted in an exterior wall or window for direct exhaust to the outdoors, or installed in a ceiling and connected to a duct running to a wall or the roof. (Small exhaust fans are sometimes installed to expel air into unused attics, but this can cause condensation.)

In kitchens, it is common practice to install a range hood or downdraft ventilator to accompany the stove. However, some ventilators can only filter cooking vapors; to be effective, range ventilators must expel vapors through ductwork to the outdoors.

Most building codes specify the minimum air-exchange rates necessary for adequate ventilation, and manufacturers' tables list the right-size fan, range hood, or other ventilator to do the job.

Heating appliances

Furnaces, fireplaces, and gas-fired water heaters need ventilation to operate properly and to prevent carbon monoxide buildup, which can be lethal. Basements, where gas-fired furnaces and water heaters are installed, should have enough fresh air for efficient combustion, but have the appliances inspected annually by a heating technician. If there is a problem, additional ventilation can be supplied by opening a window or vent, or an air-supply duct can be routed to the appliance. (New furnaces have air-supply ducts that don't need household air for combustion.)

Fireplaces and woodstoves that operate poorly lack sufficient air; slightly opening a nearby window may cure the problem. Freestanding fireplaces have air-supply ducts that run to the outside of the house.

Any home with fuel-burning appliances should have carbon monoxide detectors to warn if harmful levels accumulate. In tightly sealed homes, imbalances in ventilation can draw combustion exhaust from appliances down chimneys and into living areas, a condition known as backdrafting.

Basement or crawl-space ventilation

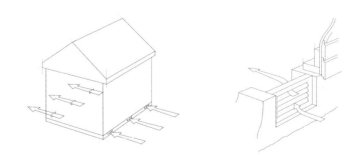

Vents are placed on opposite walls to encourage airflow.

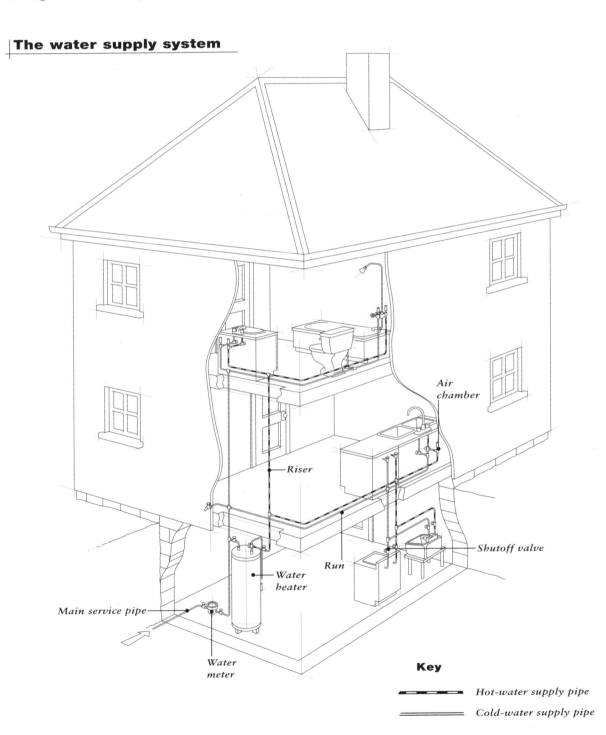

3 | Water supply systems

A home's water supply may come from a municipal water source or from a private well. Municipal water is the most common. The water is delivered around the house through a series of pipes—one for hot water and one for cold water.

The water supply system

Air chamber

Riser

Run

Shutoff valve

Water heater

Main service pipe

Water meter

Key

- - - - *Hot-water supply pipe*

——— *Cold-water supply pipe*

The plumbing system

Water flows under pressure from a main pipe to the house. Upon entering the house, the main supply pipe divides, with one segment running to the water heater, which heats water in a tank. From that division, hot- and cold-water pipes run more or less parallel on their routes to fixtures and appliances in the house.

Vertical pipes in the plumbing system are called risers. Horizontal pipes are called runs. Air chambers, installed close to certain fixtures and appliances (usually out of sight, inside walls), create cushions for the pressurized water, keeping pipes from banging or shuddering when a faucet or an appliance is turned off (plumbers call this "water hammer").

Valves throughout the system provide control, enabling sections of the plumbing—or all of it—to be shut off and drained, if necessary. The main shutoff valve to the property is usually a gate valve near the water meter, which may or may not be inside the house. If the meter is inside, another shutoff valve may also be located on the other side of the meter, near where the supply pipe enters the building. Additional shutoff valves are usually located near the water heater and adjacent to individual fixtures. Extensive plumbing systems may have shutoff valves to isolate runs to upper floors, outdoor faucets, and other outlets.

Private wells

Most private wells operate by means of a pump. Shallow wells draw water from springs and the local water table. Deep wells tap into purer water from aquifers located hundreds of feet (meters) underground. The well pump sends water to a pressure tank, usually located inside the house or next to it, in a protected shed. The purpose of the tank is to provide storage and also to supply water to the house under uniform pressure.

There are two types of pumps. Submersible pumps are lowered into the well to push water upward. They can be located at any depth. Jet pumps are installed at the surface and suck water upward from below. They are designed for shallow wells, no deeper than 100 feet (30 m).

Pressure tanks

There are two common types of pressure tanks. In a standard tank, incoming water forces air to the top, where it forms a cushion. When the pressure of the air in the tank reaches a certain level, the air cushion's springlike action triggers a switch that shuts off the pump. As water is drawn off from the tank and the air pressure decreases, the switch turns the pump on again.

The other type of tank is smaller and contains a sealed air cushion as a separate component. Water filling the tank compresses the cushion, triggering the pump's "off" switch; when the cushion expands as water leaves the tank, the pump comes on again.

Submersible pump

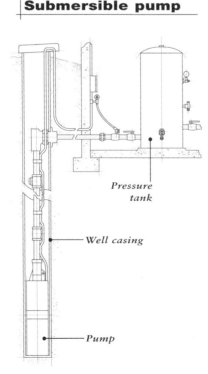

Pressure tank

Well casing

Pump

Metal pipes

In homes built before the 1950s supply pipes were made of galvanized steel and joined by threaded connections. Depending on pipe diameter, water composition, and frequency of use, good-quality steel pipe lasts 40 to 60 years before rusting or becoming blocked by mineral deposits.

Copper pipes replaced steel during the mid-1950s and were the only type installed until the 1970s. They are the most durable and may last indefinitely, except where the water is highly corrosive or there are manufacturing defects. Copper pipes are joined with solder, which contained lead until it was banned in 1988. The Centers for Disease Control do not consider lead in solder a hazard; most water contains mineral salts that coat the pipes, covering the solder.

Plastic pipes

There are several types of plastic pipes; some are not suitable for supply pipes. Some building codes may not allow using any type of plastic supply pipes; all plastic pipe is flammable and produces toxic fumes when burned. The pipes are joined by cemented connections that melt them together or by plastic or metal threaded mechanical connections.

Polyvinyl chloride (PVC) pipe is allowed for single-floor cold-water supply pipes in some areas; but chlorinated polyvinyl chloride (CPVC) pipe is preferred and is the only plastic pipe allowed for multistory use and for carrying hot water. CPVC pipe is ideal where water is "hard" (has high mineral content); the minerals don't adhere to the pipe walls.

Flexible polyethylene (PE) pipe is allowed by most building codes for carrying cold water, but is not approved for hot water, which softens it. Polybutylene (PB), which is gray in color, was removed as an approved material from the Uniform Plumbing Code in 1989, after claims of ruptured fittings.

3 Drainage systems

The wastewater generated within the house by bathing, flushing toilets, washing clothes, and preparing food is disposed of by a drainage system, which carries used water out of the house for disposal.

DWV system

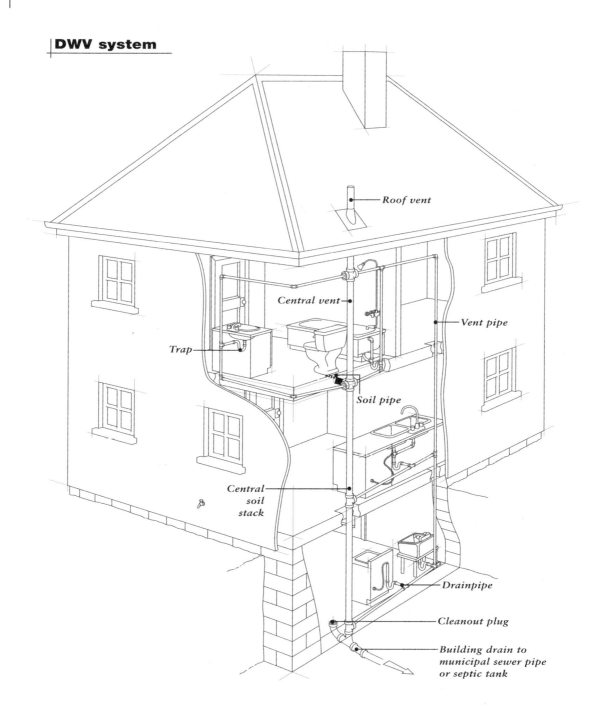

Roof vent

Central vent

Vent pipe

Trap

Soil pipe

Central soil stack

Drainpipe

Cleanout plug

Building drain to municipal sewer pipe or septic tank

The septic tank

Waste is carried to a septic tank, where bacteria break it down into effluent (liquids), sludge (solids), and scum. Effluent flows into a distribution box, then to a drainage field.

Septic tank

Distribution box

Drainage field

The DWV system

Wastewater is disposed of by a drainage system, which carries it out of the house to municipal sewer pipes, or to a private septic tank or cesspool. Plumbers call this the DWV system; the letters stand for drain, waste, and vent, which accurately describes the components. Waste water is carried off by drainpipes (these are also referred to as waste pipes). Toilet discharge is carried by soil pipes, also called stacks, which are larger in diameter.

Water in DWV pipes flows by gravity; so drainpipes are run so they slope at least ¼ inch per foot (6 mm per 305 mm). Horizontal drain sections have cleanout plugs for removing blockages. Soil stacks are vertical or run at a steep angle.

Metal drainpipes

Galvanized steel was once used for drainpipes, but it is susceptible to mineral buildup, which constricts the flow of the waste, and to corrosion. Most of this material has been replaced by copper or plastic piping. Copper waste pipe was often used in the 1950s and 1960s, and it performs quite well; many original installations are still in use.

Homes built before the 1950s may contain lead drainpipes. Any that still exist may be prone to leakage at the joints because of age, but the pipe itself is likely to be sound; it is resistant to corrosion. To prevent future leaks, lead plumbing is replaced during a major renovation if the pipes are exposed. Lead waste plumbing is not a health hazard—the water flowing through it is not used for consumption.

Plastic pipes

Due to the high cost of copper, plastic pipe has been used in construction and remodeling since the 1970s (building codes allow it to be used in waste systems). ABS (acrylonitrile-butadiene-styrene) plastic is the most commonly used for DWV systems. Black in color (which distinguishes it from white or tan PVC supply pipes), ABS pipe is simple to join by cementing sections together.

Two types of ABS pipe are available: solid and foam core. The latter is more common, especially in new houses, chiefly because of its sound-insulating properties. It consists of two layers of ABS pipe with a layer of closed-cell foam between them.

Soil stacks

Cast iron has always been popular for soil stacks, but its high cost has diminished its use. While heavy, difficult to work with, and prone to corrosion, the advantage of cast iron is its ability to muffle the noise of the water flowing through it. This makes for quieter installations and allows more flexibility in where to locate the pipes; for example, enclosing a cast-iron soil stack from an upstairs toilet in a living room wall is usually feasible; the same installation using an ABS stack can be a social disaster.

Vent pipes

Plumbing systems need air-venting to allow sewer gasses to escape, to equalize air pressure in the system so that waste flows freely in the pipes, and to maintain adequate water in the U-shaped traps at each plumbing fixture. The latter is the most important. Plumbing traps provide a water seal that prevents sewer odors and possibly pathogens from entering the house. After a fixture is used, water should remain in the trap, creating the seal. If the system is not properly vented, the water will be drawn out of the trap by a siphoning action.

Vent pipes can be of any material already mentioned. Since vent pipes carry only air, they last a long time regardless of their composition. The location of a vent pipe must be just downstream of a trap to allow air into the drainpipe and prevent a vacuum between the water running down the drain and the water in the trap. From there, vent pipes may run directly to the roof, where they open into the air; or they may connect as part of a network of pipes to centralized vents, which also exit through the roof.

In a typical small house, plumbing fixtures drain into a central soil stack, the upper portion of which functions as a central vent. Individual vent pipes rise from each fixture and connect to the central stack at a point above the height of the uppermost fixture; thus all the connected fixtures are vented but only one stack will be visible at the roof.

The electrical system is the lifeblood of the modern house, and although it is mostly concealed from view within the house structure, it is useful to understand it so that improvements and alterations can be planned sensibly and faults can be traced easily.

Household electrical system

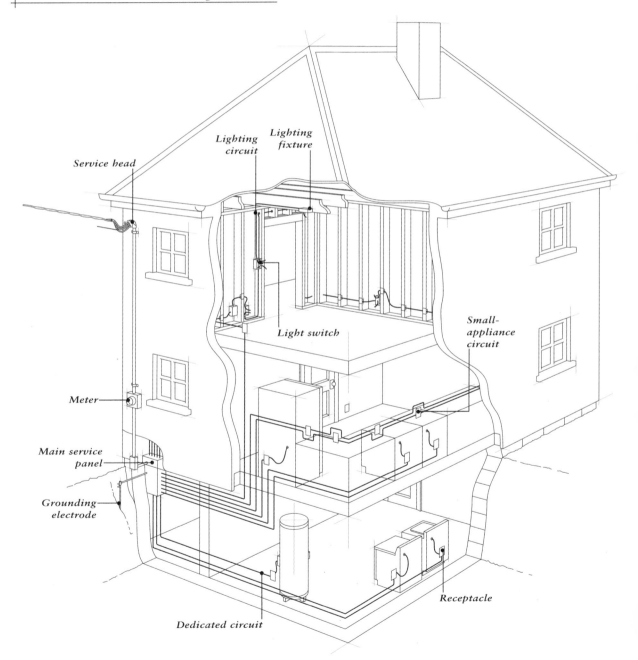

Service head

Lighting circuit

Lighting fixture

Light switch

Small-appliance circuit

Meter

Main service panel

Grounding electrode

Receptacle

Dedicated circuit

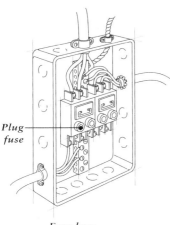

Fuse box

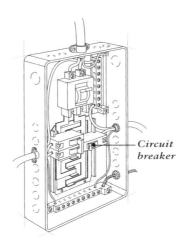

Circuit breaker panel

Entering the house

The electricity supply, or service, reaches the house through a cable from a utility pole or from underground. Most homes built since the 1950s have a three-wire electrical service, consisting of a neutral wire and two 120-volt power-carrying, or hot, wires that provide 100 to 200 amps at 120 and 240 volts. Older homes may have a two-wire service, with a neutral wire and only one hot wire; this service is inadequate, supplying only 30 to 60 amps and 120 volts.

Service supplied from overhead wires connects to a service head, a fitting mounted high on the house. From there, the electricity travels to a meter that measures electrical usage, then indoors to the main service panel, where current is distributed throughout the house via branch circuits. Underground wires lead directly to the meter.

Electricity must travel in a closed loop, or circuit, from its source (a power generating station) to a load—i.e., appliance—and back. In a lighting circuit, current flows at 120 volts through a hot wire (usually black) to a bulb, where it is converted to light. From the bulb, a neutral wire (usually white) returns current at zero volts to the main service panel and back to the source. In case of a malfunction, a grounding wire (usually green) runs with the other wires.

Grounding system

The grounding system provides an escape route for stray current from a malfunction. Electricity always flows by the path of least resistance to a point of zero voltage—the earth—and it flows through copper more readily than other materials. If the hot wire to a wall switch comes loose and touches the inside of the metal electrical box inside the wall, the box is electrically charged; anyone touching the box's metal cover will receive a shock. In a grounding system, a copper wire fastened to the box will carry the stray current to the service panel and from there into the earth. Newer receptacles have a third slot that connects to a grounding wire; this extends grounding protection to electrical items having a corresponding three-pronged plug.

Branch circuits

There are three types of branch circuits to conduct current to receptacles (wall outlets), appliances, switches, and lighting fixtures. Lighting circuits are 120-volt, 15- or 20-amp circuits supplying light fixtures and receptacles for ordinary use. Small-appliance circuits are 120-volt, 20-amp circuits supplying receptacles used in kitchens, workshops, laundries, and some bathrooms. Kitchens should have two small-appliance circuits (one of these may extend into a pantry or dining room), routed so that plugging appliances into adjacent receptacles connects them to separate circuits.

Individual, or dedicated, appliance circuits are 120- or 240-volt, 20- to 50-amp circuits, each connected to a single major appliance such as an electric range, water heater, clothes dryer, or baseboard convector.

Safety devices

Electrical systems are protected by circuit breakers in newer houses and by fuses or a combination of the two in older homes. Both devices interrupt the flow of electricity through them if more current is demanded than the circuit can supply. This often occurs when too many items are plugged into a circuit or when a faulty appliance comes in contact with a more viable path for the electricity passing through it, causing a "short circuit." Fuses interrupt current by melting internally, breaking the circuit; they must be replaced. Circuit breakers have electromagnetic mechanisms that switch off, or "trip." They can be reset after the overload condition has been fixed.

A ground-fault circuit interrupter, or GFCI, is another type of safety device. A ground fault is similar to a short circuit but on a smaller scale. However, even a small current leak can be lethal—for example, if you stand barefoot on a wet bathroom floor and pick up a faulty hair dryer. GFCIs monitor current flowing in the hot and neutral wires of a circuit. The amounts are normally the same, but if the device registers an imbalance, it interrupts the current in a split second. New circuits in kitchens, bathrooms, laundries, and other damp locations must have GFCIs.

Most homes have a central heating system that delivers warmth to rooms from a single heat source, usually a furnace fueled by oil or gas, or powered by electricity. A central air-conditioning system may be attached to certain central heating systems.

One-pipe hot-water system

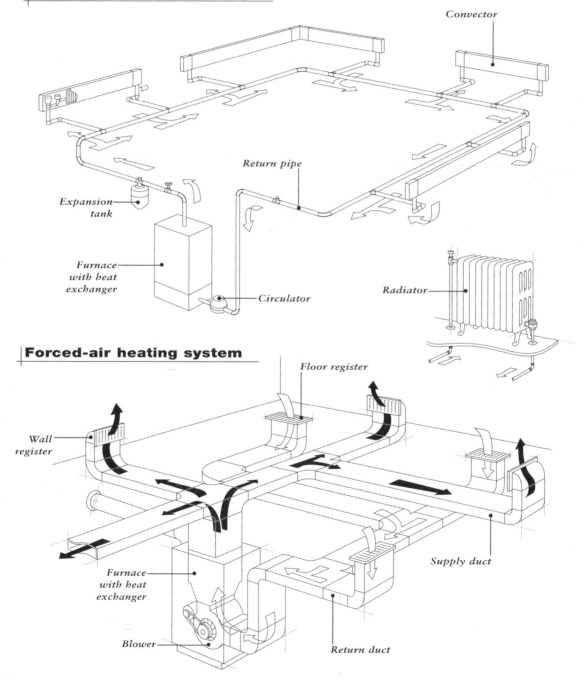

Convector

Return pipe

Expansion tank

Furnace with heat exchanger

Circulator

Radiator

Forced-air heating system

Floor register

Wall register

Supply duct

Furnace with heat exchanger

Blower

Return duct

Heating system types

The most common central heating systems are forced air (including heat pump systems), hot water, steam, and radiant in-floor heating. All function the same way in principle: air or liquid heated by a central furnace is delivered to rooms via ducts, pipes, or tubes.

Forced-air and heat pump systems

In forced-air systems, air is heated by the furnace in a chamber attached to it called a heat exchanger. A blower passes the air through the exchanger and forces it through supply ducts leading to each room in the house, where it enters through registers in the walls or floor. The registers and ducts contain shutters that can be operated manually (or electronically in the newest installations) to balance the amount of heat distributed to each room and throughout the house. Returning cool air is drawn back (aided by the blower) to the heat exchanger in a second series of ducts.

Heat pump systems are a variety of forced-air systems. A heat pump is a reversible central air conditioner—it extracts heat from outdoor air and carries it indoors for release via the same ductwork as a forced-air heating system. Most heat pumps also supply cool air to the home in summer by operating in reverse. Because heat pumps, like air conditioners, circulate refrigerant cooled to -20°F (-28.5°C), they can extract heat from outdoor air during all but the coldest spells. Heat pumps also incorporate an auxiliary electric heater to supplement extracted heat during prolonged or severe cold weather.

Hot-water systems

Water is heated in a heat exchanger—often called a boiler—in hot-water systems. Modern systems are pressurized and referred to as closed systems. A pump called a circulator forces the water through the exchanger and

Central air-conditioning system

A condenser unit supplies cool air, which is delivered throughout the house by ducts—often the same ones used to transport heat supplied by a warm-air furnace.

Duct

Evaporator coil

Outside condenser unit

Warm-air furnace

along pipes to radiators or convectors in the rooms, where the water gives up its heat before it flows back via return pipes to the heat exchanger. As the water heats, it expands, increasing pressure in the plumbing. To prevent the pipes from bursting, hot-water systems include an expansion tank containing air, which allows the water in the system to expand safely.

Steam heating systems

Steam heating was common in houses built until the 1940s. In this system, water is heated to 212°F (81°C); the steam that forms rises naturally to radiators. The water that forms as the steam gives up its heat condenses and falls by gravity back to the boiler.

Two types of pipe systems are common: the single-pipe system, in which rising steam and returning water occupy the same pipe leading to and from radiators, and the two-pipe system, in which steam circulates to radiators in one set of pipes, condensates and returns to the boiler in another set.

Radiant heating

In-floor heating systems operate like hot-water systems, but the hot water flows through tubes embedded in the floor. The tubes heat the floor, which radiates the heat into the room. Copper tubes conduct heat most effectively, but special polyethylene tubes are recommended by some experts as more durable with only slightly less effective heat transfer.

Radiators and convectors

Radiators transfer heat from a warm surface to a cooler one without significantly heating the air between them; they are found on steam systems, old hot-water systems, and in radiant in-floor systems. Other "radiators" are convectors. They heat the air, which rises as cool air is drawn behind them, and is then heated in turn.

Radiators are made of cast iron and stand about waist height. Convectors are lower in height and are often concealed in louvered cabinets or baseboard panels; they consist of copper tubing surrounded by metal fins that increase the heated area.

Reference section 4

If you've had no previous home improvement experience, talking to the professionals can be confusing at first. To help you understand the jargon that professionals often use, you'll find in the following pages a glossary of common building terms. Also included are sample budget and contract forms and a list of resources—this list supplies the addresses and other information for contacting trade associations and home improvement suppliers.

The professionals will take time to explain the details on anything that you are unclear about—don't be afraid to ask questions.

Baluster
A type of post used in a set to support a handrail along an open staircase.

Balustrade
The structure alongside an open staircase or landing, consisting of the balusters, newels, and handrail, to provide support and protection from falls as people use the stairs.

Baseboard
A decorative wood molding that runs along the bottom of the walls, covering the gap between the walls and the floor.

Below grade
Beneath ground level, whether natural or excavated.

Brace
A piece of lumber or metal attached to a structure to provide stiffness and support to its frame. It is set diagonally at an angle under 90 degrees.

Building code
The legal requirements established by the local government to regulate building construction practices.

Casement window
A type of window in which the pane swings out when opened. Some of the panes in the window may be stationary.

Casing
The wood trim that frames a door or window opening.

Caulking compound
A material applied (usually with a cartridge gun) to seal gaps between surfaces, usually of dissimilar materals, such as between a window frame and siding or a bathtub and wall; it hardens as it dries.

Circuit
The path that electricity follows from the source (the power plant) to an appliance or fixture, then back to the source. There are usually separate branch circuits within a house.

Conduit
A flexible metal pipe that is used to protect bundles of electrical wires.

Cripple
A part of a framing structure that is shorter than similar parts in the same structure. One example is a cripple stud, which is often used around a door or window opening.

Cured
A term that applies to certain materials, such as concrete, once they have hardened.

Decking
Refers to either the exterior floor structure for outdoor relaxation or entertaining or to the platform created by roof or floor sheathing.

Duct
Large pipe that transports air that has been heated or cooled by a furnace or air conditioner to various rooms in the house.

Fascia
The part of the roof at or under the eaves, visible from the front of the roof.

Finish flooring
The top layer of a floor, used mostly for decorative pur-

poses. The materials that are suitable as finish flooring include ceramic floor tiles, vinyl tiles, sheet vinyl, carpet, and wood strips. A concrete floor in an underused area may not be finished.

Fixture
Something that is attached to the building; for example, an overhead ceiling light is a lighting fixture and a toilet is a plumbing fixture.

Flashing
Sheets of metal applied in strips to weatherproof the junctions between two surfaces, such as between a chimney and a roof.

Footing
The concrete base that supports the foundation walls.

Foundation
The base of the house, starting below ground level, that supports the whole structure.

Framing
Another term for frame or framework, it consists of the parts that give strength or shape to the object it supports such as a window or a wall.

Frost heave
An upheaval of the ground or of pavement that is caused when moist ground freezes.

Frost line
The depth of the ground at which the soil freezes; it varies in different parts of the country, depending on the average winter temperature.

Furring strips
Wood strips that are attached to walls or ceilings in parallel rows; they provide a framework for attaching sheet materials for a decorative finish, such as wallboard or paneling.

Galvanized
Steel or other metals coated with zinc to prevent rusting; it is used in roofing and plumbing materials and in nails.

Girder
A large wooden or metal beam that helps support the structure above it.

Grade
The ground level.

Grading
Preparation of the ground, generally to make it level; it is usually necessary before building an addition, a patio, or an outbuilding.

Hardwood
Wood that comes from broad-leaved trees, usually deciduous; for example, ash, beech, and oak. These generally have a characteristically hard structure; however, there are some exceptions, such as balsa, a soft lightweight hardwood.

Insulation
Any of several types of materials available that is used around a room or area to limit the transmission of heat, cold, or sound. Another form of insulation, which is a nonconductive material, is used around electrical wires and connections to prevent electric shock.

Jamb
The side and top pieces of a door or window frame.

Joist
A horizontal wooden (or sometimes metal) beam; a row of parallel joists is used to support a structure—for example, a floor or ceiling.

Lath and plaster
Usually found in older houses, walls that consist of narrow wood strips, or laths, that are nailed to studs; the laths support the plaster that provides the finish for the walls.

Mastic
A type of adhesive used for setting tiles or sheet vinyl.

MDF
The abbreviation for medium-density fiberboard, a type of

board made of compressed fine wood fibers; it is usually available in 4 x 8-ft (1220 x 2440-mm) sheets.

Molding
A narrow, decorative strip of wood or other material, such as baseboard and picture rail; it comes in a variety of shapes.

Municipal
Part of or relating to an urban political government.

OSB
The abbreviation for oriented-strand board, a type of man-made board that is as strong as plywood; it can be susceptible to water damage.

Outbuilding
A building on the property that is detached from the main house; examples include a gazebo, a shed, and, sometimes, a garage.

Partition wall
An interior wall that consists of a wooden frame that is covered, usually with wallboard, to provide a smooth finish; it can be painted or decorated with wallpaper.

Platform framing
A technique for framing the structure of a house, with vertical members extending only between the floor and ceiling in each story.

Polyethylene sheeting
A type of plastic sheet that is used to protect surfaces, items, or areas as work progresses. It may also be used as a vapor barrier (see right).

Primer
The base coat used to seal the surface of the work—either carpentry, such as cabinets, or walls—before applying one or more top coats of paint.

Pull permit
The procedure involved in applying for and being issued a building permit from the local building department.

Punch list
A list of the last remaining items of work that have not been completed in a project.

Purlin
A horizontal beam that provides support for the rafters in a roof.

Rabbet
A step-shape recess in the edge of a workpiece that forms part of a joint; it is also used on an exterior door frame as a stop, which prevents the door from swinging through.

Rafter
One of the beams that form the main structural member of the frame that supports the roof covering.

Ridge vent
The continuous vent that runs along the ridge, or peak, of a roof. It works in conjunction with other vents.

Runoff
The rain or melted snow that drips off the roof, walls, or paved areas.

Sash
A part of a window, the wood frame around the glass.

Sash window
Also referred to as a hung window, a type of window with sashes, one above the other. Either both sashes or only one of them may move.

Services
A term referring to the systems in a house such as plumbing, heating, gas, and electricity.

Settling
The movement of a house that occurs when it is built on disturbed ground or that occurs when normally firm, stable ground has been undermined by excess moisture.

Sheathing
Panels or boards, usually 4 x 8-ft (1220 x 2440-mm) sheets, attached to the exterior wall or the roof framing to provide stability and strength to the structure. It also acts as a surface for attaching the finish surface such as siding or roof tiles.

Shim
A thin strip of wood that is pushed into a joint between two surfaces to fill a gap. It may be used to level an object.

Shingle course
A horizontal row of shingles, either on an exterior wall or on a roof.

Sill
A horizontal part of a frame, such as a window frame or a partition wall.

Sleepers
Wood strips attached in parallel rows over a concrete floor to provide a nailing surface for a finish flooring.

Softwood
Wood that comes from coniferous trees such as pine and cedar. As its name indicates, this type of wood is characteristically soft in nature.

Stud
One of the vertical members that make up a partition wall. They are usually spaced on 16-inch (405-mm) centers.

Subflooring
Either plywood or OSB boards attached to floor joists to provide a smooth, stable surface applying the finish flooring.

Underlayment
The material laid under the finish covering for either the roof or the floor; it provides a smooth surface for applying the finish. The underlayment for the roof also provides a waterproof barrier.

Valley
The inside corner angle formed where two sloping surfaces of a roof meet.

Vapor barrier
A material that prevents water vapors from penetrating into walls or other parts of the building. The typical materials used as a vapor barrier are polyethylene sheeting, aluminum foil and building paper.

Wallboard
Panels, consisting of a layer of gypsum plaster that is covered on both sides with paper, that are used to finish interior walls and ceilings. They are also referred to as Sheetrock, drywall, and gypsum wallboard.

Weatherstripping
Narrow strips placed around windows and doors to prevent air and moisture from entering the house. The strips may be made of metal, plastic foam, fiber, or another material.

The professional you hire will usually provide you with contracts and other forms, but reviewing them beforehand will better prepare you for negotiations about costs and labor.

Budget forms

You can adapt the form below to help plan your budget. Start with setting aside money for the necessities such as a cotingency allowance, building permits, and inspection fees. The type of materials used, which may also affect labor costs if the installation techniques are different, can then be adapted to match your funds.

This is not a complete form and you may want to add your own categories or to be more precise than the ones given here. For example, under cabinetry, you may want to list the

Budget form

	Expenses of renovation or addition		
	Room renovation	**Additions**	**Exterior improvements**
Total sum available $	**Floors** Materials $ Labor $	**Preparing the site** Materials $ Labor $	**Roof** Materials $ Labor $
Minus 10% contingency allowance $	**Interior wall construction** Materials $ Labor $	**Foundation** Materials $ Labor $	**Gutters and downspouts** Materials $ Labor $
Minus building permits $		**Frame construction** Materials $ Labor $	
Minus inspection fees $	**Interior wall decoration** Materials $ Labor $	**Roof** Materials $ Labor $	**Exterior walls** Materials $ Labor $
Minus living expenses during renovation $	**Carpentry** Materials $ Labor $	**Windows and doors** Materials $ Labor $	**Deck or patio** Materials $ Labor $
Remaining sum for renovation $	**Curtains/upholstery** Materials $ Labor $	**Insulation** Materials $ Labor $	**Fences or walls** Materials $ Labor $
Minus architect fee $	**Electricity** Materials $ Labor $	**Ventilation** Materials $ Labor $	**Landscaping** Materials $ Labor $
Minus designer fee $			
Minus contractor fee $	**Plumbing** Materials $ Labor $	**Room decoration** See "Room renovation"	
Minus specialist fee $	**Heating** Materials $ Labor $		

specific materials, such as the carcasses, doors, countertop, and hardware, separately so that you can consider substituting a less expensive material if the budget for a kitchen renovation is too high.

Estimates

Always compare estimates carefully. Price is important, but you shouldn't go only by cost; for example, a low bidder may be trying to build a client base. Different construction methods or the quality or quantity of varioius materials may also account for price discrepancies.

You should pay attention to the appearances of the bids, their level of detail, and how promptly and courteously they are submitted. Remember, you want professionals you can count on for good workmanship and service.

Estimates are not binding until they are signed or incorporated into a formal contract; so a chart that points out crucial differences between bids can be a useful tool for negotiating between bidders. Consider making a comparison chart listing the elements of each bid, including labor and materials, so that you can compare them more easily (see below).

Contracts

You can use a simple work order (see right) for small jobs, but most repairs and improvements are covered by more substantial contracts. The simplest of these are often combined on the same form as the contractor's proposal or estimate—by signing the estimate you also agree to have the contractor perform the job. There is also a standard short-form contract; more complicated contracts, which are used for large projects, can run to several pages in length.

Remember, contracts are not standardized, and all wording is negotiable. The examples shown on pages 166–167 are intended for reference only. For more on negotiating contracts, see pages 20–21.

Work order

The simplest repairs may be contracted using an elementary work order containing little more than:
• Contractor's name, address, telephone number and contractor's license number. (These are usually incorporated in the work order letterhead.)
• Homeowner's name and address
• Description of work
• Start date and date of completion
• Total amount due (usually itemized by labor, materials, and tax)
• Signatures of contractor and homeowner
Legal clauses similar to those in longer contracts (see pp. 166–167) may appear in fine print—check the back of the document.

Comparison chart

Painter A

Siding
1 coat primer, 1 coat acrylic latex paint, applied with brush and roller $495.00
Windows (10)
1 coat primer, 1 coat acrylic latex paint, applied with brush and roller $320.00
Doors (2)
1 coat primer, 2 coats acrylic latex paint, applied with brush and roller $70.00
Miscellaneous trim
1 coat primer, 1 coat acrylic latex paint, applied with brush and roller $400.00

Total $1,285.00

Painter B

Siding
1 coat primer, 2 coats acrylic latex paint, sprayed on $645.00
Windows (10)
1 coat primer, 2 coats acrylic latex paint, applied with brush and roller $360.00
Doors (2)
1 coat primer, 2 coats acrylic latex paint, sprayed on $90.00
Miscellaneous trim
1 coat primer, 2 coats acrylic latex paint, applied with brush and roller $495.00

Total $1,590.00

Painter C

Siding
1 coat primer, 2 coats acrylic latex paint, applied with brush and roller $780.00
Windows (10)
1 coat primer, 2 coats acrylic latex paint, applied with brush and roller $400.00
Doors (2)
1 coat primer, 2 coats acrylic latex paint, applied with brush and roller $115.00
Miscellaneous trim
1 coat primer, 2 coats acrylic latex paint, applied with brush and roller $650.00

Total $1,945.00

Proposal and contract

Contractor's name:
Address:
Phone:
Fax:
Lic #:

Date:

Owner's name:
Address:

Dear:_____

[Contractor] proposes to furnish all materials and perform all labor necessary to complete the following:

(Additional materials and labor may be specified in attachments to this contract.)

All of the above work (and any work specified in attachments to this document, if applicable) shall be completed in a substantial and workmanlike manner according to standard practices for the total sum of $_____.

Approximate start date when the work shall commence: _____.

Approximate date the work shall be substantially completed: _____.

Payments shall be made _____ as the work progresses to the value of _____ percent (_____%) of all work completed.

Final payment, constituting the entire unpaid balance of this contract and including the amount of all change orders, shall be made not later than 30 days after completion. Completion shall be considered to occur upon satisfactory final inspection by a building inspector; occupancy of the improvement by the owner or abandonment as defined by [applicable statute]; or the posting of a completion notice, whichever occurs first.

Any alteration or deviation from the specifications set forth in this Proposal and Contract involving increased or reduced costs of materials or labor will only be executed upon written orders for same, and will become an additional charge or a credit to the sums set forth in this agreement. Additional materials or labor for changes required by building department officials will be specified in writing and will become an additional charge over and above this contract amount.

The price quoted is for acceptance within 10 days. Any delay in acceptance will require verification of prevailing material and labor costs.

Estimate submitted by: _____

Date: _____

Acceptance

[Contractor] is hereby authorized and directed to furnish all materials and labor required to complete the work according to the terms and conditions of the Proposal set forth above (and in Attachments, if applicable), for which the undersigned agrees to pay the amount mentioned in said Proposal, and according to the terms thereof.

The undersigned further agrees that in the event the undersigned defaults or fails to make payment(s) as herein agreed, the undersigned will pay all reasonable attorney fees and costs, including collection costs, necessitated by said default to enforce this contract. Default or non-payment is defined as failure to make payments to Contractor within 30 days of the due date. Further, the undersigned agrees that for any balance due under this agreement outstanding for a period of more than 30 days after the due date, a late fee of 5% per month of the balance due shall be charged and added to any and all outstanding amounts.

The undersigned further represents and acknowledges they have fully read and understand the terms and conditions of this Proposal and Contract and fully accept each and every term and condition herein. No other promises or acts have been contracted for other than as set forth in the Proposal and Contract.

Signed: _____

Date: _____

Short-form fixed price agreement

Contractor's name:
Address:
Phone:
Fax:
Lic #:

Date:

Owner's name:
Address:

Project address:

I. Parties

This contract (hereinafter referred to as "Agreement") is made and entered into on this _____ day of _____, 19_____, by and between _____, (hereinafter referred to as "Owner"); and _____, (hereinafter referred to as "Contractor"). In consideration of the mutual promises contained herein, Contractor agrees to perform the following work:

II. General scope of work description

LUMP SUM PRICE FOR ALL WORK ABOVE: $_____

III. General conditions for the agreement above

A. Exclusions
This Agreement does not include labor or materials for the following work:

B. Date of work commencement and substantial completion
Commence work: _____. Construction time through substantial completion: Approximately _____ to _____ weeks/months, not including delays and adjustments for delays caused by: inclement weather, additional time required for Change Order work, and other delays unavoidable or beyond the control of the Contractor.

C. Change orders: concealed conditions and additional work
1. **Concealed conditions:** This Agreement is based solely on the observations Contractor was able to make with the structure in its current condition at the time this Agreement was bid. If additional concealed conditions are discovered once work has commenced which were not visible at the time this proposal was bid, Contractor will stop work and point out these unforeseen concealed conditions to Owner so that Owner and Contractor can execute a Change Order for any Additional Work.
2. **Deviation from scope of work:** Any alteration or deviation from the Scope of Work referred to in this Agreement involving extra costs of materials or labor will be executed upon a written Change Order issued by Contractor and should be signed by Contractor and Owner prior to the commencement of Additional Work by the Contractor.

D. Payment schedule and payment terms
1. **Payment schedule:**
• First Payment: $1,000 or 10% of contract amount (whichever is less) due when Agreement is signed and returned to Contractor: $_____
• Second Payment (Materials Deposits): _____
_____ $_____
• Third Payment: _____
_____ $_____
• Fourth Payment: _____
_____ $_____

• Final Payment: Balance of contract amount due upon Substantial Completion of all work under contract: $_____
Upon request by Owner, Contractor agrees to furnish Owner with Conditional Lien and Unconditional Lien Releases. All payments due under this Agreement are payable upon receipt of invoice from Contractor.
2. **Payment of change orders:** Payment for each Change Order is due upon completion of Change Order work and submittal of invoice by Contractor.
3. **Additional payments for allowance work and related credits:** Payment for work designated in the Agreement as ALLOWANCE work has been initially factored into the Lump Sum Price and Payment Schedule set forth in this Agreement. If the actual cost of the ALLOWANCE work exceeds the line item ALLOWANCE amount in the Agreement, the difference between the cost and the line item ALLOWANCE amount stated in the Agreement will be written up by Contractor as a Change Order subject to Contractor's profit and overhead at the rate of _____%.

If the cost of the ALLOWANCE work is less than the ALLOWANCE line item amount listed in the Agreement, a credit will be issued to Owner after all billings related to this particular line item ALLOWANCE work have been received by Contractor. This credit will be applied toward the final payment owing under the Agreement. Contractor profit and overhead and any supervisory labor will not be credited back to Owner for ALLOWANCE work.

E. Warranty
Contractor provides a limited warranty on all Contractor- and Subcontractor-supplied labor and materials used in this project for a period of one year following substantial completion of all work.

No warranty is provided by Contractor on any materials furnished by the Owner for installation. No warranty is provided on any existing materials that are moved and/or reinstalled by the Contractor within the dwelling (including any warranty that existing/used materials will not be damaged during the removal and reinstallation process). One year after substantial completion of the project, the Owner's sole remedy (for materials and labor) on all materials that are covered by a manufacturer's warranty is strictly with the manufacturer, not with the Contractor.

Repair of the following items is specifically excluded from Contractor's warranty: Damages resulting from lack of Owner maintenance; damages resulting from Owner abuse or ordinary wear and tear; deviations that arise such as the minor cracking of concrete, stucco, and plaster; minor stress fractures in drywall due to the curing of lumber; warping and deflection of wood; shrinking/cracking of grouts and caulking; fading of paints and finishes exposed to sunlight.

THE EXPRESS WARRANTIES CONTAINED HEREIN ARE IN LIEU OF ALL OTHER WARRANTIES, EXPRESS OR IMPLIED, INCLUDING ANY WARRANTIES OF MERCHANTABILITY, HABITABILITY, OR FITNESS FOR A PARTICULAR USE OR PURPOSE. THIS LIMITED WARRANTY EXCLUDES CONSEQUENTIAL AND INCIDENTAL DAMAGES AND LIMITS THE DURATION OF IMPLIED WARRANTIES TO THE FULLEST EXTENT PERMISSIBLE UNDER STATE AND FEDERAL LAW.

F. Work stoppage, termination of contract for default, and interest
Contractor shall have the right to stop all work on the project and keep the job idle if payments are not made to Contractor in accordance with the Payment Schedule in this Agreement, or if Owner repeatedly fails or refuses to furnish Contractor with access to the job site and/or product selections or information necessary for the advancement of Contractor's work. Simultaneous with stopping work on the project, the Contractor must give Owner written notice of the nature of Owner's default and must also give the Owner a 14-day period in which to cure this default.

If work is stopped due to any of the above reasons (or for any other material breach of contract by Owner) for a period of 14 days, and the Owner has failed to take significant steps to cure his default, then Contractor may, without prejudicing any other remedies Contractor may have, give written notice of termination of the Agreement to Owner and demand payment for all completed work and materials ordered through the date of work stoppage, and any other loss sustained by Contractor, including Contractor's Profit and Overhead at the rate of _____% on the balance of the incomplete work under the Agreement. Thereafter, Contractor is relieved from all other contractual duties, including all Punch List and warranty work.

G. Dispute resolution and attourney's fees
Any controversy or claim arising out of or related to this Agreement involving an amount of less than $5,000 (or the maximum limit of the court) must be heard in the Small Claims Division of the Municipal Court in the county where the Contractor's office is located. Any controversy or claim arising out of or related to this Agreement which is over the dollar limit of the Small Claims Court must be settled by binding arbitration administered by the American Arbitration Association in accordance with the Construction Industry Arbitration Rules. Judgment upon the award may be entered in any Court having jurisdiction thereof.

The prevailing party in any legal proceeding related to this Agreement shall be entitled to payment of reasonable attorney's fees, costs, and expenses.

H. Expiration of this agreement
This Agreement will expire 30 days after the date at the top of page one of this Agreement if not first accepted in writing by Owner.

I. Entire agreement
This Agreement represents and contains the entire agreement between the parties. Prior discussions or verbal representations by the parties that are not contained in this Agreement are not a part of this Agreement.

I have read and understood, and I agree to, all the terms and conditions contained in the Agreement above.

_____ _____
Date   CONTRACTOR'S SIGNATURE

_____ _____
Date   OWNER'S SIGNATURE

Associations

American Arbitration Association
335 Madison Ave.
New York, NY 10017
tele: (212) 716–5800
website: http://www.adr.org

Founded in 1926, this independent organization was established to resolve a wide range of disputes using mediation, arbitration, and out-of-court settlement procedures.

American Institute of Architects
1735 New York Ave., N.W.
Washington, D.C. 20006
toll free: (800) 242–9930
website: http://www.aiaaccess.com

Architects that are members of this institute remain current with professional standards through continuing education and subscription to a code of ethics and professional conduct that ensures clients, the public and colleagues of their dedication to high standards in professional practice.

The American Institute of Building Design
991 Post Rd, E.
Westport, CT 06880
toll free: (800) 366–2423
fax: (203) 227–8624
website: http://www.aibd.org

This institute has developed nationwide design standards and a code of ethics for the building design profession.

The American Lighting Association (ALA)
P.O. Box 420288
Dallas, TX 75432–0288
toll free: (800) 274–4484
website: http://www.americanlightingassoc.com

An association that consists of lighting manufacturers, distributors, representatives, and other industry-related companies, it is dedicated to providing the public with quality residential lighting.

American Society of Home Inspectors
85 Algonquin Rd.
Arlington Heights, IL 60005
toll free: (800) 743–2744
website: http://www.ashi.com

An association dedicated to building public awareness of home inspection, as well as to enhance the professional and technical performance of home inspectors.

American Society of Interior Designers (ASID)
608 Massachusetts Ave. N.E., Washington, DC 20002–6006
toll free: (800) 775–3480
e-mail: asid@asid.org
website: http://www.asid.org

A society that promotes professionalism in interior design services and designs for the workplace and home. It provides a worldwide referral service to help find the right interior designer. To find an ASID designer on the Internet use the following address: http://www.interiors.org.

Building Officials & Code Aminstrators International, Inc. (BOCA)
4051 W. Flossmoor Rd.
Country Club Hills, IL 60477
tele: (630) 799–2300
website: http://www.bocai.org

An organization dedicated to preserving the public health, safety, and welfare in the built environment through the effective, efficient use and enforcement of model codes.

Efficient Windows Collaborative
1200 18th St., N.W.
Suite 900
Washington, D.C. 20036
tele: (202) 857–0666
fax: (202) 331–9588
e-mail: ewc@ase.org
website: http://www.efficientwindows.org

A coalition of window, door, skylight, and component manufacturers, research organizations, as well as federal, state, and local government agencies and others, which is interested in expanding the market for high-efficiency fenestration, or window and door, products.

Gas Appliance Manufacturers Assoc.
P.O. Box 9245
Arlington, VA 22209–1245
tele: (703) 525–9565
fax: (703) 525–0718
website: http://www.gamanet.org

A national trade association whose members manufacture appliances, components, and related products used in connection with space heating and water heating.

Home Builders Institute
1090 Vermont Ave. N.W., Suite 600
Washington, DC 20005

tele: (202) 371–0600
fax: (202) 898–7777

The educational arm of the National Association of Home Builders (NAHB), this institute is the nation's leading source of education and training programs serving the home-building industry.

International Code Council (ICC)
5203 Leesburg Pike
Suite 708
Falls Church, VA 22041
tele: (703) 931–4533
website: http://www.intlcode.org

Dedicated to developing a single set of comprehensive and coordinated national construction codes.

International Conference of Building Officials (ICBO)
5360 S. Workman Mill Rd.
Whittier, CA 90601
tele: (562) 699–0541
fax: (562) 692–3853
e-mail: order@icbo.org
website: http://www.icbo.org

Dedicated to the promotion of public safety in the built environment, this organization publishes the Uniform Building Code and are a partner in the International Code Council, which publishes the International Building Code.

National Burglar & Fire Alarm Association
7101 Wisconsin Ave. #901
Bethesda, MD 20814
tele: (301) 907–3202
e-mail: staff@alarm.org
website: http://www.alarm.org

An association that aims to represent, support, and promote the electronic security and electronic life safety systems and services industry.

National Fire Protection Association (NFPA)
1 Battery March Park
Quincy, MA 02269–9101

tele: (617) 770–3000
fax: (617) 770–0700
website: http://www.
nfpa.org *and*
http://www.sparky.org
This association's mission is to reduce the worldwide hazard of fire and the affect it and other hazards have on the quality of life. It provides scientifically based consensus codes and standards, research, training, and education.

National Kitchen and Bath Association (NKBA)
687 Willow Grove St.
Hackettstown, NJ 07840
tele: (908) 852–0033
website: http://www.
nkba.org
The NKBA provides expert advice and planning guidelines for remodeling the kitchen and bathroom; it also offers a list of approved kitchen and bathroom design forms.

National Lead Information Clearinghouse
toll free: (800) 424–LEAD
The goal of this organization is to educate the public on the health hazards associated with lead. Ask for the free brochure "Reducing Lead Hazards When Remodeling Your Home."

National Roofing Contractors Association
324 Fourth St., N.E.
Washington, D.C. 20002
tele: (202) 546–7584
website: http://www.
nrca.net.
An association that provides roofing information, it educates and conducts programs to enhance the professionalism of the roofing industry, and it provides consumers with the best available technology and business practices.

National Wood Window and Door Association
1400 E. Touhy Ave.
Suite 470
Des Plaines, IL
60018–3305
tele: (847) 299–5200
fax: (847) 299–1286
Promotes the interests and high standards of the window, skylight, and door industry.

Southern Building Code Congress International, Inc. (SBCCI)
900 Montclair Rd.
Birmingham, AL 35213
tele: (205) 591–1853
website: http://www.
sbcci.org
An organziation that provides educational, technical, and administrative support to governmental departments and agencies engaged in building codes and their administration and enforcement.

Cabinets
Aristokraft
One Aristokraft Sq.
Jasper, IN 47546
tele: (812) 482–2527
tele: (812) 634–2838
website: http://www.
aristokraft.com
A leading manufacturer of quality kitchen, bath, and home cabinetry. It offers over 40 different styles, from the traditional beauty of oak to the radiant elegance of cherry.

HomeCrest Cabinetry
P.O. Box 595
Goshen, IN 46527
tele: (219) 535–9300
fax: (800) 737–1500
e-mail: hcinfo@home
crestcab.com
website: http://www.
homecrestcab.com
Offers affordable choices in construction options, building materials, door styles, and finish colors.

IXL Cabinets, a division
of Triangle Pacific Corp.
16803 Dallas Pkwy.
Addison, TX 75001
toll free: (800) 527–5903
fax: (214) 887–2434
e-mail: info@ixl
cabinets.com
website: http://www.
ixlcabinets.com
Offers a number of kitchen cabinets styles in a variety of materials, including cherry, oak, maple, thermofoils, and laminates.

Omega Cabinets
1205 Peters Dr.
Waterloo, IA 50703
tele: (319) 235–5700
fax: (800) 328–8529

e-mail: sales@omega
cab.com
website: http://www.
omegacab.com
Provides cabinets with solid wood doors and frames and plywood sides; finished maple dovetail drawers with undermount guides are among their standard features.

Countertops
Avonite, Inc.
1945 Highway 304
Belen, NM 87002
toll free: (800) 428–6648
fax: (805) 864–7790
e-mail: sales@
avonite.com
website: http://www.
avonite.com
Avonite solid surface, or synthetic stone, is available in a range of unique and diverse solid colors and patterns.

Formica Corporation
10155 Reading Rd.
Cincinnati, OH 45241
toll free: (800) FORMICA
fax: (513) 786–3024
e-mail: bill.rousch@
formica.com
website: http://www.
formica.com
Recognized innovator in the surfacing industry, this company's product range includes

laminates, solid surface materials, wood surfacing, metal laminates, solid metal surfaces, and flooring materials.

Nevamar Laminate
8339 Telegraph Rd.
Odentom, MD 21113
tele: (410) 551–5000
fax: (410) 551–0357
website: http://www.
nevamar.com
Supplier of decorative surfaces, including high pressure laminates, decorative acrylics and engineered veneer.

Nocera Art Tile
HCl Box 1374
Milanville, PA 18443
tele: (570) 729–7946
fax: (570) 729–7317
website: http://www.
art-tile.com
Designers and makers of hand-fashioned architectural tile for interior and exterior use; this company can also provide custom-made work.

Prémoulé
2375, Dalton
Sainte-Foy, PQ GlP 3S3
toll free: (800) 463–5297
tele: (418) 652–1422
fax: (800) 667–7234
e-mail: thermo@
premoule.com
website: http://www.
premoule.com
Manufacturers of cabinet doors and postformed HPL countertops.

PrimeWood
2217 N. Ninth St.
Wahpeton, ND 58075
toll free: (800) 642–8780
tele: (701) 642–2727
fax: (701) 642–2431
Manufacturers of wooden and laminate countertops, wooden doors, door frames and surrounds, and wooden cabinet and cabinet doors.

Rynone Mfg. Corp.
P.O. Box 128
N. Thomas Ave.
Sayre, PA 18840
tele: (717) 888–5272
fax: (717) 888–1175
Manufacturers of laminate countertops.

Closets
Closet Maid
650 SW 27th Ave.
P.O. Box 4400
Ocala, FL 34478–4400
toll free: (800) 874–0008
fax: (352) 867–8583
website: http://www.
closetmaid.com
Offers a complete line of wire storage products suitable for any home.

Poliform
150 East 58 St.
New York, NY 10155
tele: (212) 421–1220
tele: (212) 421–1290
website: http://www.
poliformusa.com
Italy's leading manufacturer of high-end closet systems, bedrooms, libraries, dining rooms, and kitchens.

Decks

Heritage Vinyl
1576 Magnolia Dr.
Macon, MS 39341
tele: (800) 473–3623
fax: (662) 726–4054
website: http://www.
heritagevinyl.com
Vinyl decking and speciality outdoor products.

Doors and windows

Americana Building Products
P.O. Box 1290
Salem, IL 62881
toll free: (800) 851–0865
fax: (618) 548–2890
e-mail:
sales@americana.com
website: http://www.
americana.com
Supplies standard and custom-sized window awnings and patio covers, screen and glass wall enclosures, carports, walkways, entrance awnings, and pavilions.

Eagle Window & Door
375 E. Ninth St.
P.O. Box 1072
Dubuque, IA
52004–1072
toll free: (800) 453–3633
tele: (319) 556–2270
fax: (319) 556–4408
website: http://www.
eaglewindow.com
Supplies awning and casement windows, as well as French and patio sliding doors in aluminum-clad or wood.

Great Lakes Window
P.O. Box 1896
Toledo, OH 43603–1896

tele: (800) 666–0000
tele: (419) 666–5555
fax: (419) 661–2926
website: http://www.
greatlakeswindow.com
Manufacturer of all-vinyl custom windows and patio doors.

Hayfield Window & Door Co.
P.O. Box 25
Industrial Park Rd.
Hayfield, MN 55940
tele: (507) 477–3224
fax: (507) 477–3605
Supplies windows and doors.

Hurd Millwork
575 Whelen
Medford, WI 54451
toll free: (800) 2BE–HURD
fax: (715) 748–6043
e-mail: hurd@midway.
tds.net
website: http://www.
hurd.com
Produces energy-efficient wood, aluminium-clad wood, and vinyl windows and patio doors.

Huron Window Corp.
345 Mountain St. S
Morden, MB R6M 1J5
tele: (204) 822–6281
fax: (204) 822–6343
website: http://www.
huronwin.com
Has high performance, energy efficient windows for new construction and renovation.

Renaissance Old World Door Co.
743 Sanborn Pl.
Salinas, CA 93901–4532
tele: (831) 759–0558
fax: (831) 759–2635
website: http://www.
carving.com
Hand-aged entry and interior doors with the look and feel of gracefully aged antiques. Can be made to order—hand carving is also available.

The Woodstone Co.
P.O. Box 223
Patch Rd.
Westminster, VT 05158
tele: (802) 722–9217
fax: (802) 722–9528

website: http://www.
woodstone.com
Provides fine custom wooden windows and doors.

Flooring

Columbia Forest Products
222 S.W. Columbia
Ste. 1575
Portland, OR 97201
toll free: (800) 654–8796
website: http://www.
columbiaforestproducts.
com
North America's largest manufacturer of hardwood plywood and veneer, this company produces flooring and veneer raised panel doors.

Domco Tarkett Inc.
4103 Parkway Dr.
Florence, AL 35630
toll free: (800) 465–4030
website: http://www.
domco.com
Hard surface flooring manufacturer, producing resilient sheet and tile, laminates, and hardwoods.

Granville Manufacturing Co. Inc.
Granville, VT 05747
tele: (802) 767–4747
fax: (802) 767–3107
website: http://www.
woodsiding.com
Manufactures primarily wood siding and flooring.

Historic Floors of Oshkosh
911 E. Main St.
Winneconne, WI 54986
tele: (920) 582–9977
fax: (920) 582–9971
e-mail: info@historic
floors.com
Produces decorative hardwood standard and custom inlays, including borders, medallions, and parquet flooring. Many designs, wood species, sizes, and shapes are available for use in new or existing floors.

M.L. Condon, Co.
250 Ferris Ave.
White Plains, NY 10603

tele: (914) 946–4111
fax: (914) 946–3779
Supplies domestic hardwoods, softwoods, and plywoods with the ability to custom manufacture moldings and millwork.

Protective Products
1205 Karl Cour,
Suite 116
Wauconda, IL 60084
toll free: (800) 789–6633
tele: (847) 526–1380
fax: (800) 880–7141
e-mail: sales@protective
products.com
website: http://www.
protectiveproducts.com
Surface protection and dust control products for carpets and floors, hardwood, tubs, tile, cladding, windows, countertops and more.

Renaissance Old World Door Co.
743 Sanborn Pl.
Salinas, CA 93901–4532
tele: (831) 759–0558
fax: (831) 759–2635
website: http://www.
carving.com
Hand-planed aged flooring with the look of aged floors in classic European estates.

Heating and fireplaces

Electro Industries
2150 W. River St.
P.O. Box 538
Monticello, MN
55362–0538
toll free: (800) 922–4138
fax: (612) 295–4434
Products include warm flo® "smart heat" pump controller and radiant underfloor heating comparison.

Heatilator, a division of Hearth Technologies Inc.
1915 W. Saunders St.
Mt. Pleasant, IA 52641
tele: (319) 385–9211
tele: (319) 385–5862
website: http://www.
heatilator.com
Manufacturers of a full line of gas- and wood-burning fireplaces and accessories.

The Majestic Products Co.

1000 E. Market St.
Huntington, IN 46750
toll free: (800) 525–1898
tele: (219) 385–9211
fax: (219) 356–9672
website: http://www.
majesticproducts.com

Supplier of gas- and wood-burning stoves and fireplaces, and a range of accessories.

Napolean Fireplaces (Wolf Steel)

24 Napolean Rd.
RR1 (Hwy. 11 & 93)
Barrie, ON L4M 4Y8
tele: (705) 721–1212
fax: (705) 722–6031
website: http://www.
napolean.on.ca

Canadian manufacturers of wood-, gas-, and oil-burning fireplaces, inserts, and stoves.

Superior Fireplace Co.

4325 Artesia Ave.
Fullerton, CA 92833
tele: (714) 521–5233
website: http://www.
superiorfireplace.com

A leading manufacturer of factory-built wood-burning and gas-burning fireplaces, including the world's first catalytic gas fireplace.

Kitchens

Heritage Custom Kitchens, Inc.

tele: (717) 354–4011
fax: (717) 354–0169
website: http://www.
HCK.com

A high end, custom manufacturer of old world, traditional and contemporary cabinetry for kitchens, baths, and other rooms of the home.

Paints

Benjamin Moore & Co.

51 Chestnut Ridge Rd.
Montvale, NJ 07645

tele: (201) 573–9600
fax: (201) 573–6673
e-mail: benjamin
moore@att.net.
website: http://www.
benjaminmoore.com

Manufacturers of premium quality paint and architectural coatings.

Dean & Barry Co.

970 Woodland Ave.
Columbus, OH 43219
toll free: (800) 325–2829
tele: (614) 258–3131
fax: (614) 258–3530
e-mail: dbpaint@dean
andbarrypaint.com
website: http://www.
deanandbarrypaint.com

Carries a full line of paint and coatings products with well respected names.

Pratt & Lambert Paints

toll free: (800) 289–7728
fax: (216) 566–1655
website: http://www.
prattandlambert.co

The choice of many top designers and architects, produces acrylic paints with unmatched levels of titanium dioxide for magnificent color.

Duron Paints & Wallcoverings

10406 Tucker St.
Beltsville, MD 20705

tele: (301) 937–4700
fax: (301) 595–3919
e-mail: webmaster@
duron.com
website: http://www.
duron.com

Manufactures architectural and light industrial coatings and distributes paints, sundries, and wallcoverings.

Stone, concrete, and masonry

Cold Spring Granite Co.

202 S. Third Ave.
Cold Spring, MN 56320
toll free: (800) 328–5040
fax: (320) 685–8490
website: http://www.
coldspringgranite.com

Offers a complete line of landscape and paving materials, including granite sawn or split-edge pavers, retaining walls, curbing, tiles, and slabs for countertops.

Perma.Crete® Products

501 Metroplex Dr.
Ste. 115
Nashville, TN
37211–3127
toll free: (800) 607–3762
tele: (615) 331–9200
fax: (615) 834–1335
website: http://www.
permacrete.com

Resurfaces concrete, masonry, aggregate, steel, and asphalt and provides a new, architectural load-bearing surface. Can be used for vehicular surfaces, driveways, and building exteriors.

Pet-mal Inc.

Architectural
Representatives &
Distributors
830 Atlantic Ave.
Baldwin, NY 11510
tele: (516) 867–4573
fax: (516) 867–4691
website: http://www.
Petmal.com

Direct primary resource for over 70 different slates, sandstones, and quartzites for flooring, countertops, walls, and finishes.

Tiles

Designs in Tile

P.O. Box 358
Mt. Shasta, CA 96067

tele: (530) 926–2629
fax: (530) 926–6467
e-mail: info@designs
intile.com
website: http://www.
designsintile.com

Specialists in custom-made, historic, Victorian and late 19th-century tiles and murals.

Laufen U.S.A. Ceramic Tiles

6531 N. Laufen Dr.
Tulsa, Okla 74117–1802
tele: (918) 428–0608
fax: (918) 428–0695
e-mail: hdonovan@
laufen.com
website: http://www.
laufen.com

Manufacturer and distributor of glazed ceramic tiles for wall, countertops, and floors; distributor of natural stone tiles and slabs.

Meredith Collection

PO Box 8854
Canton, OH 44711
tele: (330) 484–1657
fax: (330) 484–9380
e-mail: info@meredith
collection.com
website: http://www.
meredithtile.com

Hand-carved molds and 19th-century presses are used to make relief tiles.

Terra-Green Ceramics

1650 Progress Dr.
Richmond, IN 47374
tele: (765) 935–4760
fax: (765) 935–3971
website: http://www.
terragreenceramics.com

Manufacturers of ceramic tiles for flooring, countertops, walls, and finishes.

Wallcoverings

York Wallcoverings, Borders & Fabrics

750 Linden Ave.
York, PA 17404
tele: (717) 846–4456
fax: (717) 843–8167
e-mail: intl@york
wall.com
website: http://www.
yorkwall.com

Manufacturers of a broad range of wallpapers, borders, and coordinated fabrics with unique colors and designs.

t

tackless strip 40
termite infestations 74–75
terracing 121
terrazzo 121
toilet
　installing 53
　removing 52
transverse brace 78
tree roots 118–119
trusses 85

u

utility room 62–63

v

varnishes 37
ventilation 150–151
　and condensation 74–75
　rules and regulations 75
　sunrooms 94
　waste plumbing 155
　in windowless rooms 81
Veterans Administration
　(VA) 23
vinyl floor coverings 41
　asbestos in 42–43
　laying 43
volatile organic
　compounds (VOCs)
　36–37

w

walkways 121
wallboard 137
wallcoverings 38–93, 54
walls
　boundary 124, 125
　cavity 149
　exterior 111, 134–135,
　　135
　insulation 72, 149
　knee 84–85
　load-bearing 57, 78, 137
　partition 56–57, 81
　plaster 136–137
　removing 78–79
　retaining 121
　stick built 136–137
wardrobe units 59

warranties 30
washbasin 51
　installing 53
　removing 52
washing machine 62–63
waste disposal unit 47
waste water disposal
　154–155
water heaters 67
water supply systems
　152–153
wells
　dry 131
　water supply 153
windows
　awning 139
　casement 138, 139
　dividing rooms 57, 81
　dormer 25, 85
　double-hung 138
　hopper 139
　horizontal sliding 139
　insulation 73
　jalousie 139
　maintenance 111
　moisture proofing 147
　picture 139
　replacing 112–113
　securing 114
　skylight 85
　see also glazing
wiring, electrical 68–69
wood finishes 37
wood flooring 41
wood framed houses 135
workshop 106–107

y

yard improvements
　120–121

z

zero-clearance fireplace 70,
　132–133
zone heating 70
zoning ordinances 14

Acknowledgments

Photographic credits

page 1 Camera Press/Mel Yates; 2 Houses & Interiors/Verne; 3 Elizabeth Whiting & Associates/Rodney Hyett; 4 (left) Stock Market, 4 (center) Houses & Interiors, 4 (right) Camera Press; 5 (top left) Ikea, 5 (top center left) Camera Press, 5 (top right) Houses & Interiors/Roger Brooks, 5 (top center right) Elizabeth Whiting & Associates/Rodney Hyett, 5 (bottom left) International Interiors/Paul Ryan, 5 (bottom right) Houses & Interiors; 6 (top) Camera Press, 6 (center) Mainstream/Ray Main (Behr/Mill Hill), 6 (bottom) View/Dennis Gilbert (Architects: Ingram Avenue, London); 7 (top) Corbis, 7 (center) View/Chris Gascoigne (Architects: Gerrard Taylor Associates), 7 (bottom) Thermador Professional Series available from the American Appliance Centre, Enfield; 8–9 Elizabeth Whiting & Associates/Rodney Hyett; 10 Stock Market/Pete Salutos; 11 Corbis; 12–13 Mark Wilkinson Furniture; 15 International Interiors/Paul Ryan (Designer: J. Saladino/S. Casdin); 16–17 The Stock Market; 19 View/Dennis Gilbert (Architects: James Melvin and Gollins Melvin Ward & Partners, refurbishment by Sauerbach Hulton); 20–21 Robert Harding Syndication/Inspirations/Russell Sadur; 22 Mainstream/Ray Main (Behr/Mill Hill); 23 Interior Archive/Henry Wilson (Owner: Florence Lim); 25 International Interiors/Paul Ryan (Designer: Jason McHoy); 27 Mainstream/Ray Main (The Maples, Adderbury); 28 Elizabeth Whiting & Associates/Rodney Hyett; 30–31 Jerry Harpur (Designer: Diane Wakelin, San Francisco); 32–33 Camera Press; 34 Houses & Interiors, 34–35 Houses & Interiors; 36 Camera Press; 37 Camera Press; 38 (top left), 38 (center left), 38 (center right), 38 (bottom left), 38 (bottom right) Andrew Sydenham/Marshall Editions, 38 (top right) Farrow & Ball; 39 (left) Houses & Interiors/Jake Fitzjones, 39 (center) Arcaid Simon Kenny, 39 (right) Elizabeth Whiting & Associates/Nadia Mackenzie; 40–41 Mainstream/Ray Main (Orange Juice, Kilburn); 42 (top left) Amtico, 42 (top right) Fired Earth, 42 (center left) William Lomas Carpets/The Chatsworth Collection, 42 (center right) Amtico, 42 (bottom left) Kahrs (UK) Ltd, 42 (bottom right) The Original Seagrass Company; 43 (left) Elizabeth Whiting & Associates/Brian Harrison, 43 (right) Elizabeth Whiting & Associates/Tim Imrie; 44 Elizabeth Whiting & Associates; 46 Andrew Sydenham/Marshall Editions; 48 (top right) Corbis/Richard Fukuhara, 48 (top right) Kirkstone Quarries Ltd., 48(center left and center right) Andrew Sydenham/Marshall Editions, 48 (bottom left) Fired Earth, 48 (bottom right); Junckers, 49 (left) Interior Archive/Fritz von der Schulenberg, 49 (center) Elizabeth Whiting & Associates/Rodney Hyett, 49 (right) Elizabeth Whiting & Associates/Tom Leighton; 50–51 View/Dennis Gilbert (Architects: Ingram Avenue, London); 52 (top) House & Interiors/Mark Bolton (Catherine Gray Bathroom), 52 (bottom) Andrew Sydenham/Marshall Editions; 53 (left) Arcaid/Richard Bryant (Designer & Architect: Spencer Fung), 53 (right) Tony Stone/David Hantzig; 54 Camera Press; 55 Elizabeth Whiting & Associates/Lu Jeffery; 56–57 Camera Press; 58 Sharps Bedrooms; 59 Robert Harding Syndication/Mike Jones; 60 Andrew Sydenham/Marshall Editions; 61 Options Fitted Furniture of Mitcham, Surrey; 62 Elizabeth Whiting & Associates; 63 Elizabeth Whiting & Associates/Rodnet Hyett; 64 CURVOFLITE STAIRS AND MILLWORK, INC.; 65 International Interiors/Paul Ryan (Architects: Hariri & Hariri); 66 View/Chris Gascoigne (Architects: Gerrard Taylor Associates); 68 Mainstream/Ray Main (Park Road, London); 69 (left) Elizabeth Whiting & Associates/Rodney Hyett, 69 (right) Mainstream/Ray Main (Room Sets, Abbotts Langley); 70 Gazco Living Flame Gas Stores; 71 Anglia Fireplaces & Design Ltd. (01223) 234713; 73 Corbis; 75 Gen Ex Kitchen (available from the American Appliance Centre, Enfield); 77 Thermador Professional Series (available from the American Applicance Centre, Enfield); 79 Interior Archive/Andrew Wood (Designer: Leonie Lee Whittle/Snap Dragon); 80–81 View/Peter Cook (Homes for the Future, Glasgow, Kirkstone Quarries); 82 View/Peter Cook (Architect: Fiona McLean), 82–83 Mark Wilkinson Furniture; 84 Elizabeth Whiting & Associates/Rodney Hyett; 85 International Interiors/Paul Ryan (Designer: Marjolyn Wittich); 86 Andrew Sydenham/Marshall Editions; 87 House & Interiors/Roger Brooks; 88–89 View/Dennis Gilbert (Architects: Chance de Silva); 90 Ikea; 92 International Interiors/Paul Ryan (Designer: John Saladino); 95 Corbis; 96–97 Corbis; 99 Houses & Interiors/Mark Bolton; 100 Elizabeth Whiting & Associates/Rodney Hyett; 101 Elizabeth Whiting & Associates/Rodney Hyett, 102–103 Arcaid/Nicholas Kane (Architect: Shahriar Nasser, Regent's Park Glass Extension); 104–105 Houses & Interiors/Roger Brooks; 107 Jerry Harpur; 108 (left) Clive Nichols (Clive and Jane Nichols), 108–109 Houses & Interiors; 110 Elizabeth Whiting & Associates/Michael Dunne; 113 Corbis; 114–115 The Stock Market/Don Mason; 116 Jerry Harpur (Phillip Watson, Fredencksburg, VA); 117 Jerry Harpur (Design: Oehme & van Sweden Associates); 119 Elizabeth Whiting & Associates/Jerry Harpur; 120 Garden Picture Library/Brigitte Thomas; 122 Houses & Interiors; 123 Houses & Interiors/Roger Brooks; 126–127 Camera Press/Greg Waugh (Australia Brisbane); 160–161 The Stock Market/Michael Keller; 162, 163, 168, 169, 171, 172, 173, 174 Bruce Mackie/Marshall Editions; Front cover Tony Stone Images /Joe Polollio (top left), Camera Press Ltd (top centre), The Stock Market/Pete Saloutos (top right), International Interiors/Paul Ryan (Designer: John Saladino) (bottom left), Houses & Interiors (bottom right)

Illustration credit

All illustrations are by Patrick Mulrey

Acknowledgments

Contracts (pp. 166–167) are by courtesy of Gary Ranson, *The Contractor's Legal Kit*; Journal of Light Construction Books, 1996. The publishers would like to give special thanks to Kuo Kang Chen